SIR JOHN AMORY'S STAGHOUNDS

Richard Lethbridge (MBE)

with best wishes

26-11-2012

SIR JOHN AMORY'S STAGHOUNDS

RICHARD LETHBRIDGE MBE

ryelands

First published in Great Britain in 2012

Copyright © Richard Lethbridge 2012

All rights reserved. No part of this publication may be reproduced,
stored in a retrieval system, or transmitted in any form or by any
means without the prior permission of the copyright holder.

British Library Cataloguing-in-Publication Data
A CIP record for this title is available from the British Library

ISBN 978 1 906551 34 6

RYELANDS
Halsgrove House,
Ryelands Business Park,
Bagley Road, Wellington, Somerset TA21 9PZ
Tel: 01823 653777   Fax: 01823 216796
email: sales@halsgrove.com

Part of the Halsgrove group of companies.
Information on all Halsgrove titles is available at: www.halsgrove.com

Printed in China by Everbest Printing Co Ltd

CONTENTS

Introduction	9
Acknowledgements	11
Sir John Amory's Staghounds	19
Mark Amory's Collection	143
Captain Harry Amory's Staghounds	149

Overleaf: *Meet at South Molton Station.*

PHOTO
E. ASKEW.

JOHN AMORY'S STAGHOUNDS S'HOLTO

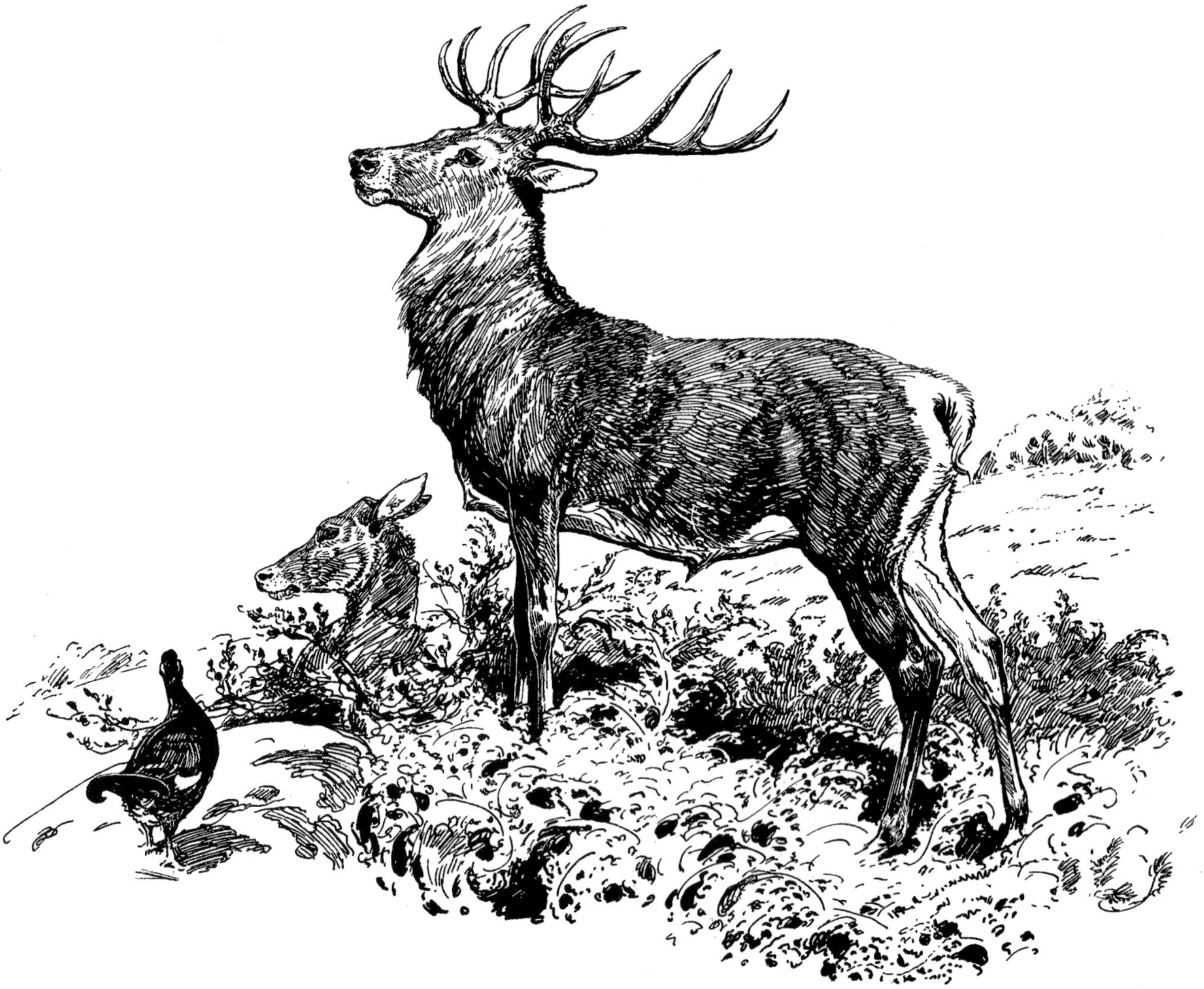

INTRODUCTION

IN THE YEAR 2000 I wrote a book on the Tiverton Staghounds, followed in 2002 by one on the parishes of Chittlehamholt, Warkleigh and Satterleigh. Then in 2004 by one on the Barnstaple Staghounds. With the passing of time I thought it necessary to bring out another Staghunting one that would appeal to the hunting fraternity, and I have come up with the runs of Sir John Amory's Staghounds and Captain Harry Amory's Staghounds. These hounds were established in 1896, and this arrangement continued until 1911 when Ian Amory decided to relinquish his duties of hunting the hounds and become huntsman of the Tiverton Foxhounds. This gave an opening for Ian Amory's brother Harry to take over the hunting of the Staghounds, which from then on became known as Captain Harry Amory's Staghounds. This continued until 1915 when Harry went to war and the Staghounds had a new man at the helm of the ship, namely Mr Charley Slader from South Molton; they then became the South Molton Staghounds. 1919 saw another change when the four Yandle brothers from Bampton near Tiverton alternately hunted the hounds and from then on they were known as the Tiverton Staghounds. They continue in strength today, and trail hunt under the new hunting act. Some of the runs of Sir John Amory's Staghounds were printed in my Tiverton Staghound book, and as I scanned through the old papers I could see there was enough material to do a whole book on the runs of these hounds. When they were established Queen Victoria was still on the throne, and there were no horse boxes, so hounds had to be hacked to the meets and returned home the same way. With lengthy runs sometimes hounds would not reach their kennels until very late in the evening. When moving off from the meets the pack would be kennelled at a nearby farm. With meets down at the Chulmleigh end of the country they would come down with the horses and hounds the night before. In accounts of two meets the correspondent tells us that they were stabled the evening before at the Fox and Hounds at Eggesford. Sometimes we see that hounds and horses were transported by train – what a luxury this would have been, but I guess this had to be paid for and something they could not do each time. On occasions the deer would be captured alive and liberated on another day, something we find strange and fascinating to comprehend today. But these were different times and I think we would have loved our hunting even more if we had been alive then. One such occurrence is described in an account of a run from Okehampton and capturing the stag alive at Hatherleigh, only to be taken in a cart back to the George Hotel for the night. Regular invitation meets in the Devon and Somerset Staghounds country around the Haddon, Bury and Dulverton districts were common and the Carnarvon Arms a favourite place to meet, with more than once the hounds arriving by train. Meeting in the Devon and

Somerset country for a week had Sir John Amory's Staghounds staying with Mr Sanders the Master at that time at Exford. When hunting the Barnstaple district they were the guests of Mr Basset at Westaway with hounds, horses and hunt servants staying there. Meets occurred also in the Quantock country and also on Dartmoor. Roping and killing the deer with a knife was a brutal approach then, but something that was accepted. We owe so much to the correspondents at the time for giving these gems of information, for now a hundred years later barely any "handed down material" is available. In some of the reports South Molton Road Station is mentioned: it was later renamed King's Nympton Station because people would often get off here thinking they were coming into South Molton itself. With some 215 runs in this book, 56 are invitation meets in the Devon and Somerset staghunting country. To complement all of the runs 153 images are also included. I hope you enjoy reading this book.

Found Bycott, killed Lapford. 28th September 1907. Presented to Tom Yandle by Ian Amory.

ACKNOWLEDGEMENTS

FIRSTLY I WOULD LIKE TO SAY a big thankyou to the Amory family (descendents of Sir John Amory) who have given me their support and approval for the book to be published, without this I would not have been able to continue. So thanks go to Sir Ian, Mark, Michael and Charles Amory. Also to Penny Whitefield who has been extremely helpful to me regarding the collation of this book, guiding me on the right line when using my laptop. Also to Ken Povey for his help in downloading my photos onto computer, and to Terry Gable for enhancing this book with her wonderful sketches. Other sources of photos and illustrations are from Shirley Bray, M. J. Sheperd, Tom Bartlett, Terry Moule and the *Illustrated Sporting and Dramatic News*. Finally to Halsgrove Publishing for their assistance in the making of this book. Because much of this book consists of transcriptions of contemporary reports printed in the *Tiverton Gazette* and the *North Devon Journal*, to a large degree spelling and punctuation have been retained to convey the original flavour of the material.

Richard Lethbridge

After a day's hunting in Dulverton, the stags head was displayed in a shop window in the evening.
Sketch by Terry Gable

Stag Hunting Poem By James Merson

Oh, for the sound of the horn on a fine hunting morn;

When a crack of the whip, and the cry of a hound

Announces from his lair the stags first bound.

Behold what music, so thrilling and enchanting.

At least for those who have a taste this way,

While the cry of the pack, now ahead striding.

Makes life worth living, if only for a day.

So another has joined the list.

Of those gone before. May those in future, when put to the test.

Run as stoutly, as those of yore.

The hart in his heart loves roaming at leisure.

Enjoying the fruits of the earth.

But when pursued by hounds, and deprived of that pleasure.

Huntsman whipping the hounds off.

Life succumbs to the inevitable, in times of stress or death.

With prominent eyes like saucers.

Being the keys of his mind.

He speeds along o'er hill and dale, swamps and rivers.

Until driven to surrender for sport, the encouragement of horse breeding and horsemanship,

as well as for the food of mankind.

Of all sport, it is the best.

For visitors when coming West.

In addition, the scenery is beyond description.

When turning one's head, in either direction.

A close encounter of stag and hound.

The 1900-1901 Baily's Hunting Directory
gives an account of Sir John Amory's Staghounds

Master – Sir John Amory, Knighshayes Court, Tiverton, Devon.
Secretary – Lewis Mackenzie, Esq., Tiverton.
Huntsman – Ian Heathcoat Amory, Esq.
Whippers-in – A. de Las Casas, Esq., and J. C. de Las Casas, Esq.
Harbourer – T. C. Yandle, Esq.
Twenty five couple of hounds.
Kennels – Hensleigh, Tiverton (telephone from P.O. Hensleigh).
Telegraph Office and Railway Station – Tiverton, one and a half mile distant.
Days of Meeting – Wednesday and Saturday.
The country which lies in Devonshire, covers an area about 30 miles long by 20 miles wide; it consists of about 40 per cent pasture, 50 per cent moorland, 5 per cent plough, and 5 per cent woodland. There is no wire. The Tiverton, Mr Bathurst's, the Dulverton and Mr Tremlett's Foxhounds hunt portions of the territory.
The best centres are: Tiverton, Dulverton, Witheridge and Bampton.
A private pack, the property of the Master.
Sir John Amory's Staghounds were established in 1896, at the suggestion of the Master of the Devon and Somerset Staghounds, to hunt the country into which the deer were spreading, and which lies beyond the limits of the Devon and Somerset regular territory; the latter pack not being able conveniently to hunt it.

Hunting trophies. Deer slot with clock presented to Percy Yandle from Captain Harry Amory. Found Haddon, killed Half Penny Bridge 10th January 1914. Arthur Heal's silver hunting horn and a slot presented to Tom Yandle by Harry Amory 11th October 1905, found Nethercott.

The quarry.

Hounds pursuing stag in river during a hunt with the Devon and Somerset staghounds.

Hounds and stag in the river.

Ian Heathcoat-Amory on his horse.

Sir John Amory's Staghounds in Mid and North Devon

1896-1915

The following article is from a piece written by the late Philip Everard and published in *Hunts and Huntsman of the South West* published in 1908.

THE HISTORY OF the pack goes back to 1896 when in February of that year at a meeting of the Devon and Somerset Staghounds a formal compliant had been made by Sir E. H. Dunning – then Mr Dunning – of Stoodleigh Court, Tiverton Devon, as to the somewhat inadequate arrangements for hunting the Stoodleigh district, in view of the fact that the Red Deer had increased considerably of late years in that neighbourhood, while, the deer was constantly being augmented by fresh deer being driven over the line of the Devon and Somerset railway from the Haddon strongholds, and other large coverts. For some time previously, successive Masters of the Devon and Somerset Staghounds had felt the difficulty of hunting the district, between the town of Tiverton and Dulverton station, with sufficient regularity, the distance from kennels being very great, and there being already more than enough material, much nearer home, to be dealt with. It was at this junction that Mr Ian Heathcoat Amory came forward with proposals which readily solved the difficulty. He was able to announce the conclusion of negotiations with Mr E. H. Dunning which provided for the capture of a certain number of deer each year, and Mr R. A. Sanders, Master of the Devon and Somerset Staghounds, in April, 1896, reported that he had come to an arrangement with Mr. Amory for hunting the country to the south of the Devon and Somerset line of railway, which runs nearly due east and west between Barnstaple and Taunton. This slice of country was then formally lent to Mr Amory by the hunt committee, with liberty of course, to follow his deer across the railway to the north of it. In the following year this scheme was extended, by giving Mr Sanders authority to invite Mr Amory to hunt on the north side of the railway. Following on the meeting of 1896, Mr Amory was not long in getting a pack together, and beginning to harry the deer, and, in the five seasons next following, his pack accounted for one hundred and fifty-one deer, of which fifty-seven were taken in the country lent to him, while sixty-six were the result of a serious of invitation meets in the in the Dulverton district of the Devon and Somerset Staghound country, while fourteen were taken from the Barnstaple coverts, and fourteen more from the Quantock herd. Since then Sir John Amory's pack, hunted by Ian Amory, has been at work regularly in its own country, and by invitation in the Dulverton district, and has long ago reduced the Stoodleigh herd to a manageable proportions, but it no longer travels afield to the Barnstaple country or the Quantocks, the former no longer hunted, and the Quantock Hills having for the past six seasons owned a resident pack. In 1902, Mr Amory's level of sport was well maintained, his season's record amounting to twenty-eight stags and sixteen hinds, and in the following year his total was almost the same, except that hinds preponderated. In 1904, deer had become somewhat scarcer, owing to several seasons of regular hunting, and only thirty-two were taken, but, at the annual meeting of the Devon and Somerset Staghounds hunt committee in May, 1905, which was a record year in the annuals of wild deer hunting, Mr Amory's tally amounted to forty- six. In 1906, the numbers were somewhat less, and made a total of thirty-four deer. Throughout these years, Mr Ian Amory has carried the huntsman's horn, and for the greater part of the time has relied on the services of amateur whippers-in, the Messrs de Las Casas and Captain H. Heathcoat Amory being his chief supporters. Mr Amory was the first to vary the time honoured custom of using only dog hounds for deer hunting, on account of their superior size. So satisfactory did his experiment of using a mixed pack appear, that it has been largely followed by the Devon and Somerset Staghounds, and other packs, in recent years. This pack has always been hunted without subscription, except for the purpose of providing a fund for the compensation of deer preserving farmers, whose crops suffer from the ravages of the deer, and the thanks of the countryside are due to Sir John Heathcoat Amory, for the maintenance of an establishment which has kept wild deer hunting alive and prosperous in a wide district where it was threatened with discontinuance.

The following two books mention Sir John Amory's Staghounds:

An extract from *Staghunting on Exmoor* by Philip Evered published in 1902.

A noble beast, from the Stoodleigh coverts, taken by Mr Ian Amory with Sir John Amory's Staghounds near chain bridge in the autumn of 1897, weighed, when cleaned and dry, no less than 333 lbs, which, reckoned according to the custom of the country, would amount to 16 score 13 lbs. This I believe to be the record weight, for the west country at any rate, if not for the British Islands. The Scotch method of weighing being of course entirely different and would have included all that had been removed from this woodland giant. This stag's horn measured round outer curve from burr to tip the notable length of 39 1/2 inches.

An extract from the book by Fred Goss *Memories of a Stag Harbourer* published in 1931.

Long cross country runs have occurred especially after Christmas. I remember one deer we found in Hele Ball wood above Jury, close to Dulverton, that ran to Milverton before being killed, a run of a good many miles, the run was with Sir John Amory's Staghounds and Mr Albert De Las Casas, who usually acted as honorary whip, he was hunting them on that day in the place of the Master who was ill. On looking back I think some of the happiest days in my life were those when harbouring was at its busiest and when hunting seemed at its zenith. It included a period in which, in addition to harbouring for the Devon and Somerset Staghounds four days a week I was often employed in harbouring for Sir John Amory's Staghounds on the other two. In this way I have several times harboured six stag in a week. Meets for Sir John Amory's hounds were often held by invitation in the Haddon and other neighbouring districts, for these I was generally asked to harbour a stag. Later on, Miller and then Lang, the present harbourer for the Devon and Somerset, used to harbour for them. On leaving for military service Colonel Harry Amory gave many of his hounds to the Devon and Somerset, the remainder being looked after and hunted during the difficult war years by Charlie Slader of South Molton. On Mr Slader giving them up they became the Tiverton Staghounds of today passing into the hands of the Yandle family, sons of the late Tom Yandle, whose keen sportsmanship all country deeply respected. I have in my possession a highly valued memento of the five hundred deer killed by the Sir John Amory pack, in the form of one of the stag's tusks mounted as a safety pin. And also another happy reminder of this period in the shape of a silver mounted blotter presented to me by Sir Ian Amory and Colonel Harry Amory, and on it inscribed "In memory of a many a good mornings harbouring and many a good days hunting 1896- 1915". I remember in one spring staghunting season a young stag behaving with extraordinary coolness in face of hounds. The meet was with Sir John Amory's Staghounds at Cuzzicombe Post, and I had harboured a young stag in West Molland wood. While tufting for him I was riding through a wood just in front of Ludovic Amory who was that day hunting hounds, when I suddenly saw the stag I had harboured lying just below using an old charcoal pit. We stopped our horses to look at him and waited, expecting the tufters, which were close at hand, to put him up. Seeing he was observed and there being no undergrowth in the pit to serve as any sort of concealment, the stag got up but did not offer to move away. At that moment the tufters came level with the pit, but it so happened some ran above it and some below it, none of them chancing either to scent or see the stag, There the stag stood quite still watching the hounds passing him, realising no doubt that his chance of escaping their notice lay in not moving. So far as all those tufters were concerned the stag was not correct, but unfortunately for him one tufter had lagged behind and in following the rest he went straight through the pit thereupon he came right on the stag who then thought it time to leave.

Fred Goss, Harbourer for the Devon & Somerset Staghounds and also for Sir John Amory's Staghounds.

A BIOGRAPHY OF SIR JOHN AMORY

We are indebted to Sir John Amory for establishing his staghounds in 1896, and at that time he also had a pack of harriers named after him which he formed in 1859 that hunted the hare. In 1914 he died aged 85, a graphic account of his life is relayed through the papers at the time given below.

Sir John Heathcoat-Amory, Bart, was born on May 4th 1829, and was the eldest son of Mr Samuel Amory, of the Priory, Homerton, Middlesex, and of Portland Place, London, who married in 1826 Anne, second daughter of Mr John Heathcoat, the distinguished inventor and founder of the lace industry in Tiverton. Mr John Heathcoat's career, one of the most remarkable in the annals of the British commerce, is set forth at some detail in a well known book by the late Dr Smiles – *Self-Help*. He is there referred to as a man of great natural gifts of sound understanding, quick perception, and a genius for business of the highest order. With these he possessed up-rightness, honesty, and integrity, qualities which are the true eulogy of human character. The gifts and qualities of his famous Grandfather were inherited in no small degree by the Grandson, who after being educated at University College, London, became closely associated with John Heathcoat in the management of the great industrial establishment which from 1816 to the present day has been one of the chief factors in the prosperity of Tiverton, and the name of John Heathcoat & Co. is a synonym for enterprise and efficiency in the market of the world. On his father's side also Sir John was of notable decent. His Grandfather – Samuel Amory, the elder was a London banker, who died in the last year but one of the eighteenth century. He in his turn was the son of one Thomas Amory, Doctor of Divinity, of Taunton, who was born in 1700. Those interested in tracing out links with the past may note that a period of 207 years from 1700 to 1907 is covered by four lives in direct lineal succession. It was Sir John Amory's misfortune to lose his mother before he was five years old. She died at the age of 26 on January 1st 1834, and is interred in St Peter's churchyard, where also, 23 years later, her husband, Mr Samuel Amory, was laid to rest. Mr John Heathcoat had two other daughters, the younger of whom, Mrs Caroline Brewin died in May, 1877, at the age of 67, and the elder, Miss Eloise Heathcoat, in December, 1880 at the age of 75. On April 6th, 1863, Sir John (then Mr Amory) was married at St James' Piccadilly, London, by the Lord Bishop of Oxford, to Miss Henrietta Mary Unwin, daughter of Mr William Unwin, of the Colonial Office in London, for some time private secretary to the fourteenth Earl of Derby, "the Rupert of debate". Lady Heathcoat-Amory's mother was a member of a noted family in Scotland, being the eldest daughter of Mr James Murray Grant, of Glenmoriston and Foy. After her husband's death Mrs Unwin settled at Tiverton, where she died at the age of 90 in September, 1904.

Mr and Mrs Heathcoat-Amory were blessed with the following sons and daughters. Mr Ian Murray Heathcoat-Amory, J. P. born April 16, 1865, and married June 6, 1893 to Alexandra Georgina, daughter of the late Admiral Seymour, of Kings Lynn; Mr Harry William Ludovic Heathcoat-Amory, born June 7, 1870, married November 1, 1898, to Evelyn, only daughter of Mr E. J. and the Hon. Mrs Stanley, of Quantock Lodge, Somerset; Mr Ludovic Heathcoat-Amory, born May 11, 1881, married on July 12, 1911, to Miss Mary Stuart Bannatyne, of Haldon; and three daughters – Mrs Charles Carew, married October 15, 1891; Mrs Louis de Las Casas, married April 22, 1899; and the Hon Mrs Lesley Butler, whose marriage took place in July 1907. The additional surname and arms of Heathcoat were assumed by Sir John (then Mr Amory) by royal license dated February 28 1874, and three weeks later a baronetcy was conferred upon him by Her Late Majesty Queen Victoria on the recommendation of the Rt. Hon.W. Gladstone.

Sir John Heathcoat-Amory on his horse.

In Parliament

For seventeen years Sir John Heathcoat-Amory represented the borough of Tiverton in the House of Commons. He was first returned in November 1868 with the Hon. George Denman as his colleague. That election was unopposed. It was not, however Sir John's first appearance on the hustings. Eleven years previously, at the public nomination Lord Palmerston and Mr John Heathcoat as members for the borough. Mr Heathcoat, then elderly and in failing health, was represented on the hustings by his namesake and grandson. In 1872, Mr Denman having been made a judge, the Rt. Hon. W. N. Massey became Sir John's colleague in the representation of Tiverton – an association which lasted until Mr Massey's death in 1881. During that period there were two fiercely contested elections at Tiverton – the first in 1874, when Sir John Amory headed the poll with 677 votes, Mr Massey came next with 624, and Sir John Walrond (Grandfather of the present member for the Tiverton Division) was at the bottom with 605. After much pressure Sir John Walrond again came forward in 1880, and was once more defeated, the numbers being: Amory, 743; Massey, 699; Walrond, 590. On the death of Mr Massey Lord Ebrington (now Earl Fortescue) was chosen as the Liberal candidate; and thanks largely to Sir John Amory's influential support, was returned by a substantial majority. When in 1888 the borough of Tiverton was for electoral purposes merged in a division of the county of Devon, Sir John Amory decided to retire from parliamentary life.

The services rendered by Sir John Amory while M. P. for Tiverton to the Liberal cause were highly appreciated by Mr Gladstone, then the leader of the party. Though Sir John very rarely spoke in the House, his wide knowledge of affairs, great experience, and sound judgment gave to his opinions great weight. When occasion required, as was proved in various election campaigns, he could speak with force, fluency, and effect. Thanks largely to his staunch advocacy of Liberal principles, the borough of Tiverton was for many years regarded as a safe Liberal seat for two members; the only Conservative member from 1832 to 1885 being Sir John Walrond, who in 1865 gained a seat by three votes and retained it three years. The baronetcy conferred on Sir John Amory by Mr Gladstone in 1874 was a fitting reward of loyal and faithful service. After his retirement from Parliament Sir John Amory, like many other sound Liberals, found himself unable to follow his old leader in the advocacy of Home Rule for Ireland; and for some time he was a Liberal Unionist. When however, tariff reform came to the front, Sir John once more ranged himself with the Liberal party, and became President of the Tiverton Divisional Liberal Association.

The First Meeting to Discuss Plans to Establishing a Pack of Staghounds for the Tiverton District.

April 26th 1896

A meeting of gentlemen interested in Staghunting was held at Tiverton Town Hall on Tuesday to receive a statement from Mr Ian Amory, as to the terms of which he has decided to collect a pack of Staghounds, and hunt the country south of the Devon and Somerset railway. There was a large and representative gathering, and the business-like and enthusiastic manner in which the proposals were taken up is sufficient guarantee that Staghunting in the Tiverton district will become an established success. There were present Mr Ian M. Heathcoat-Amory, M.H., Mr W. C. L. Unwin, M. F. H., Mr F. R. Henson, M.H., Major Braddon, Messrs. C. Carew, Hugh March-Phillips, J. R. Hollond, L. Mackenzie, T. O. Lazenby, A. de Las Casas, C. de Las Casas. L. de Las Casas, C. D. Harrod, Hill, E. C. Nicholetts, B. Bayley, W. H. Vinnicombe, J. F. Pugsley, T. Clarke, J. F. Ellerton, W. H. Martin, T. Row, H. Giles, C. J. Irving, J. T. Periam, H. C. Saunders, W. Goodland, M. Goodland, J. Farrant, C. R.K. Webb, E. M.Moyle, C. W. Nelder, W. Thorne, T. Ferris, G. Haydon, &c. Mr Holland was voted to the chair, and at once called upon Mr Amory to make a statement. Mr Ian Amory said: - I think that the meeting may be glad to know how the circumstances arose which have led to the formation of a separate pack of Staghounds to hunt this country. You are aware that, thanks to the active support of the landowners and of the tenant farmers in the Stoodleigh country, the deer have increased very much there of late years. Mr Dunning, realising that, in the interest of his tenants, this rate of increase could not go on indefinitely, asking the Master of the Devon and Somerset Staghounds to hunt the country more regularly and to undertake to kill a certain number of deer in it each year. This Mr Sanders, after consulting the committee, found himself unable to do, owing to the demands made on him by the rest of his large country. Mr Sanders then asked me if I would undertake to hunt all the country south of the Devon and Somerset Railway. Mr Dunning and the other landowners having expressed their approval, and having giving most generous subscriptions towards the fund which it will be necessary to raise for the compensation of farmers whose crops may be damaged by the deer, I have undertaken to do this- (cheers). I propose to get together a small pack of Staghounds. I have been lucky enough already to be given four couple of very good looking hounds, most of them given me by Mr Unwin from the Tiverton Foxhounds- (cheers). There are as yet very few stags in our country old enough to run so that it will not be necessary to begin hunting until well on in November, when we shall begin hind hunting and probably keep at them until the beginning of April, after which we could put in two or three weeks at the stags. Tiverton will not be called upon to subscribe towards any of the ordinary expenses of hunting the country (cheers) but I do hope that those amongst us who have the interest of hunting at heart will subscribe such a sum as will enable the committee to guarantee the farmers, to whom we owe so much against any loss they may suffer by the preservation of the deer (cheers). Mr Unwin said after Mr Amory's speech they could judge how very necessary it was, if the deer were to be preserved in the neighbourhood, that they must have a second pack of Staghounds to hunt them. He congratulated Mr Amory upon the manner in which he had come forward to support these pack of hounds (Hear, Hear). It was thought by some that the interests of Foxhunting might suffer in that district by reason of the starting of Staghounds. He (Mr Unwin) did not think so. There was plenty of room for both packs (Hear, Hear). He congratulated Mr Amory on his pluck in coming forward and he wished him every sort of luck. He hoped would show them as good sport with his Staghounds in the future as he had with his harriers in the past. He moved that the following form a committee: Sir John Amory, General Spurway, Messrs C. Carew, N. Chichester. J. W. Coulson, G. J. Cruwys, W. C. L. Unwin, T. C. Daniel, E. H Dunning, Dunsford, J. R Hollond, A. de Las Casas, L. Mackenzie, E.M. Mole, E. C. Nicholetts, and J. F. Pugsley. Mr Mackenzie seconded. They were all sensible advantages which would accrue to the neighbourhood from the generous conduct of Sir John and Mr Amory in taking up staghunting on this side of the Devon and Somerset line (Hear Hear). Landowners and tenants were also to be congratulated, because they had undoubtedly suffered in the past from the lack of a sufficiently extended and generous deer damage fund, but it seemed as if their time was at last come. He thought it was extremely important that the meeting should fully understand that Sir John and Mr Amory undertook the whole cost of their new hounds. Therefore whatever subscriptions were given would be devoted entirely to compensating the tenants for the damage done to their crops by the deer- (cheers). It was absolutely necessary that this deer damage fund should be a generous one- (Hear Hear). The resolution was carried, and the meeting terminated. The committee afterwards met to transact business, when Mr L. Mackenzie was elected secretary and Mr E. C. Nicholetts treasurer.

The First Meet of Sir John Amory's Staghounds

Oct 1896

The opening meet was held at Stoodleigh Court, the residence of E. H. Dunning, with the new Master, Mr Ian Amory and his two whips Mr Albert and Manuel de Las Casas, who arrived punctually at ten o'clock with 14 couple of hounds. A large number of staghunting friends assembled, and a most warm and hospitable welcome was given to everyone by Mr and Mrs Dunning. The day promised to be fine and a balmy south west wind and heavy dew seemed signs of a scenting morning. The harbouring had been excellently performed by Tom Yandle, and a warrantable stag was found within a few minutes of the tufters being thrown in Stuckeridge Wood, just above the old kennels opposite Black Copse. Hounds at once began to bustle along, driving through this long cover down to Chain Bridge, and from thence opposite Duvale, away to Cove Bridge and leaving Emmerford on the left, nearly to New Bridge. Here the tufters were stopped and the hounds, which had been left at the new kennels were soon fetched, and rattling down to the Stoodleigh Drive, were put in just below Hatherland Wood North. Soon after getting into the wood hounds divided, and a hind was seen to be the cause, after some delay Ian Amory got his hounds together and laid on the stag, which had been seen making his way back to Stuckeridge. Passing down the Iron Mill Stream we crossed the Exe to Wonham House and away as if for Bampton, but turning back through Highleigh Wood South to Wonham again and the Stuckeridge Coverts, where he turned up four fresh deer. This proved fatal to sport and as hounds had been running for four hours and the ground was seriously foiled, they were called off and taken home. Mr Ian Amory who acted as huntsman is to warmly congratulated on his first day's sport with a fresh pack, only five couple being old hounds, everyone was pleased with their day's sport with the new venture.

Dec 2nd 1897

Sir John Amory's Staghounds met again at Chelfham, near Barnstaple, on Tuesday. There was again a large field present including the Master Ian Amory, Messrs De Las Casas (2), Mr C. H. Basset, Mr J. Harper, Mr R. Lake, Mr W. Penhale, Mr Pitts Tucker, Mr T. Copp, Miss Hurst, the Misses Chichester (Pilton), Mrs Hugh Toller, Mrs Eyton, Messrs Stanley Heard, Oatey, Hutton, Q. Tamlyn, S. Petter, Fry, Southcombe, J. Alford, H. Turner, Taplin, L. Cooke, C. Cooke, Speke, Arnold Thorne, jun., Mervyn Ridd, J. Parminter, B. Fanshawe, Vickery, & c. Mr Comer Clarke came to the meet with the news that he had several deer lying in his woods at Smithapark. Tufters were no sooner in than a fine stag was roused, as also a bevy of hinds. The wood indeed, appeared alive with deer. Some of the tufters followed the hinds, whilst others stuck to the stag, which held a course up the valley, somewhat in the same direction as that on Saturday. He ran parallel to the Lynton Railway, which unfortunately, he seemed disinclined to cross, without which a moorland run is impossible. After going some distance the deer struck to the left for Tidycombe, the steep ascent being very trying to the horses. He crossed the coach road to Lynton, and turned into Lady Chichester's woods at Arlington. Under Eastdown House, for some

Arlington Court where on a few occasions, the stag and hounds entered the grounds.

Bratton Fleming Station on the Barnstaple to Lynton railway – this line was crossed by Sir John Amory's Staghounds on many occasions.

reason, he turned sharply back, and came down the water to Woolly Wood, just opposite Loxhore Cott. The pack was fetched from Chelfham and fresh tufters thrown into the wood, when the stag was speedily refound. He again pointed up stream. The pack raced him through the woods at a tremendous pace up to the fish pond in the Arlington grounds, where he took to the water, which covers a space of about seven acres. Hounds followed, but the deer proved to be a bold swimmer. After a while a boat was manned, Lady Chichester's keeper taking the lasso. Mr W. Smith, of Eastdown, was at the oars, and followed manfully and strongly for a considerable time, but the deer managed to keep at rope length ahead of the boat. At last he was lassoed, taken to land, and quickly dispatched. He proved to be a fine stag, with brow, bay, tray, and two on top on each side, being probably five years old. Mr Ian Amory may well be satisfied with his two days' sport, and the neighbourhood of Barnstaple owes a debt of gratitude to Mr Basset for the interest he has taken in getting the deer (which have for a long time been doing considerable damage) hunted.

Jan 29th 1898

On Saturday a capital run was enjoyed by a large number of sportsmen, when hounds paid another visit to within the precincts of Tiverton. The meet was at the Manor House, Oakford, those present in addition to the Master including Mr W. C. L. Unwin, Miss March Phillipps, Miss Amory, Messrs. de Las Casas (4) Misses Spurway (2) Messrs Hollond (3) T. Yandle, F. Butt, Beedle (Sydeham), and many others. Owing to the fact that hounds have been rattling the Stoodleigh and Stuckeridge covers about so much lately it seemed as though the hinds had moved off. Most of the likeliest covers were drawn without result, and at a quarter to three hounds were taken to Champells Cliff. Here four deer were found and the pack settled on the line of one which made for Ash Cross. From here she struck off for Stoodleigh Kennels then made her way down to the Iron Mill Stream, from thence going to Chain Bridge and down the Exe by Cove Bridge. Turning, the quarry then went away to Hangmans Hill, then returned to Cove Bridge. Hounds afterwards carried the line to Steart, down by East Stoodleigh, then to the Exe, and passing by Emmerford, went on to Newbridge. Easterlands was the next point, after leaving which the hind came to Worth, passing close by Worth stables. From here she made her way to Prescott, then to Hensleigh, and passing through Hensleigh cover went away down to Ashley and on to Custom Wood. It was by this time quite dark and the day ended.

Feb 5th 1898

Sir John Amory's Staghounds met at Chelfham Mills, near Barnstaple, on Wednesday, by invitation. The field was a large one, considering the inclemency of the weather, there being no less than 80 horsemen and horsewomen present. Among them were the Master and huntsman, Mr Ian Amory, the two whips, Messrs de Las Casas, Mr C. H. Basset, Mr Orlando Chichester, Miss Hext, Miss Pitts-Tucker, Miss Perse (Oare), Mrs F. H. Toller, Miss Crang, Mrs Penhale, Miss Smith, the Rev. F. W. and Mrs Toms, Messrs R. Lake, A. F. Seldon, G. H. and Mrs Gould, Comer Clarke, W. Penhale, F. W. Taplin, Cole, H. Turner, Stanley Heard, German, F. Elliott, M. Squire, W. L. Ashton, W. Speke, Tamlyn, List, and others. During the day the wind blew nearly a gale, and at frequent intervals there were heavy showers of hail and rain. The pack was kennelled at first at Chelfham Mills. Sir Arthur Chichester's keeper reported that a number of hinds were in Woolley Wood, but

Hounds getting comfortable while they are on their journey to the meet.
Sketch by Terry Gable

Mr Comer Clarke arrived soon afterwards brought the news of a single hind being in Smithapark. Preference was given to the latter, and the pack was taken on to draw the wood. The hind, however, had moved on to Tidycombe, where other deer were known to be lying. So the pack was again put in Tidycombe Farm. Immediately, on the tufters being taken into the wood, three deer were found, and came down the valley at a rattling pace (two hinds and a calf) in full view of the field, pointing for Smithapark. The pack was brought out and laid on, and we ran at a tremendous pace through Loxhore down to the River Yeo. The deer turned up the river and into Woolley Wood, where other deer had been harboured in the morning. The pack was consequently stopped and put up at Loxhore Cott, and the tufters taken into the wood. A hind was soon roused, and made directly for the Arlington Cover. Heavy squalls of rain and hail now came on and obliterated nearly every trace of scent. This caused great difficulty, and a large number of deer being soon on foot caused a good deal of delay and trouble in singling out a hind. After a time, a deer again came down the valley along by the river Yeo. It was uncertain whether it was a male deer or a hind, but being late in the day the Master determined to give the field a further gallop, and the pack was laid on just above Loxhore Cott. The scent improved. The deer ran at a good pace through Sir Arthur Chichester's covers at Youlston, turning right handed we came to Youlston Old Park and raced the deer back again to Shirwell Mills, when he once more came down the water and into the stream, just opposite the new viaduct at Chelfham, on which the new Lynton and Barnstaple railway line runs. He there jumped up in view of the pack, and raced up for several miles, nearly to Lady Chichester's fishpond at Arlington, when all trace of him was lost. The light having begun to fail, the sport was abandoned for another day.

March 31st 1898

Sir John Amory's Staghounds met at Chawleigh on Wednesday, including Mr Ian Amory (Huntsman), Messrs Las Casas(2), J. B. Lake, and several other gentlemen from Tiverton, Major Dunning (Lapford Wood), Miss Poyntz (Bradford Lodge), A. W. Luxton (Brushford), Tucker, C. Mortimer (Morchard Bishop), Peacock (Lapford), F. Webber (Chulmleigh) and many others. Stags having been slotted in Foxes Cover earlier in the morning the tufters were first put in there, and immediately three stags were afoot. Two of them being small, were allowed to get away. The other proved to be a grand stag, and he made away towards Chenson, and then on to Toneyfield. Turning up over the hill, he reached Hansford Farm. Thence he made away across country to Pouncers, then turned to the right, and ran on near Burridge and Burridge Moor. The tufters had been hunting the stag up to this point, the riders being able to get near them, but here the huntsman managed to whip them off and put the hounds on. The stag had led them down over the hill into the valley, then up near Affeton Castle, and on close to the village of West Worlington. Then he took over the hills to Broads Moor, East Worlington, and turned to the left passing through Meshaw. Next he made away up the bottom to Yarde Wood, Roseash, on through Ash Moor and away to Rackenford Moor, the hounds going splendidly all the way. Then he went towards Tiverton passing Spurway Mill, through the Stoodleigh Covers, on to Chain Bridge. Then he turned back over the hill to Stuckridge and crossed the River Exe, ran up to Wonham, near Bampton, turned back again to the river, and near Oakford Bridge was killed. The stag was a magnificent animal and had given over 3¼ hours hard riding without a check, and the kill was about twenty three miles away from the starting point. Some of the riders had to go nearly thirty miles to reach their homes.

April 2nd 1898

Sir John Amory's Staghounds met at Exford on Friday, where Mr Amory (with the hounds and horses) is now the guest of Mr Sanders, the Master of the Devon and Somerset Staghounds. On Saturday they met at Hawkcombe Head. The weather was bitterly cold, and a strong north east gale was blowing. In spite of the inclement weather a large field turned out meet Mr Amory on this his first visit to the forest side of the Devon and Somerset country. Deer were reported to be lying in one of the deep valleys close to the meet. The pack was therefore taken on and kennelled at Culbone Stables. Seven couple of tufters were taken out and found two big stags. They were stopped on these and laid on the line of four hinds which they drove down to the big woods on the cliffs between Porlock Weir and Ashley Coombe giving them no time to dwell. Here they found two of them up to the moor and out over the forest by Hawkcombe Head, where the run began in earnest. Two nights' sharp frost had made the moor ride very hard; it rattled under the horse's hoofs in a most unpleasant way. One or two people gave it up and went home, others left the moor and followed the road which was in a much better condition. Of those who followed hounds three soon had occasion to wish they hadn't, however their horses were soon caught and no damage was done. Meanwhile hounds were racing out over the forest, over the shoulder of Dunkery, round just above Exford, and back by Aldermans Barrow and Oareford. They gave the hind no time to look for other herds of deer that must have been lying in some of the coombes near which they passed. The line then taken by the deer was near enough to Culbone Stables for the whips to slip back there for the remaining half of the pack, which they brought smartly on and it was not long before the deer was killed in a big coombe leading down to Porlock Weir after a capital run of three and a half hours.

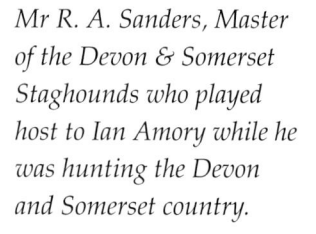

Mr R. A. Sanders, Master of the Devon & Somerset Staghounds who played host to Ian Amory while he was hunting the Devon and Somerset country.

September 24th 1898

From the opening meet at Chawleigh on Saturday, three stags had been harboured in Leigh Wood, where they would have been found in due course, if a nut picker, ignorant of the harm that he was doing, had not wandered into the covert immediately after the harbourer, who, work completed, had gone home to a well-earned breakfast. Shortly after eleven o'clock Mr Ian Amory took the pack back to Chawleigh Barton, and having kennelled them in Mr Baker's farm buildings, took two and a half tufters with which he proceeded to draw Leigh Wood. The field, confident of a quick find, had taken up their position on a hill overlooking the covert. To their surprise however, half an hour passed without a sound to denote that the deer had been mixed. Shortly the Master appeared with the tufters at the opposite end of the cover to that at which he had gone in, showing that it had been drawn blank so confident, however, was the harbourer that the deer were there that the cover, a fairly large and wonderfully thick one, with a great growth of under-cover in it, was most carefully drawn again. Then the hounds were taken all round the cover, but could hit no line. By this time it was nearly one o'clock. Tufters were then taken back to kennel and eight couple of fresh hounds taken out. With them the cover was again drawn from end to end, but the result was the same.

Sketch by Terry Gable

Western Wood was next drawn, then Chawleigh Barton Wood. It was not until all this country had been drawn (three o'clock in the afternoon) that the confession of the nut picker was reported and word brought that the three stags had left the covert about 9.30, and had gone up-stream towards the Worlington coverts. There the hounds were taken on the chance of the stags having waited in one of the neighbouring woods, but nothing could be made of them, and at 4.30 the Master gave the word for home. The one bright spot in a disappointing day's work was the cordial hospitality and the keen and sportsmanlike interest shown by all the inhabitants of the Chawleigh district. Chawleigh hospitality has become proverbial, and extends from Mr Thomas Baker who provides lodgings for the hunt servants, stabling for the horses and kennels for the hounds, and the other owners and tenants of the land who with west country hospitality make the deer and the hounds and their followers all feel equally welcome and at home while they are upon their land, to the keepers who – good sportsmen that they are – vie with the farmers in doing what they can (and it is much) to help forward the sport of others.

Oct 1st 1898

Sir John Amory's Staghounds met at Ash Cross on Wednesday in tropical weather, which accounted for the fact that there was little or no scent. There was a very large field out including the Master Mr Ian Amory, Mr J. R. Hollond, Miss Hollond, Mr and Mrs T. O. Lazenby, Mr Renton, Mr N. Chichester, Misses Chichester (3), Mr E. C. Nicholetts, Mr J.

Jarvis-Bailey, Miss Blake, and many of the neighbourhood. Among those on foot were the Misses Dunning (2), and Master Dunning. Owing to a recent accident, the first whip, Mr Albert de Las Casas was unable to be present, many regrets being expressed at his absence, everyone wishing him a speedy recovery. His duties of first whip was undertaken by Mr Louis de Las Casas. Three stags had been most satisfactorily harboured by Mr Tom Yandle in Stuckeridge South Covers in spite of great difficulties, owing to the hardness of the ground. Selecting the largest of the three, hounds ran him for about half an hour, but could never press him. Soon after hounds raised a hind, and at once pursed her. They were, however, taken back, but all efforts to get on the line of the hunted stag were fruitless. The rest of the day was vainly spent in trying to find another stag, and at 4.30 hounds were taken home. The day was one of disappointment for both hounds and field, as owing to the dry weather, there was very little scent.

The meet on Saturday was at West Worlington, the weather being still very hot and the ground hard. Among those present were the Master Mr Ian Amory, Mr Harry Amory, Miss Stanley, Mr Renton, Mr Jarvis- Bailey, Messrs Webber, Baker, Smith, sen, and jun, G. Zelly, J. Zelly, F. Andrew, J. Butt, and many others. Cobley Wood was first drawn, but it was found that the stags had moved out. Some other covers being drawn, three stags were roused. Tufters were then stopped and hounds laid on. The best of the three stags singled himself out, and ran over Cuddenhay Moor by Lutworthy Plantation to Meshaw Moor, where he turned to the left, and went nearly out to Meshaw Village. Doubling back by Romansleigh, the stag passed Midhay Moor, going through the wheat plantation on to Huntacott, Sydenham and into Chawleigh Wood, where he waited in the little Dart river. Here he was fresh found and turned away left handed going down past Eggesford Station, and into the Big Lapford Woods. Here fresh deer were started, and as it was found impossible to do any more with the hunted stag, hounds were called off, and at a quarter to five they started on their 19 miles journey home. This was a very hard day for the hounds who were running fast for over two and half hours. The stag was probably only four or five years old, or he would not have been able to stand before the hounds so long. We are informed that as the ground has become so hard, these hounds will not go out again until after the rain.

Oct 1st 1898

Sir John Amory's Staghounds on Tuesday attempted a revival of staghunting on Dartmoor. It is said that stags have been fairly numerous on the fringe of the moor for several years past, but they were nowhere to be seen on Tuesday, and the day was a complete failure. Before it was announced that the staghounds were coming to the south of the county to revive the hunting of the stag, which had been unknown on Dartmoor for at least half a century, there were several stags to be seen about. One man pointed out a field of turnips in which he had seen a fine stag only a week ago, and the keepers and others working on the land all spoke of having seen red deer about in the Buckland Woods of late. One old resident in the district says stags have been there for ten years past. They have been carefully harboured by Mr Bastard and the other landowners in the neighbourhood, with the hope that the red deer would become as popular on Dartmoor as on the smaller moor between Dulverton and Lynton. Mr Bastard has in his beautifully situated residence at Buckland half a dozen antlers from Dartmoor stags, all picked up within the last few years, and the Hon. R. Dawson, residing at the other side of the Dart, has three. These are all proofs of the presence of wild deer on Dartmoor. A year or two ago one of Mr Bastard's tenants had the hardihood to shoot one of the stags because of the damage it had done to his crops, and he was severely reprimanded. The farmers of the district have not learnt to love the red deer as their brethren on Exmoor do. There, thanks to the liberal administration of the damage fund, the farmers always welcome the presence of a stag; but on Dartmoor there is no such fund, and, up to the present, no compensating enjoyment in the nature of a hunt. Consequently, Datmoor farmers have not yet learnt to look upon the presence of the deer with pleasure. One farmer expressed the hope that they would find a stag and "kill'un" because of the damage done. But no stags were found. None had been seen in the district for a week. They had apparently cleared out as soon as it was announced that the staghounds were coming

Mr Amory the Master of the hounds, arranged for two meets in the Buckland drive and Holme Chase district as an experiment. He brought the hounds down on the Saturday, and kennelled them at the Hon. R. Dawson's place, at Holme. On Monday tufters were out looking for the deer, but no trace could be found. On Tuesday the first meet was held at Welsfor Cross, two miles from Ashburton, up, up, always up a steep hill, being the trysting place. Before eleven o'clock a considerable crowd had gathered in the road at the cross, for it was a lovely morning, with the air clear and bracing, and every indication of a fine day. It was an interesting crowd. Large numbers were on foot, almost as many were in brakes and carriages of varying description, and scores of ladies and gentlemen from all parts of South Devon were on horseback. The Master of the South Devon Foxhounds, the Masters of local packs of Harriers were there, the bulk of the farmers from all the country around were there on animals ranging from a shaggy Dartmoor pony to a well bred hunter. Rev. H. W. Thornton, a well known hunting parson, was there all the way from North Bovey; Prebendary Wolfe, who had driven over from his Manaton residence, was welcomed by a wide circle of friends. The Misses Carew had driven over from Ilfracombe, Miss Divett from Bovey, Miss Tudor was there from Lustleigh, the Misses Taylor of Torquay and Widecombe; Mr Pernley Tanner, Mr G. H. Hext, Newton Abbot; Mr H. Steele, Mr E. Tucker, Mrs R. Abraham, Major Tucker Mrs R. C. Tucker, Mr A. C. Loveys, Mrs and Miss Loveys, Mrs E. Tucker, the Messrs Amory, Rowe, Princetown, Mr Burnard, Mrs Burnard, Mr Lawrence Burnard, Mr K. A. Lake, Mr Yelland, Mr Poaden, and scores of others.

The Reverend W. H. Thornton, who was present at the Meet on Dartmoor.

Mr Ian Amory punctually rode up at the head of the hounds, with Messrs Las Casas acting as whippers-in. They passed through the crowd, although the narrow road was nearly blocked, and road on to the field on the left, from where magnificent views of the country for miles around could be obtained. The air was so clear that the channel beyond Teignmouth and Babbacombe was plainly seen, and on the other hand the view extended over a wide stretch of the moor. Mr Amory informed our representative that no deer had been seen, and that he feared their visit would not result in much hunting. Despite this gloomy outlook, however, Mr Amory tried the Buckland Woods and the woods on the other side of the Dart, but without success, There was only this conclusion – that it was a magnificent day, and that the scenery was some of the finest to be found anywhere in the British Isles.

As Mr Amory considered no sport was likely to accrue from a further trial of the covers, the meet arranged for Gallantry Bower on Friday was abandoned.

Nov 5th 1898

Sir John Amory's Staghounds met at Lydeard St Lawrence, on Wednesday, to hunt some of the deer that had crossed the line and were reputed to be lying in Mr Trollope's wood at Crowcombe Heathfield. There was a very large field out to meet the hounds, consisting probably of not less than 100 horsemen. Five couple of tufters were laid on, and a young stag was immediately found in the big covert, They ran him sharply round the coverts four an hour and a half, but finally compelled him to break away into the open. Tufters were now called off and the pack laid on, but the scent was bad, and hounds were unable to press him. He went away over Willetts Hill and on to Nettlecombe. Then left handed back towards Wiveliscombe, and on to Rawleys Cross. Hounds now got on terms with him, and after a couple of hours up and down the valley he was killed in a shallow pond close to Rawleys Cross. He proved to be a fine young stag, with his uprights only. In response to a generally expressed wish that hounds should come again, the scene of the meet was at Lydeard St Lawrence on Saturday. When the pack reached the meet the harbourer was unable to report the presence of deer. They seemed to have moved off on Wednesday when hounds were running through the covers. After two hours futile drawing of all the covers in the neighbourhood, Mr Sanders suggested that the Master should cross the line and draw for a deer on the Quantocks. The pack were therefore moved along into Birchen Wood where a stag and four or five hinds were roused. Hounds were stopped from these and laid on the trail of the stag, running him fast down over the hill and along the Crowcombe Village, down at the back of the woods almost to Quantock Lodge. Here other deer were found to be in front of hounds, and after some difficulty they were stopped and taken back to the line of the stag. He then led hounds over the Stowey road and along the whole length of the Quantock Hills to St Audries. Here he turned back across the hill and went into the big woods with hounds close behind. It was, however, growing too dark to do any more good and hounds were therefore stopped and taken home, after a run of two and a half hours. This was rather a disappointing finish, as it time had allowed the chances were that the stag would have been killed within the next half an hour

Mr C. H. Basset, from Westaway, Barnstaple – who kennelled Sir John Amory's Staghounds when they were hunting the Barnstaple District.

Oct 29th 1898

The meet on Saturday was at Chelfham Bridge near Barnstaple, in the same misty sort of weather as had prevailed there throughout the past week. There was a large field out to meet the Master Mr Ian Amory and the whips Messrs Las Casas (3). Amongst those present were Mr C. H. Basset, Mrs Curzon, Miss Hurst, Mr and Miss Smith, Mr Comer Clarke (in whose covers the deer are made so kindly welcome), Mr Lidston (a sportsman of many years experience), Mr March-Phillipps, Miss Coulson, Messrs J. F. Pugsley, Penhale, Speke, and many others on wheels and on horseback. Owing to the lack of scent the harbourer had been unsuccessful in finding a good stag, and it was decided to draw Mr Comer Clarke's coverts at Smithapark. Here several hinds were found, but hounds were at once stopped from these. The wood was again drawn, and two young stags went away, but as neither of them was good enough to hunt, the pack was taken back again. Soon after another stag was roused, but this one also proved a failure. Directly after news reached the Master that a stag had been seen in the woods bordering on the River Yeo. The pack were at once

Westaway House – the home of Mr C. H. Basset.

taken down and in a few minutes a fine stag was roused. Scent, however proved to be very indifferent, and after having run the length of the covers down towards Barnstaple and back, he made his way into Miss Chichester's covers at Arlington. Hounds were therefore called off and sport was at an end for the day. The large field present highly appreciated the endeavours of Mr Amory to show sport by bringing the hounds into this part of the county to hunt the deer which the farmers are so loyally preserving in spite of the many difficulties that stand in their way. A wish was universally expressed that later on in the season these hounds should again visit the neighbourhood and hunt the hinds. During the week that the pack has been at Barnstaple hounds, horses, and men had been the guests of Mr Basset, of Westaway (a former Master of the Devon and Somerset Staghounds) whose hospitality and the help he gives all forms of sport have become proverbial in North Devon.

Dec 10th 1898

Sir John Amory's Staghounds met at Aldridge Mill on Saturday. Mr Yandle had been unable to harbour any hinds. The pack was kennelled in Mr Cole's stable near Aldridge Mill, and with a larger pack than usual of tufters the Master drew Waspley Wood on the chance of hinds being there. But hounds soon roused a young stag and ran him hard into Bickham and out at the higher end, where they were stopped and taken back to draw for a hind in Sydeham. They had almost drawn the wood when they again found the same stag, and this time managed to slip away before the whips could get at them, and scent, was so good that they could not be caught until they were between Rackenford Moor and Knowstone. Here all but the leading two couple were caught and stopped. After this some of the Rackenford covers were drawn, then Blatchworthy. Rifton, Rhyll, Wheatland, and Town Wood were tried, but nothing except another stag was found, until at three o'clock a hind and calf were moved in Chample's Cliff. And with the whole pack on good terms with them they led us at racing pace by Ash Cross, Rifton Wood to Tidderson Moor, then right handed to Rackenford Moor, across it and down over Harestone Moors they ran at such a pace that horses could scarcely live with them. Here they turned right handed, and unfortunately the hinds picked up a stag, and with them led us back over Bickham Moor and through all the Stoodleigh covers to the Exe above Chain Bridge. It was now almost dark, so hounds were stopped and taken home. We have been asked to say that as the hinds have moved away from the home coverts, the meet will not take place on Saturday 10th, as advertised at Spurway Mill, but will be at Witheridge at 10 o'clock.

Dec 15th 1898

Followers of Sir John Amory's Staghounds enjoyed two excellent days' sport last week. On Wednesday they met at Bury Village, and as hinds were reported to be in the Deer Park the pack was kennelled on Haddon Moor. No sooner were the tufters into covert than they roused a fine stag; they were quickly stopped from his line and thrown into covert again, and this time they found a single hind; she broke at the further end of the covert and went out over Skilgate Common with the hounds almost in view, took one turn down over the fields towards Skilgate Village and back on to Haddon Moor, along the south side of this and into the big covert by Wynne corner. Soon after entering this covert she ran into a herd of several deer, and hounds divided. They were soon, however, got together again, and ran one of the hinds hard the whole length of the moor and on Skilgate Common, but in spite of being driven along at her best pace with the hounds close to her, she would not leave the covert, and by Exton Lodge turned in again. The Master as he passed the keeper's cottage picked out a few more hounds and laid them on. With the increased pack she was driven out over towards Clatworthy, and back again into West Hill. One more turn into Haddon, and out again by West Hill to Kingsbrompton, and on as if for Bridgetown. The Mater now came galloping back for the pack, and took them by Baronsdown into the Exe Valley, where he met the tufters running hard down by the river, and laying on the pack they soon settled to business, and ran her at a great pace down by Hele Bridge to Weir, and up again by Bury to the Higher Lodge, Baronsdown, and on through the whole length of the coverts to the Deer Park, where she turned right handed, and came on to the open Moor again. But hounds were pressing her too hard, and she soon had to turn down hill again, and in the water between Clammer and Harford she was killed after a first class run of three and a half hours.

No sooner were the last rights performed than it was reported to the Master that a hind that had been run hard by some of the hounds had gone by Baronsdown down into the Exe Valley, he decided therefore to lay the pack on to her line, and, although she had gone on some three quarters of an hour more, they were able to own to it, and after running it slowly down to the Exe, they brought her back up over the hill into Haddon again, down to Bury, out into the Exe Valley again, and under Baronsdown she was killed. Both these hinds were big ones, and were fairly run up, and the Master is to be congratulated on so satisfactory a performance.

On Saturday the meet was at Aldridge Mill and an even better day was in store for us than we were blessed with on Wednesday. The pack was kennelled in the building between Aldridge Mill and Spurway Mill which is so kindly placed at Mr Amory's disposal by that good sportsman Mr Cole of Warbrightsleigh. Bickham and Sydenham woods were first drawn, but the deer had evidently moved out of these covers and in Warpley they were found. Tufters first found a male deer from which they were quickly stopped. Then they found a fine hind and with her they went away on the best of terms, through Little Warpley Wood and near enough to the place the hounds were kennelled to enable the Master to whip them out and lay them on without the loss of two minutes. It was quickly apparent what scent was like; hounds dashed away and ran as if they were viewing their deer by Wheatland, Ash Cross, Mr Dunning's kennels, and the Garden of Eden to Chain Bridge, down the water and through the woods by Steart and

Emmaford almost to Worth, right handed by Washfield to Loxbeare and on to Calverleigh Cross, down to Cruwys Morchard and away to Witheridge, on over the rough moor to Bradford Ponds, and on past them to Rackenford, where at 3. 30 she was killed. It was then, for the first time, discovered that it was a male deer. Where we changed no one seems to know. The last place the deer was seen was going into Emmaford covert, and here hounds were certainly running a hind. Probably they changed in the coverts between that place and Washfield. Anyhow, the run was a grand one; hounds were running hard for four and a half hours, with only one check of a few minutes at the water by Bradford, and lucky were the few people out of the large field who started who were able to see the end of this great run

Jan 29th 1899

Sir John Amory's Staghounds met on Wednesday at Wonham by invitation, when a large and representative field were most hospitably entertained by Mr and Mrs Hollond. Amongst those present at the meet were The Lord Chancellor and Lady Halsbury, Viscount Tiverton, and Lady Evelyn Giffard, Mr Mackenzie (the hon sec of the hunt) and Mrs Mackenzie, Mrs Amory (on wheels), Mr and Mrs Harry Amory, Mrs and Miss Lazenby, Mr Renton and Mr Gerald Renton, Mr Ludivoc Amory, Misses North Row (2), Miss Spurway and Miss Hawthorn, Miss Coulson (2), the Rev. H. F. Holmes, Mr and Mrs Watkins Mr Moore (Dulverton), Mr John Daniel, Mr T. C. Yandle, Mr J. Selley, Mr Frank Yendell, Mr Haydon (Stoodleigh), Mr Tarr, Mr Jarvis Baily, Mrs Macalister, Mr R Hollond, Mr Nicholetts, Mr Troyte, Mr A. Blake and Miss Blake, Mr Pethick, Mr Down (Bampton), besides many more. Mr Yandle reported a deer in in Westbrooke Wood. The pack was sent on to Mr Cole's building near Spurway Mill, and tufters were put in at the north end of the covert. They soon found the deer, and ran down to Chain Bridge and out over the hill by Bampton to Exe Bridge. Here, turning left handed, they came down through Wonham Wood and across the Exe to Heightley Bridge. Tufters were now stopped, and the Master galloped off for the pack. At 12.30 the pack was laid on and ran up the valley at a good pace for about a mile, when they brought the line down to the water at the junction of two streams. Here hounds were at fault, and could own to nothing more until they had been cast up one of the streams for quite three miles. At this junction things looked critical, and just when it seemed likely that this long cast had been all in vain, and that the deer had gone up the other stream, we were rejoiced to hear first one hound, then another, pick up the line and run it cheerfully away over the big rough moors towards Anstey Station. The crisis in the day's sport was now over, and at an ever increasing pace hounds ran parallel to the Devon and Somerset Railway, past Anstey, and on to Molland Station, within 200 yards of which they fresh found their deer and ran back almost to Yeo Mill, near which they crossed the railway and the river, and then turning back again went up through the big coverts opposite Molland Station, and out on to Molland Moor. Hounds were now close to their deer, who led them at a great pace past Cuzzicombe Post, and across the moor as if for Hawkridge, but turning short of this was killed in a deep combe on the Anstey side of the hill, and after a wonderfully good run of three and a half hours, the greater part of which was very fast, while the early part, which was slow, was made interesting by the clever and persevering way in which the older hounds worked the water. Hounds and the greater part of the field had a seventeen mile trot home.

On Saturday the meet was at Bury Village, and in spite of very rough weather, a good day's sport was enjoyed. Hounds and horses went from Tiverton to Dulverton by special train. The pack was kennelled at the keeper's cottage on Yeaddon Moor. The tufters were taken out and four deer were at once found in the Deer Park. Most of the hounds went away with one of the hinds, and ran her down through the Great Woods, nearly to Clammer, and across the Haddeo and up through Haddon Wood, and out over Skilgate Common. Here tufters were stopped and the pack having been laid on, ran the line into Sir John Davies' coverts at Bittiscombe. Out of these coverts they brought the hunted hind and four fresh ones, all of which they raced back to Haddon. The leading hounds stuck to the hunted one and ran her to Bury, and out into the country for a bit, but she came back again into the big coverts, up and down which they ran her for a long time. Once or twice they changed on to fresh deer, but were stopped and laid on again upon the right line. Finally they fresh found her in the water under Harford Cleave, ran her up to the Deer Park and down the entire length of the coverts, almost in view. At Bury she stood to the water, and in the Exe, between Weir and Perry, she was killed. A very fine hind and a satisfactory ending to a hard day's work.

Feb 18th 1899

Sir John Amory's Staghounds met at Aldridge Mill on Saturday. Amongst those who were out we noticed Mr and Mrs Lazenby, Mr Renton, Mr Hollond, Miss Spurway, Mr Yandle, Mr John Selley, Mr Frank Yendell, Mr Cole, Mr Heywood, Mr J Blake and Mrs Blake, Mr Dunsford, Mr Baily, Mr Loosemore, Mr Beedell, Mr Channing, and several others. The harbourer reported that he had been unable to harbour a hind in any of the home coverts. It therefore became necessary to draw the most likely ones in the chance of finding some hind that had not happened to come out to feed during the night, and had thereby given the harbourer no clue to her whereabouts. The pack was, as usual, kennelled in Mr Cole's building near Spurway Mill, and with five and a half couple of tufters Mr Amory proceeded to draw Wormsworthy covert and Champles Cliff, and on down the valley, until just above Hangmans Hill hounds hit upon a line, and in a short time found their deer and ran him to Chain Bridge and up to Stuckeridge, down through Stuckeridge north cover, across the Exe, and on close to Mr Hollond's house, through the Wonham coverts, and down to the Exe, back again and out over as if for Bampton. Changing his mind, he came down to the river again and crossed it just below Exe Bridge, and went away with hounds close to him by Riphay Barton to Brushford, across the Devon and Somerset Railway, and into Aller Wood across the Barle and into Pixton Park, through which hounds raced almost in view, and down to the Exe just below Hele Bridge. Up the water and into Exe Cleave he went in view of the leading horsemen. There tufters were stopped, and as it was too far from where the pack was kennelled to make it possible to get them on in time to do any good it was decided to go back to Stoodleigh and draw again. Fresh hounds were taken out, and the woods between Chain Bridge and Halfpenny Bridge and the Steart Coverts were drawn without result; and it was not until hounds were thrown into the covert opposite Barrels House that any deer were found. Here they raised two stags, one a very good one and the other a small one. They ran together up the valley to Aldridge Mill and into Wheatland. Here Mr de Las

Casas met us with the pack, and they were laid on, on good terms with the deer, who went nearly to Mr Luxton's farm and then turned left handed back into the Iron Mill Stream valley, up to Stuckeridge and down into the Exe, down stream nearly to Chain Bridge, where hounds bayed him; and it was apparent for the first time what a magnificent stag he was, carrying as he did all his rights and three on top each side. As it would have been contrary to the spirit of the rules of staghunting to kill such a big stag at this time of year hounds were called off and taken away to draw again. At 4 o'clock a single hind was found in Stuckeridge covert, and she, after being rattled round the coverts for half an hour or so, apparently made up her mind that it would be wiser to leave them. Leave them she did, much to the surprise of most of the field, who forgot until too late to follow her example. From Stuckeridge, by Steart, East Stoodleigh, Dry Hill, Eastaps, Hatherland, and Washfield, hounds raced her until at Worth they were within a hundred yards of her. Down to the river just below the bridge she went, but hounds were so close to her that she dared not go in, and turning short back she led them over the park by Prescott to Broomhill, and then right handed almost up to Hensleigh, across the long drag and on by Coombe Butler to Duxmoor and Calverleigh Cross, and back again in Calverleigh Copse. Here, as it was 6.15 and quite dark, the Master stopped the hounds and took them home.

Feb 25th 1899

Thanks principally to Mr C. H. Basset, Sir John Amory's Staghounds have been again hunting on the Barnstaple side, the hounds being, as usual, kennelled at Westaway, the Barnstaple residence of Mr Basset. A very good beginning was made on Tuesday, when, in splendid weather, the meet took place at Chelfham, about four miles from Barnstaple. There was a large field. Deer were reported lying on the wooded spur of the hill, exactly opposite the meeting place, and in sight of the viaduct. Mr Amory took three couples of tufters, and three deer were almost immediately on foot. Pointing for a short distance down the valley towards Barnstaple, they turned sharply to the right, going up to Youlston Old Park and back through Long Timber Wood to Cot Hill, and through Cot Wood crossing the stream to Deerscombe at a good pace. The deer then pointed for Smithapark Woods, crossing the Lynton road on Loxhore Cot Hill, through Mr Comer Clarke's Covers and back again to Loxhore Cot Wood. Here the hind had left the two stags behind her. She was closely followed by the tufters, almost in sight and ran through the woods down the valley nearly to Barnstaple, turning shortly back by Kingdon Gardens, and coming down to the River Yeo and through the marches, when she again went up to the cover, through Coxleigh Wood and over the open fields at Sepscott, where she was viewed by the whole field. The pack was now brought up by Mr Amory and laid on. The hind by this time shewed signs of giving in, but unfortunately the hounds, in again going through the covers towards Loxhore Cot, changed on again to two stags and a hind. In coming through Cot Wood the deer separated, the pack keeping to the line of a fine stag. For a time he ran the same line as the hind in the morning to Smithapark, where he came down the Bratton Stream, being killed a few yards above the bridge at Bratton Cross. It was now four o'clock, the hounds having thus been running almost without a check for five hours. Both hounds and horse had apparently had enough. The stag had all his rights of brow, bay tray, and two on top on each side, his antlers shewing signs of having engaged in many a combat.

The hounds met half an hour later on Wednesday morning, and were again kennelled at Chelfham Mills. A report came that deer were lying in Woolley Wood, and no sooner were the tufters in than out came a three year old deer, accompanied by a male deer.

These were allowed to pass by, and the tufters were stopped. In another five minutes a second stag was out – a five or six year old. The tufters were stopped and within another ten minutes a grand stag was turned out, and, pointing for the Warren, the tufters were laid on, there being no hind in the cover, With a breast-high scent, they raced him through the Warren, past Cot Wood, and Long Timber, down the valley past Chelfham Bridge, where the pack was now taken out by the Master. At a rattling pace they went down to Collar Bridge and joined the tufters. They ran through Coxleigh Wood, and went on to Kingdon Gardens, and turned up to Roborough. At Kingdon Gardens a couple of young deer divided the pack, and the Master, holding on with his lot, went over Roborough and on to just at the edge of Westaway, crossing the stream under Westaway. Thence the stag went straight over Tutshill Wood, turning to his left, and sank the hill into a pond beyond Mr Goss's Anchor Mills. He then pointed his head for Upcott, went over Poles Hill, across the Braunton road on to the Marches. Here the whips brought up the portion of the pack that was divided, and, carrying a good head over the Marches, the stag got on to the bank of the Ilfracombe Railway, near the river, evidently intending to take a dip in the Taw; but the platelayers on the line caused him to alter his movements, and he continued along the Marshes and got close to Heanton Court, where he turned up the hill, close by Mr Sanders' farm at West Ashford. He then took to the road, and so ran pretty near to Heanton Church. When near the church he turned sharply to the right, and laid up in a larch plantation. This sudden turn caused a short check, which the hounds worked out beautifully, and presently with a crash they fresh found him in the larch plantation. They then never let him out of sight, and finally took him in a stream at Wrafton-in-the-Marsh on Mr Reed's farm. Although thoroughly beaten, he was able to defend himself, and he was secured after great difficulty by means of a rope, and being hauled partly up the wall beside of the stream he was dispatched by Mr Basset, the last rites being performed by Mr Joe Blake. The field gradually came up from different quarters, all expressing themselves exceedingly pleased with the run. From the time we found to the time we killed was only one and a half hours.

Feb 28th 1899

These hounds had two very good days sport on Wednesday they found plenty of deer in Haddon, and after a long days work killed one in the Haddeo, just above Bury. On Saturday they found a one horned stag near Witheridge, and had a very fine run of three hours after him; running him across the river and the South Western Railway, then back to the river again two miles to the north of Eggesford House. The hounds had a journey of over 20 miles home, and reached their kennels at nine o'clock.

March 4th 1899

Sir John Amory's Staghounds had a grand moor run on Friday. The pack were again put up at Chelfham near Barnstaple thanks to Mr Hill. Two hinds were supposed to be in Woolly Wood, and Mr Ian Amory was determined to try for them. He drew Woolly, however this proved blank, finally a three year old stag was found opposite Chelfham. The tufters ran this at a great pace to Woolly into Arlington, where he put up five hinds. One of these, with a calf, came back over Woolly, sank the water opposite Loxhore Cot, and with the tufters close at her, ran down the valley. The pack were laid on as she passed Chelfham Bridge. Below the railway she doubled back to Youlston covers, past Long Timber, when she made another double down the valley, and turned up by Lower Loxhore. Here she was fresh found, and ran at a very strong pace through Smithapark,

Tidycombe, and the adjoining wood, across the fields opposite Wistland Pound, past The Friendship Inn, heading for the moor by way of Chapman Burrows. This was right into the Exmoor country, and the field having a fine moor run. The hind was killed in the Doone Valley

Saturday was the last day of the four meets of Sir John Amory's Staghounds in the Loxhore Valley. It was a lovely morning, and a very large number of people, both mounted and dismounted assembled, at Chelfham Bridge near Barnstaple, to meet Mr Ian Amory. The pack in spite of three hard days' work that week, were looking fresh and quite ready for another such a run as the moor gallop they had on Friday from the same place. The hounds on Friday went out over Exmoor to Badgworthy, near Oare, where they killed a six year old hind after one of the best and fastest runs seen in modern days from this valley. Of course, this great run was subject of much conversation at Saturday's meet, and, with hopes of a similar gallop, the days work began by drawing Woolley (a very favourite covert for the red deer), with the tufters, who soon had a hind on foot she pointed straight for the Arlington Covers, which here are divided from those of Youlston by a small stream, and soon put up fresh deer, making plenty of work for the tufters. After bucketing various deer about for half an hour they drove a four year old stag away by himself on the eastern side of Arlington to Smithapark, and on to Wislandpound Farm to the cattle creep, not far from the Friendship Inn. This looked like going out from Exmoor, but something turned our stag, as he doubled right back, making for Woolley, through which he went to the water below Loxhore Cot and continued down the whole line of coverts. The pack, which had been taken on, here joined, and raced him down to Raleigh Wood, where he turned down to the meadows into the Yeo Valley, being killed by Snapper. The hounds having to leave in the afternoon, the Master did not draw again. Four days' hunting in one week, with four deer killed, not forgetting the great run on Friday, made Mr Amory's visit to the Loxhore Valley noteworthy.

Badgeworthy Wood & the Doone Valley.

March 11th 1899

The fixture for Sir John Amory's Staghounds on Wednesday last was at Haddon. Although there was a very sharp frost during the night, thanks to the bright, sunny morning, the going was fairly good and a large field turned out to meet the pack at the keepers lodge. Goss the Harbourer, took the Master with five and a couple of tufters to the Deer Park, the top of the Haddon covers. Soon herds of deer were seen in all directions, and after several rings round the Haddon and adjacent covers, a single hind was viewed under Baron's Down. Mr Amory quickly had the tufters on the line, and fresh found her in a little patch of gorse. She ran back to Haddon, up through the cover, and the whole length of Haddon Hill on to the keeper's lodge, where the pack was laid on. She then pointed for Venn Cross on the Devon and Somerset railway. Here some men turned her sharp back; she ran on and skirted to the right of Morebath village, and on to Burston Farm, then down to the Exe, and keeping to the water, passed the chemical works, under the railway bridge to the marsh below, where she was killed. Time 3 hours and 45 minutes. Most of those present at the meet were in at the death, and were highly pleased with the day's sport.

On Saturday the meet was at Gidley Arms near Meshaw. There was again a large field present including most of the farmers in the neighbourhood, who are staunch deer preservers. Deer had been seen about four miles away at Bycott, where Mr Amory trotted off with the pack. After kennelling, three couple of tufters were laid on a line, which they ran down the valley to Chittlehampton, where the hounds came up with the deer, seven in number, in a small cover. They headed back towards Bycott Farm where one singled himself out. The tufters were stopped and the pack laid on. Scent being good, they raced the deer on to Week Moors, through Week plantations pointing towards Witheridge. They ran on to Affeton Barton, where a slight check occurred. Mr Amory, getting his hounds together, soon put them on the line again, when they ran through the Worlington covers and down stream nearly to Stone Mills. Turning to the left they broke over the hill pointing towards Punsford Farm, which they crossed, heading for Lapford Forches, where they swung to the right, and on to Lapford Wood, where hounds were stopped, having changed on to fresh deer, and failing to again get on the line of our hunted stag. It being now four o'clock, the order was home. Hounds and horses had a hard day's work, having been kept going from 11.30.

A red deer stag in the river.

March 18th 1899

Sir John Amory's Staghounds met at Haddon on Wednesday among those present were Mr Renton, Mr Dunsford, Mrs Lazenby, Messrs de Las Casas (4) Mrs Patten, Messrs, Hancock (Wiveliscombe) (3), Mr Capel, Mr Hollond, Miss Macalister, Miss North Row, Mr and Mrs Henson, Miss Spurway, Miss Hawthorne, Miss Blake, Mr J. Blake, and many others. The pack were kennelled at the keeper's lodge, Goss, the Harbourer, took Mr Amory with five couple of tufters to West Hill Wood, where several deer were soon on foot. A hind was viewed on Haddon Hill, which the tufters ran on through the Haddon covers nearly to Bury, where she crossed the road and back through the covers opposite Haddon on to the Deer Park, and then to Skilgate Common, giving us hopes of leaving for the open country; but turning back, she again went into Haddon, where, getting with other deer, she ran with a hind and calf the whole length of Haddon Hill towards Bury, where she again singled out and the pack were laid on just above Bury Village. They ran back to West Hill, through Haddon, where fresh deer were continually getting up before hounds, and it seemed impossible to keep a line, but after persistent perseverance on the part of Mr Amory the hounds were got on the line of an apparently beaten hind, which ran through Storridge, back to and over Haddon, and on to Morebath where she was killed just above the fishponds of Mr Harrod, at 4.40pm. It was a long tiring day, both for horses and hounds, they having been kept continually on the go from 1.30.

On Saturday a good field turned out to meet the pack at Spurway Mill. Those present were the Master (Sir John Amory), Mr Ian Amory, Messrs, A. and E. de Las Casas, Mr, Mrs, and Miss Lazenby, Misses Spurway (2), Mr Renton, Miss Amory, Miss Molly Amory, Miss Coulston, Mr R. Beedell, Mr Tom Yandle, and two sons, Mr Channing, Miss Hawthorne, Mr Worth, Mr Dunsford, Mr J. Blake, Miss Blake, Mr March-Phillipps, Messrs Snow brothers (2), Mr T. Bellew, Messrs T. Haydon and son and a great many others. Miles, the harbourer, reported that a herd of deer were moving on towards Rackenford. Hounds being kennelled, Mr Amory trotted off with three and a half couple of tufters and laid them on a line. Just beyond Broadmead Cot we very soon came up with a herd of 13 deer lying in Withy Croft; they made off over Lower Meadown on to Sydenham, where they divided, four of them turning back towards Meadown cover, where the tufters ran. One deer now singled out and ran through Trowcombe Wood, Warbrightly Covers to Aldridge Mill, where the pack was laid on. The deer pointed for Coleford Water, but turning, ran back to the valley under Aldridge Mill and right down to Chain Bridge, through the covers to Cove, where he ran a ring back to Duvale, turning sharp back to Cove again on to New Bridge, through Washfield Covers, taking the water at Fairby, he ran down the river to Lithecourt and on under Worth House, through the lawn, skirting Palmers village, on to Lurley. Then over Mr J. Butts and Courtenay Farms, pointing for Loxbeare Barton, through which we ran close by the farmhouse, then to Gibbett Moor down to Blatchworthy Covers, under Rifterwood to Coleford Water, going down stream to Aldridge Mills, again running down to Chain Bridge, where our deer went to water and was killed after one of the best runs of the season. Time, three and a half hours. One of the most prominent during the run, and who was also in at the death, was the worthy Master, Sir John Amory.

April 1st 1899

Sir John Amory's Staghounds met at Marsh Bridge near Dulverton on Tuesday last, and the few who braved the elements were rewarded by a first rate day's sport which indeed, was no more than they deserved, for the weather was so bad that it seemed probable hounds would not even put in an appearance at the fixture, much less hunt. There was a piercing north east wind, tempered at some frequent intervals with heavy snowstorms, which, while they lasted, made it impossible to see hounds, unless one was almost in the middle of them. Small, indeed, was the field which met the Master and whippers-in on their arrival at the meet, consisting as it did of four farmers of the right sort and your present correspondent. Others in later on, but never during the day were there as many as twenty people with the hounds. The pack was kennelled at Higher Coombe, the residence of Mr W. L. Webber, a staghunter and good friend of deer of many years standing. Six couples of hounds were taken out, and with them we trotted on to South Hill Cover, a small larch covert on the edge of Winsford Hill. No sooner were tufters in on one side than a large herd of deer were seen to leave on the other, and made for the allotments. There could not have been fewer than thirty five deer in the herd mostly hinds, so far as I could see through the blinding snow storm that was then raging. Tufters were soon out after them, and in the covert below the keeper's house on Winsford Hill they separated four hinds from the herd, and the majority of the tufters settling on to their line, drove them across the moor into the Devils Punchbowl and up the steep face on the opposite side, along the length of Winsford Hill, at the extreme end of which they almost ran into several more deer, possibly part of the large herd we had run into the allotments; but fortunately they did not join them, but bore round the edge of the moor as if for the Barle Valley, left handed again, and back over the heather into the allotments. Here hounds bustled about a good bit, and finally forced one of the largest hinds away by herself. Over Ashway Side and down to Tarr Steps they ran her almost in view, across the Barle and over the ridge by Hawkridge, almost up to Slade Bridge, then down stream under White Rocks, close past a herd of stags, down the whole length of the coverts fringing this great valley to Marsh Bridge. Here tufters were stopped and the pack laid on; the hind had turned short back and had made her way into the Barle Valley coverts again. Hounds quickly settled to work and fresh found her in the company of two or three others. They were however, soon stopped off the fresh deer and laid on to the line of the hunted one; she then turned down stream, and making her way over Court Down, led us into the valley of the Exe through Exe Cleave, and down to the river by Barlynch Abbey. Here ensued a very pretty piece of water work. The Master cast hounds down stream for a short distance, but apparently soon made up his mind that she had not gone down, and made a long cast up stream. Hounds seemed to understand perfectly what was wanted of them, and, half the pack on each side of the water, they raced up the river, until near Chilly Bridge they hit off the line where the hind had left the water, quite a mile above where she entered it, and running straight up through the end of the steep covert, fresh found her on the top, and raced her back, sometimes in and sometimes out of the covert, until they brought her down to the river again, just above Hele Bridge. Down the water she went, with hounds close to her to Weir. Then across the main road, up through Bury Wood and on to Morebath; but hounds were pressing her too hard, and she was forced to turn down again, and, with hounds almost in view, she made for the Exe, and was killed just above Exebridge at 4.15, having been found at 11.45. By this time the snow was covering the ground. It looked as if we were in for a heavy downfall, so those of us who lived at a distance were glad enough to start on our homeward journey, and by the time your correspondent reached home snow shoes would have been more use to him than the tired hunter he was riding.

April 15th 1899

Sir John Amory's Staghounds met again in their own country on Saturday last after some weeks hunting in the Devon and Somerset, where they have been very successful, having killed, I hear, no less than 20 deer north of their own boundary. A large field, numbering between 80 and 100 horsemen, turned out to welcome them on their arrival at West Worlington. At eleven o'clock the Master appeared with the hounds, who looked in the pink of condition and certainly none the worst for the hard work they have been doing lately. The Harbourer reported seven stags to be in Weekson Wood, and thither hounds were taken, being kennelled at Week Farm. The deer were soon found, and tufters settled on to a fine stag and ran him in full view of the whole field to Week Cover and back to Bycott. Here tufters were stopped and the pack was brought on, and getting away on good terms with him they ran at a pace that was too great for many of those who were out by Stone Moor, Chawleigh Barton Wood, Chulmleigh, to the big covers opposite Eggesford House, the residence of Lord Portsmouth. When he had led us almost to the end of these covers, he seemed to change his point and turned sharp back. Hounds were not to be put off the line by this manoeuvre, but, working out the double as closely as a pack of harriers, they drove him back past Eggesford Station, across the river, and away by Chulmleigh. Here the pace was even faster than ever and it was all that most of us could do to see which way the best mounted members of the field were going, and they in their turn were hard put to it to keep the Master in sight, and how he managed to keep in touch with his hounds at the pace they were going, over this most difficult country, was a matter of wonder to all of us. However he did manage to do this, and after the fastest two hours run that it has ever been my good fortune to ride through, he reached the River Mole with his hounds by South Molton Road Station, and found the stag in the water in front of them. The stag went down the river for about a quarter of a mile and so into the Taw. Here he was taken. The next business was to get home, hounds must have had over 20 miles back to kennels, and your correspondent not less. "Mid Devon."

May 13th 1899

The number of deer killed far exceeds that of any previous year, the Devon and Somerset and Sir John Amory's Staghounds have together killed 176 head. When one thinks of the fears excited when Lord Ebrington in one season killed 101, and one is amused to reflect how groundless they were, and how right the noble Master was, to act upon his own opinion, and to refuse to be influenced by those (and they were many) who warned him that he was reducing the deer to a number far below what was necessary if hunting was to continue. I fancy I can see and hear some of our deer regular old followers in their clubs in London, saying,"Ah! This can never last", but I venture a prophecy, even in my own country, and I undertake to say that, at all events for another year it will last, and that it will be quite safe and even advisable that a similar number should be accounted for next year. A letter or two has lately been written to the papers about the cruelty of spring hind hunting. It is a pity that people, totally ignorant of the conditions of the sport, and the enormous difficulties associated with carrying it on, should not seek information from trustworthy sources before rushing into print. As a staghunter of over forty years, I feel entitled to speak on this subject with some authority, and I made bold to assert that the sport as at present conducted is as humanely managed by both Masters as it is possible for it to be, and I go further and say I cannot think of any mode of reducing the deer (although I am quite acquainted with the details and effects on netting and shooting), which would, from the point of humanity, be, on the whole, as an improvement on the present method. If the writer of one of the above mentioned letters were to pay us a more protracted visit, and get into communication with the farmers, he would know why our respected correspondent "Snowstorm" constantly states in his reports the number of deer killed; it is the point of greatest interest to our local farmers. On the way home from hunting, what is the first question asked by the man one meets?- whether it be tenant, farmer, or labourer (and whichever he may be you may be sure that he has the true west country love of and almost veneration for staghunting). It is "Did 'ee kill un?" If that is satisfactorily answered, the next question may be "Had 'ee a good run?" But the order and relative importance of the two questions is never varied.

One cannot in the face of present circumstances be too grateful to Mr Ian Amory for the help given by his most sporting pack, and it is gratifying to see how warmly Mr Sanders has accepted this aid, and, by his frequent presence and help, has done much to assist the visitors in his own country; this shows how friendly and how sportsmanslike are the relations existing between the two Masters. With the two packs as now conducted we may look forward to much good sport in the future, and in the course of only two or three years a less arduous time of it for the hunt servants and officials. The special train run by the G W R during the season for the benefit of the Tiverton contingent have proved most useful, and have been highly appreciated; our thanks are due to the officers both at Tiverton and Dulverton for their courteous and prompt attention to our wants.

Friday, April 28th was Mr Amory's last meet for the season at Mounsey Hill Gate by invitation, and a good number of his followers were present, including Messrs de Las

Casas(3), Renton(2), Mackenzie(2), Poyntz(4), Mr Unwin, M. F. H., Miss March-Philipps, Mrs Bellew, Mr and Mrs Lazenby, Miss Chichester, Miss Slack, the Misses North Row, Messrs Dunsford, Coulson, Evered, Moore, Le Gassick Bellew, Harding, Lovelace, Tarr, Tucker, Thomas, Brokenhurst, Mr and Mrs Rook, S. Moore, Webber, Moore, jun., Moyle Pethick, Pugsley, Pring, and several others, Hounds were kennelled at Higher Combe, and four and a half couples of tufters taken to the allotments, where in a few minutes four deer were afoot before them; these ran in a ring to the Punchbowl, and disturbed there a herd of eleven, which led us out nearly to Comer's Gate, but ultimately, a hind was separated, which made for the keeper's cottage, and away to South Hill, where the pack was laid on. Being close to the hind, we ran at a good pace past Siderfin and Monschanger to Broford and Chilly Bridge, where she tried several dodges, and started a fresh herd, but the leading hounds were close to her, and they fairly pushed her out and down stream to the weir above Barlynch Abbey where she was killed at one o'clock after a fast hours work. Meanwhile, three couples of hounds were running another hind above us, so Mr Amory put on the pack again at once, and hounds ran well to Hele Bridge, and across back through Exe Cleave to Chilly Bridge, up past Broford and South Hill, across to the Barle at Bradley, running down the Parsonage Down, and under Hawkridge to Castle Bridge, where hounds fresh found their hind in the water. We went away over Molland Common to Molland Moor Gate, and away to Gourt Farm, where this second hind was killed at about three o'clock, after two hours run without a check

September 23rd 1899

About 200 horsemen, cyclists, and pedestrians attended the opening meet of Sir John Amory's Staghounds at Stoodleigh Court on Saturday. All were hospitably entertained by Mr E. H. Dunning, J. P.,C. C., refreshments being supplied in the dining hall and on the lawn. Those present included the Master Mr Ian Amory, the whips Messrs A. and J. C. de Las Casas, Mr E. H. Dunning, Mrs Dunning and party (in carriage), Misses and Master Dunning, Mr and Mrs L. de Las Casas, Mr H. Amory, Mr J. R. Hollond, Miss Hollond, Mrs Froude Bellew, Mr F. B. Dunsford, Miss Poyntz, Miss Nelder, Miss Francis, Miss Coulson, Miss Macalister, Mr and Miss Lazenby, Mr and Miss Chichester, Dr and Mrs Barnes (Petworth), Mr and Mrs Pethick, Mr and Mrs J. Jarvis-Baily, Mr S. Webber, Mr F. Reed (W. Australia), Mr and Mrs W. T. Watkins, Mr G. Cosway (Dewsbury), Mr W. J. Llewellyn and Miss Llewellyn and party, Miss Moore, Mr and Miss Renton, Mrs Ellerton and party, Mrs Moysey and party, Mr J. Blake, Miss Blake, Mr W. H. Lancaster, Dr Welsford, Rev. E. M. Russell and party, Mr T. Hayton, Mr J. Farrant, Miss Walker, Messrs Rowcliffe, Ayre (2) Hallifax (2), Long, Channing, Butt, and many others. Six couples of hounds began tufting about 11.30 in Bradley Wood it was known that a fine stag and some hinds were hidden. The stag, a particularly large one, was roused and forced into open country, eventually making its way to Stuckeridge, crossing the lawn close to Stuckeridge House. The quarry then went over into the Exe Valley, and it was thought that it

Mr J. C. de Las Casas – one of the whips of Sir John Amory's Staghounds.

would come round again towards Anstey, as stags have frequently done on previous occasions. The pack was therefore unkennelled and taken towards Anstey, but nothing of stag or tufters was seen. There was a strong wind blowing and the country was very difficult, and no one was up with the tufters, which were seen, when without a field and half of the stag, near Dulverton Station, by Mr Nelder, who stopped them, put them in the Carnarvon Arms, and rode off towards Anstey. The pack was next taken to Dulverton, but they could not own the scent, and what had promised to be a fine day's sport was abruptly brought to a termination. The stag, it was afterwards discovered, had made towards Haddon instead of Anstey. During the run an unfortunate and unavoidable accident occurred. The horse ridden by Mr Frank Reed (a visitor from Australia staying at the Palmerston Hotel, Tiverton) bolted as the result of its bit breaking, and collided violently with the animal ridden by Mr J. C. de Las Casas, one of the whips. Mr Las Casas was thrown heading from his saddle and fell heavily to the ground, but beyond the severe shaking he was uninjured, and was able to remount. Mr Reed was unhurt, and neither of the animals appears to have been injured.

Sept 30th 1899

The first meet this season of this popular pack in the Barnstaple district took place on Saturday at Chelfham Bridge about four miles from Barnstaple. A little rain had fallen in the early hours auguring well for good scent, and although the wind was rather cutting and the clouds showed an occasional tendency to discharge themselves, the air was crisp and delightfully bracing. By eleven o'clock there was a large crowd of horsemen, cyclists, and pedestrians, with a plentiful sprinkling of carriages. Among those at the meet mounted, besides the Master Mr Ian Heathcoat-Amory were Messrs de Las Casas (whips), Mr C. H. Basset, Captain Curzon, Miss Curzon, Mr E. J. Soares, Mrs Eyton, Mr W. H. Speke, Mr Nicholas Snow (Oare), Captain Laurie, Mrs F. H. Toller, Miss

Tom Yandle from Riphay near Dulverton, who came down with Sir John Amory's Staghounds and was harbourer for them while they were in the Barnstaple district.

Blake and Mr Blake (Tiverton), Messrs J. Comer Clarke, S. N. Heard (Bideford), D. J. C. Bush (South Molton), W. E. Pitts-Tucker, A. F. Seldon, H. Incledon-Webber, J. Incledon-Webber, J. Cole (Bideford), R. Clogg, F. Clogg, R. Longstaffe and C. Longstaffe (Morthoe) G. Litson, J. List, C. H. Sperry (Isle of Wight), Smyth Bros (Wistlandpound), J. Fry, Gillard, A. M. A. Bernus (Frankford), R. Penhale, Raby (Sen. and Junr), W. L. Ashton, Chamings (Coxleigh), J. Berry, Ash, Ridd and S. Reavell. The Master lost no time in setting the field in motion. The tufters were taken away to Mill Wood. It was not until ten minutes past one that the tufters were successful in their quest, though a three year old had been turned out previously. The stag which went away was a fine eight year old. He at once pointed for Marwood. Here there was a slight check, but a cast near the church resulted in the recovery of the scent, and a rattling gallop resulted towards Braunton and over Braunton Common. The stag made his way through the village of Wrafton by the post office, closely followed. He was eventually found in Wrafton Marsh, near Mr Perryman's house. The end was not yet, for he gave a great deal of trouble before being killed by going up and down the stream. He finally succumbed about a quarter past four in sight of a goodly portion of the field.

Sir John Amory's Staghounds concluded their brief visit to Barnstaple on Monday. Again the meet was at Chelfham, and the field was very large. There was little doubt as to sport, as many stags have been viewed in the covers adjoining the Yeo. The tufters were put into Pitt Mill Wood, and quickly roused a deer, and the pack was immediately laid on. He made for Smithapark and Button Covers. Here a change over undoubtedly took place, as the pack divided. A five year old now went away, and after two or three doubles returned to Smithapark, and headed toward Lower Loxhore. He was plainly viewed in the stream near Bratton Cross. His course was now down through the Marches and covers, pointing for Shirwell. He went through Youlston Covers, and traversed the bottoms to Pitt Farm and on to Pilton Bridge. Here he was within Barnstaple Borough, which he never left. Doubling back up the valley, he went through Frankmarsh and across Derby road and jumped the high wall of the meadows adjoining the cemetery. He then ran down to Derby proper, and returning to Zephyr Cottage he tried to jump the cemetery wall, but fell back. He eventually was taken in Mr Bryant's poultry yard, adjoining the high road and cemetery, and proven a fine stag, with brow, bay, and tray, and two and three on top.

Riders waiting to board the Barnstaple and Lynton train.

Oct 28th 1899

Sir John Amory's Staghounds met at Chelfham near Barnstaple, on Tuesday. There was a very large field. A heavy stag was roused in Coxleigh Wood. After taking to the stream for some time, he returned to cover, and it is conjectured, turned out a five year old, which at once headed for Exmoor by Whitefield and Longstone. Time was lost in getting up the pack at such a distance, but the line was maintained to Oare Oak, on the Somerset side of the moor. It was now getting dark and Mr Amory called off, after a clinking run of four hours

Nov 4th 1899

The second meet in connection with the latest visit of Sir John Amory's Staghounds to the Barnstaple district was at Chelfham on Friday. The weather was very unfavourable, with the result that the field which met Mr Ian Amory and the whips (Messrs de Las Casas) was not so large as that of Wednesday. The neighbouring covers were drawn without success, but there was a find at Smythapark. Getting away promptly, the stag travelled round Arlington, and then made off in the direction of Barnstaple. When just the other side of Roborough it turned, and doubling back headed for Loxhore, where it was eventually killed. It was a very fine specimen. For the concluding meet on Saturday the hounds were kennelled at Loxhore Cott. It was a fine morning, and the field on this occasion was a large one. The tufters were taken to a warren belonging to Sir Edward Chichester, at Shirwell, where a hind was soon roused. She made up under Bratton on to Smythapark, where a stag went away and pointed towards the moors. Laid on under Wistlandpound, the pack crossed the Bratton road, and afterwards proceeded in turn to Longstone and Woodbarrow. Here the stag which had apparently taken a rest was caught up and it dashed off just in front of the hounds. Travelling at a great pace, the course lay through Oare Oak, Brendon, straight to Mr Nicholas Snow's Deer Park. Here the field had the satisfaction of witnessing a large herd of deer, but sport for

Woody Bay Station.

the day was at an end, the stag having become merged with the herd, and showing no inclination to restart. The run, however, had been a capital one, having lasted without a break for a couple of hours. Mr Amory returned to Tiverton with the hounds a little later in the day.

Nov 25th 1899

Mr Amory took the staghounds to Higher Coombe on Saturday for hind hunting. There were a good number of sportsmen present, but owing to the thick, hazy day, they did not see very much sport. A number of deer were seen near Higher Coombe, but turned out to be nearly all stags. Eventually the tufters got on the line of a hind and hunted to Hawkridge, and on to Winsford Hill and Comer's Gate. The line was carried down the Barle Valley to Tarr Steps, and thence to the Allotments on Winsford Hill. Here the pack was laid on, at three o'clock, and went down to the Barle Valley again. Unfortunately the quarry joined a number of stags which were lying near by, so hounds were called off and taken home.

Dec 2nd 1899

Mr Ian Amory journeyed with his hounds to Ash Cross on Saturday, and there were present Messrs de Las Casas (2), Mr E. H. Dunning, Mrs Dunning and party, Mr and Mrs Lazenby, Capt Amory, Mr and Miss Blake, Mr S. Webber, Mrs Watkins, and many others. Hounds were kennelled at Spurway Mill, and Mr Amory with six couple of tufters drew the covers by Hangmans Hill. A hind and calf were soon on foot, and the hind ran to Chain Bridge, but eventually turned back to where she was found. She then set her head for Spurway Mill, and led tufters through Waspleigh and Throwcombe to Sydenham, where they were stopped and the pack was laid on. Scent was exceptionally good, and the pace over Rackenford Moor was a cracker. The quarry then made for Hayesdon and then pointed for Knowstone, but seemed to change her mind, turned back to Hayesdon Moor and headed for Bickham. After leading hounds nearly to the Red Deer, she almost made Brushford, and skirting the Devon and Somerset Railway turned to the right and ran down by the Exe to the covert under Hightclere Weir, where she soiled. Mr Amory stopped the hounds to get the pack together, and subsequently laid on again by Highclere Mill, and ran through the covers down to Wonham, crossed the road and river by Wonham over Stuckeridge, across the road above Chain Bridge and through the covers opposite Duvale, when hounds got on terms with her, brought her to bay in the Exe where she was killed.

Jan 13th 1900

Sir John Amory's Staghounds met at Ash Cross on Saturday. A large field turned out to meet them, amongst them we noticed besides Mr Amory and Mr A. de Las Casas and Mr J. C. de Las Casas, Mrs Ludovic Amory, Mr Dunning, Misses Dunning (2), Mr Frank Dunning, Misses Chichester (3), Mr Lazenby, Mr Dunsford, Mr Blake, Miss Blake, Miss Spurway, Mr Bailey, Mr Yandle, Mr J. Yandle, Mr Selley, Mr Butt, Mr Headon, Mr Blackmore, Mr Pring, Mr W. Haydon, and many others. Hounds were kennelled in Mr Cole's buildings near Spurway Mill, and with five couple of tufters Mr Amory proceeded to draw Rifton Wood. Several deer were soon in front of hounds, and one was singled out and driven by Blatchworthy to Waspley Wood, and down the valley near Spurway

Mill, where tufters were stopped, and the pack laid on at 11.30. Hounds ran down the valley nearly to Chain Bridge, and after several turns round the large Stoodleigh coverts went away to the left of Oakford and on almost to the Red Deer; then a right handed turn and hounds ran at such a pace that not many of us knew exactly how we got there, but we found ourselves at the Exe by Heightley Weir, with the pack streaming away on the opposite side of the river. On we went by Riphayes to Brushford, then turned right handed and crossed the Devon and Somerset Railway by Dulverton Station, across the river on to Morebath. Up the big Coombe by Mr Harrod's fishponds they ran it such a pace that it was all the horses could do to live with them into the Pitscombe Covers and down the valley for a couple of miles; then to the left and away almost to Chipstable, then right handed to Waterrow Bridge, where this strong deer was killed. It was one of the best runs of the season, lasting just four hours from the time tufters first found, with no check to speak of. "Triviator."

Jan 20th 1900

The meet was at Ash Cross, Stoodleigh, on Wednesday, and among those present were Mr Ian Amory, Messrs de Las Casas, Mr and Mrs T. O. Lazenby, Mr F. Dunning, Miss Dunning, Miss Chichester, Miss Blake, Miss Spurway, Messrs Renton, Hollond (2) Yendell, and many others. No deer had been harboured, but a single hind was discovered below Aldridge Mills. The tufters drove her round the covert, up by Colford Bottom, and back by the kennels, where the pack was laid on. Hounds at once got her away at a good pace through Waspleigh and on to Sydenham, back through the valley to Coleford Water, and then on past Chain Bridge and Oakford Bridge. Down the valley once more the hind went, and reaching Cove Cleave made through the Cleave in the direction of Knightshayes. Then on to Van Post, and reached Palfreys where she was dispatched in the farmyard.

Feb 10th 1900

On Wednesday the meet was at the Gidley Arms near Meshaw, a large number of ladies and gentlemen being present. The tufters worked through Week Covert, finding a couple of hinds at half past eleven. After driving them up through Bycott for some distance they came back to Cheldon. Here the tufters were stopped, and the pack laid on. Running down the Cheldon Valley to Chulmleigh, then back again and up the road, the pack went in the direction of Lapford Coverts, after passing Thelbridge and Eggesford. Then the deer separated, the largest hind coming back towards Chulmleigh, with hounds hard on her track. She went up the valley to Worlington, through Barrons Wood and Witheridge down to Merrifieldhayes. Then down to the Cruwys Morchard Covers by the water and over Holmead Farm, past Sidborough, and into Rifton Wood. Although hounds were close to their quarry fresh deer were put up. And before the pack could be got together again it was too dark to continue. The run was one of the fastest this pack has had for a long time

March 3rd 1900

The weather was so bad on Tuesday at Ash Cross that Mr Ian Amory had serious thoughts of giving up for the day. It cleared, however, and a pretty day's hunting was the reward. The pack was kennelled at Aldridge Mills, and with five couple of tufters two hinds were found at Rifton, and went away across the moor through Blatchworthy, Witnoll, Tidderson Moor, Hilltown, Cruwys Morchard, Merryfieldhayes, and back over

Hounds and stag in the river.

Taking out the tufters from farm buildings.

nearly the same line to Rifton, down to Coleford Bottom and Aldridge Mills. The tufting was the best of it, the pace out and back being a "cracker". The pack was laid on at the mills, and came away down the valley. Then up towards Stuckeridge and down by the bridge, away down the valley to Chain Bridge and up over to Steart; back to Halfpenny Bridge, past Duvale, and on down to the valley to Emmerford, where this fine hind was taken at about two o'clock. Amongst those out were the huntsman Mr Ian Amory, the whips Messrs de Las Casas, Captain Amory, Mr Hill, Miss Hawthorne, Miss Spurway, Mr Haydon, Mr Yandle, Mr Renton, Mr Dunsford, and Miss Chichester.

These hounds met by invitation at Haddon on Saturday at 10.15, but it was 11.30 before operations could be commenced, for a thick fog enveloped the moor. With six couple of tufters Mr Amory tried the deer park, and found a couple of hinds, which went away down as far as Bury, and one came back over Haddon Hill. The pack was laid on, and eventually the hind, which went down to the water, was taken at Harpford Mill. A second hind was found in the deer park, and did as everybody hoped she would – raced away over Skilgate Common, then on to Battiscombe, by the ponds, over to Chipstable, through the coverts, and away to Wiveliscombe, which she passed on the left, and was killed at 5 o'clock at Woodlands, a farm about three miles beyond Wivesliscombe. A very find hind indeed. Those who enjoyed this fine day's sport were Mr Ian Amory, Messrs de Las Casas, Mrs Simpson, Mrs Bellew, Mr Brown, Mr Hill, Mr Gilham, Mr Renton, Mr Nelder, Mr Earley, Mr Tapp, Mr Woodberry, and a few others.

These hounds met at Haddon on Tuesday morning. It was impossible to start hunting until noon, when, unfortunately a large number of the field had left for home. Then tufting commenced with five and a half couple of tufters in Haddon Wood, and a hind going away over the moor went the whole length of Haddon to Stuckeridge, where the pack was laid on. Here the hind went away left handed and passing Upton ran as far as Withiel Florey, where the field heard of Cronje's surrender. Hounds raced their quarry down to Bury Village, and climbed the top of Haddon Hill, killing at Bury at four o'clock.

March 10th 1900

On Saturday the staghounds journeyed by train to Dulverton to hunt Haddon, where Mr Amory was met by a good sporting field. Five couple of tufters were laid on at Haddon Wood, where a hind had been harboured, and she was soon moving down to Bury. She came back through the whole length of Haddon Coverts, and then the pack was laid on. Making a big ring close to Withiel Florey and Kings Barton, the hind ran once more into Haddon Wood, where a short check ensued. Hounds soon picked up the line again and went off by Harford Cleeve, past Bury Village and up over the hill, as if going to the Exe Valley. Here the quarry turned right handed and came down to the water again, with hounds close behind her. She went straight up the valley, and was taken about half past two just above Harford Mill. The pack was subsequently laid on a hind which was seen going over Haddon Hill, but as they ran into a lot of stags, and hounds were whipped off for the day.

March 17th 1900

The staghounds met at Haddon on Saturday, a good field being out. Amongst them were Mr Ian Amory, Messrs de Las Casas (2), Renton Capel, Miss Hawthorne, Miss Spurway, Miss Blake, Messrs J. Blake, Hill, Harley, Tapp, Woodberry, Nelder, and others. Fred Goss the Harbourer had a single hind lying in a fir plantation, and four couple of tufters sent her off over Haddon Hill and back into Haddon Wood, right through the Deer Park, where she doubled back to Harford Cove and on through Haddon. The pack was laid on at Upton at 11.30, and going through Upton Village, across the rough moors, turned right handed and came back to Skilgate Common. Here the hind was fresh found, and went straight down to Sir John Davie's property, ran the whole length of the coverts, and then turned back right over the same line to Haddon down by Bury Village, and back to Harford, over the hill to Skilgate Common. Then coming back by the Deer Park and ran the whole length down to Bury, meeting her fate here at 4 o'clock.

Sir John Amory's Staghounds are again paying a visit to Barnstaple, the pack being kennelled at Westaway, where Mr Amory, the Master, and Messrs Las Casas, the whips, are the guests of Mr C. H. Basset. The meet on Tuesday was at Chelfham, near Barnstaple, and there were present a great many on horseback, including several ladies, and others in carriages or on bicycles. The pack were left at the mills, and Mr Amory with two couples of tufters proceeded to Youlston Wood, where it was reported by Sir Edward Chichester's keeper a large number of deer were lying. The moment the tufters entered five hinds and a stag were aroused. Four of the hinds went back over Youlston Park to Coxleigh, while a hind and the stag went up the valley towards Cot Hill. Both deer ran through Cott and Woolly Woods on the top of Loxhore Cot Hill, and thence towards Wistland Pound, still being run by the tufters. Afterwards crossing the Lynton railway embankment they entered the Forest of Exmoor, from where, had the pack been laid on, a grand run would have been obtained. But owing to the Devon and Somerset Staghounds pack meeting at Highbray on Wednesday, Mr Amory decided not to interfere with Mr Sanders' sport. The stag was turned left handed down the Kentisbury Valley and towards Eastdown. Meanwhile the pack was brought up by Mr Las Casas and laid on at Rectory Cott near Loxhore. They subsequently ran into Wooly Wood, where unfortunately were a large number of deer, and it now late in the day and Mr Amory decided to collect his and proceed homeward.

March 24th 1900

The meet on Wednesday was at Loxhore. There was a good assembly, but not so large as on Tuesday. The hounds were kennelled at Loxhore, and Mr Amory took the tufters to Long Timber Wood, where a stag was soon found. He came down to Bratton Cross, where he was turned still further down the valley by a steam roller. He soiled in the Bratton stream, and then turned up the valley towards Stoke Rivers. The tufters were stopped, and the pack laid on. The hounds ran at good speed through Stoke Wood, turning left over the hill to Button Wood, and through Mr Comer Clarke's, Smithapark, on to Loxhore Cot, to Eastdown Rectory, going nearly up to Eastdown Church. He turned short back coming down the water under Woolly Wood, to Loxhore Cot, where he was killed in one of the cottager's gardens. He was a good stag, probably about six years old, with two on top on each side, and all his rights.

On Saturday Sir John Amory's Staghounds met at Spurway Mill, Stoodleigh. With four couples of tufters, Mr Ian Amory drew for a hind seen at Waspleigh in the morning, and hounds hunted a deer to Rifton, where it ran several rings around the cover, and came down towards Chain Bridge, where the pack was laid on at about 12.30 at the keepers cottage. Hounds ran down towards Chain Bridge, but turned right handed, and came back towards Aldridge Mills again. The deer then went on Rackenford Moor, and across towards Knowstone, over Knowstone Moor, and right on to Creacombe, where the hunted game wheeled round left handed and came back to within a stone's throw of Witheridge Moor, across Temple Bottom, on past the blacksmith's shop, and away by Witheridge Church. Thongsleigh was next passed, and then down the valley to Huntland Wood, where hounds fresh found, and hunted one by Seven Crosses and down towards the River Dart, but the deer seemed to change its mind and turned left handed, and came down to the Exe instead to Ashley. Here it remained swimming up and down for about half an hour. Mr Mark Goodland, junr., of Tiverton, who was present, pluckily swam in after the deer and dispatched it. And with assistance brought the deer to land, he being none the worse for his wetting. It was one of the grandest runs of the season, the point being over ten miles, and the deer was running for six hours.

Sept 22nd 1900

Sir John Amory's Staghounds met at Stoodleigh Court, as usual on the opening day of the season – Saturday last, The large field that turned up at the meet were received by Mr and Mrs Dunning with the utmost hospitality. A hunt breakfast was provided, and full justice was done to it by many hungry sportsmen. About 11.15 hounds looking in the pink of condition and a credit to their kennel huntsman, moved off and were kennelled in that most convenient of buildings near Spurway Mill, belonging to Mr Cole, of Warbrightsleigh. Mr Amory took out five couple of tufters and drew Wormsworthy Wood. Soon hounds were heard running something, but when they came out with two hinds in front of them they were quickly stopped and taken back to draw again. Within a few minutes they were at work, and this time it was seen that two stags were before them. Sticking to one of them they ran him down to Hangmans Hill and then up the valley again to Rifton Wood. Here, unfortunately, they were found to be running a hind. So they were stopped and a long time was spent in trying to find the stag again. Several other deer were roused, and it was seen that scent was wonderfully bad; hounds could hardly run through two covers without losing the line. After many fruitless efforts to find the stag that had been roused in the morning tufters were changed, and a fresh start made. The large woods running down to Chain Bridge on both sides of the valley were drawn, but nothing old enough to run was found. It was not until five o'clock that a good stag was found at Warbrightsleigh Wood. The pack was laid on, and ran him at a great pace by Rifton and Rhyll Woods to Mr Dunning's bathing pond, and into which he jumped, followed by many of the hounds, and out of which he only just succeeded in scrambling – after a sharp encounter with Captain Amory – in time to save his life. From here, with the pack at his heels, he led the field to Cove Bridge and down to Emmaford, across the river and railway, up through Mr Unwins covers and on by Cove House to Bampton Down; right handed to Huntsham Court, through the grounds and on – evidently pointing for Wiveliscombe, much to the joy of Mr Hancock, who was already, no doubt, looking forward to a good finish within a few minutes ride of his house. But time was against him; and it was already 7.25 and almost dark, so the Master stopped hounds and gave the word for home. Just before hounds were stopped, the stag was viewed no distance in front of them; and if there had been another half hour's daylight, probably a most satisfactory ending would have been put to this good run. As it was, hounds had worked hard and run well, and they could not have reached their kennels much before half past nine.

Oct 6th 1900

These hounds met at Chawleigh on Friday last. The hounds and horses went on over night and were most hospitably put up by Mr Baker, of Chawleigh. The meet was arranged there in consequence of reports which had been received of the presence in that neighbourhood of a very old stag that the harbourer was unable to discover any signs of his having visited his old haunts the previous week. He had evidently shifted his quarters a few days before the advent of the hounds. Mr Amory therefore decided to trot on to Cheldon and draw for some stags that the harbourer had found there. Hounds were kennelled at Mr Webber's farm at Cheldon Barton, and five couple of hounds were taken out as tufters. After about an hour Mr de Las Casas came back for the pack and they were laid on a four year old stag on Affeton Moor. It was quickly apparent that scent was first rate, and at racing pace the hounds ran him by Cottonhays and Lutworthy covers past the Gidley Arms to Rose Ash, here they turned left handed and ran nearly to South Molton; then right handed almost to Molland Station, near which they crossed the line and killed him. The hounds returned home by train.

Oct 13th 1900

These hounds met at Spurway Mill on Saturday. There were out Mr Ian Amory (Master), Messrs, Las Casas (2), Mrs and Master Jack Amory, Messrs and Miss Renton, Misses and Mr W. E. Chichester. Mr and Mrs Jarvis Baily, Colonel Griffiths, and many others, including a number from the Dulverton country, and a host of farmers. The pack was kennelled at Aldridge Mills, and with five couple of tufters went in search of a big stag harboured in Stuckeridge North. After a lot of dodging, this stag went away towards Ash Cross, where the pack was laid on at about 12.15. He turned left handed, and came down the Iron Mill Stream to Chain Bridge, and on through High Wood to Halfpenny bridge. He passed Cove siding and made away to New Bridge, through Mr Unwins coverts and right into the village of Cove where he created considerable disturbance and gave a farm servant a rare fright. Hounds bustled their stag on through the orchard down across the railway and up the river to the Exeter Inn, through the coverts and back again to the Iron Mill Stream, where, unfortunately, they changed deer and ran through High Wood and the Steart coverts before they could be stopped, Meanwhile the hunted stag had made good his escape. Another stag, probably the largest in the Stoodleigh country, was found at Stuckeridge North, and hounds ran him right down past Emmerford, where Mr Amory found they had hinds before them, in consequence of which and the approaching darkness, he decided to make for home, after a most interesting day's hunting.

October 27th 1900

Sir John Amory's Staghounds had an exceptionally fine days sport on Friday which included Mr Ian Amory, Messrs Las Casas (2) Captain Amory, Mr, Mrs, and Miss Lazenby, Mr Renton, Mr Corbett, Messrs Chichester (2), Misses Chichester (2), Mr and Mrs Baily, Miss Blake, Messrs Webber, Pring, Zelly, Yandell, and a crowd of sporting farmers. Mr Amory kennelled the pack at the usual place Aldridge Mills, which Mr Cole of Warbrightsleigh, so considerately places at his disposal, and, taking five couple of tufters, drew Steart Wood for a big stag harboured there by Mr Yandle. After some time getting this fine deer away, he made off by Cove to Chain Bridge and on by Oakford Bridge to Leigh. Here all the tufters were stopped with the exception of "Whynot", who ran the deer across the river through the Wonham coverts and back to Highleigh again. The pack was then laid on just above Leigh, and hounds ran hard passed Oakford onto

Bickham Moors and Swineham Hill, where they turned and came back over Broadmead and still at racing pace down the valley to Langridge Farm, and on down the Exe once more. It was a grand gallop, and those lucky enough to be in it have something to remember for many a day. Here in the Exe Valley the deer was met by that good sportsman Captain Amory, and of course he lost but little time in holloaing hounds on. Soon the deer was being bayed but he succeeded in breaking away, ran the whole length of the Wonham Woods, crossed the river at Stuckeridge Bridge, ran through the Stuckeridge coverts across the iron mill stream, and down by Halfpenny Bridge to Cove once more, where hounds set him up, and he was subsequently taken. He was a fine deer with three and two atop. The Devon and Somerset Staghounds met on the same day at Winsford, and found a stag close to the secretary's house (Mr Everard's, Milton Rocks), and after a good run came right down into the Stoodleigh country into the Leigh covert just as Sir John Amory's Staghounds were leaving it with their stag. It was lucky for the sport that the Devon and Somerset stag turned up through Steart but just as Sir John Amory's hounds killed their stag the Devon and Somerset were below at New Bridge but a few hundred yards distance, and they ran their stag till dark and did not kill. Such a singular occurrence as two packs of staghounds meeting at such distances and running their respective deer into the same covert within a few minutes of each other is probably unparalleled in the history of the chase.

Nov 3rd 1900

A grand day's sport followed the meet at Haddon on Wednesday, and there were out Mr Ian Amory (The Master), Messrs Las Casas (3), Captain H. Amory, Dr and Mrs Mackenzie, Messrs Renton, Misses North Row, Mr J. Baily, Mr Corbett, Mr F. Dunsford, Messrs Snow, Yandle, Clatworthy, Hurley, and many others. A good stag, soon found, led us around Skilgate and the allotments, and back to Haddon. Running hard along the valley past Bury, he came down to the Exe Valley by Hele Bridge, where Mr Amory laid the pack on. The stag then took a line through Exe Cleave and Stockham Wood past Chilly Bridge, and through Red Cleave, where he came down to the water and then beat up stream to Bridgtown, where he was soon taken, a good stag with very fine points. As it was still quite early, only two o'clock, Mr Amory decided to try for a stag seen earlier in the day close by, and he soon succeeded in laying on the line of a deer on Court Down. He ran down to the Exe at Chilly Bridge and back again to the Barle Valley, where he went nearly up to Tarr Steps and back again to Marsh Bridge, through Burridge Wood, close to Dulverton, and back over Northmoor Summer House, down to the Barle, and, again, up the valley to Ashway, where he beat up and down, and was taken just before 5 at Three Waters. He had all his rights and two a top each side. Mr Amory was heartily congratulated on having provided such grand sport, and the hope was expressed on all hands that he would bring his pack to the district again at no distant date.

Nov 17th 1900

These hounds met at Duvale on Tuesday, and a good number were at the meet, including the Master (Mr Ian Amory), Captain and Miss Amory, Messrs Las Casas (3), Mr Renton and son, Mr Corbett, Miss Chichester, Mr Hill and many others. Mr Amory took five and a half couple of tufters and drew Town Wood, and then Champles Cliff, where two deer went away by Ash and to Rifton and Blatchworthy, on to Tidderson Moor and Hill town, where they turned to the right and came across Rackenford Moor, on to Beaples Hill and close to Ash Moor. Here the tufters were stopped by Mr Amory, Captain Amory in the meantime having gone back to Duvale for the pack, a good six miles from where the tufters were stopped. A storm of wind and rain came on. Hounds could hardly own the line, and finally the deer ran the pack out of scent.

On Friday the meet was at the Carnarvon Arms Dulverton, the field including Mr Ian Amory, Messrs Las Casas (2), Mr Renton, Mr Bailey, Mrs Watkins and party on wheels, Mr Bellew, Mrs Bellew, Mr Froude Hancock, Mr Yandle (Perry) Mr and Mrs Lazenby, Messrs, Woodbury, Moore, and many others. We first drew Bury Castle with seven couples of tufters, and it was not long before a stag and hind came out and crossed the river to Pixton and Aller Wood. We brought the hind to the Exe into Exe Cleave. After a bit of dodging about she came back to Weir and lay up in a little fir cover. Here the pack was laid on. Finding it too hot for her, she crossed the road by Hele Bridge, over Baron's Down into Haddon, and back to the Exe again by Bury Castle, into Pixie Copse, where we had a lot of deer up. Hounds however, stuck to their hunted hind, drove her up the river as far as Chilly Bridge, and back again as far down as the chemical works at Exebridge, where the hounds ran up to her. Breaking away again she came back through Pixie Copse and Bury Castle to Hele Bridge, up over to Barons Down, into Haddon back again along the top to Chilly Bridge, and up the river nearly to Milton Rocks, where this good hind was taken at 4.30.

Nov 24th 1900

On Saturday Mr Ian Amory responded to the invitation of the Devon and Somerset Staghounds, and took his hounds to Hele Bridge. With seven and a half couple of tufters he tried Pixie Copse, and there found a lot of deer, five or six of which went over the hill into Haddon, came back to Bury Castle, where one went away up the Exe Valley, through Exe Cleave and Stockham to Red Cleave and on to the allotments on Winsford Hill, where the pack was laid on. It was obvious scent was good, for hounds simply raced to Comer's Gate, and down to Withypool Village. They came down the Barle Valley, where they fresh found their hind just above Tarr Steps, over Hawkridge, and down to Marsh Bridge, where a herd of deer were roused and consequently hounds had to be stopped and taken home.

Dec 22nd 1900

These hounds met at the Carnarvon Arms on Saturday and enjoyed an exceptionally fine day's sport. The special train conveying hounds and horses and several sportsmen from Tiverton reached Dulverton Station at 9.55. It was then raining fast, and the prospects of a fine day were anything but bright. Hounds and horses were soon unboxed, and after a few minutes law Mr Amory kennelled the pack in Mr Nelder's stable, and drew out five couple of trusty tufters. A move was then made to Pixie Copse and three hinds were quickly found. Tufters ran them into Rookwood and across to the Barle, then back by the edge of Pixton Park to Hele Bridge, where one hind left the others and went into Exe Cleave. Tufters stuck to the other two and ran them well for about half an hour backwards and forwards between the Barle and the Exe Valley. Then one of them made into Haddon, but as she was not the largest of three, tufters were stopped and Mr Amory went back for the pack, with which he drew Rookwood for the remaining hind. She was presently found, and breaking cover in view of the field was seen to be an old and very fine deer. The weather had now greatly improved, and hounds gave her but little time to continue the dodging tactics she had pursued with the tufters, but drove her with the dash for which these hounds are celebrated to Dulverton Station and on by Coombe to the Barle Valley, where no doubt she relied on finding other friends to take up her work, but she was given no time to look after them. Hounds were too close to her, and she was compelled to run straight through these covers and make her way with all haste by Highercombe to Winsford Hill and on to the allotments. Here she found a herd of fresh deer and promptly joined them, but Mr Amory, who was close to the leading hounds saw the manoeuvre and also saw her after travelling some distance with them- leave the other deer. And was thus able to direct the hounds on to her line and avoid all complications. From here she turned over Winsford Hill and led us by South Hill and Red Cleave to the Exe Valley and down by Chilly Bridge and Exe Cleave to Hele Bridge and Weir; then over the hill to the Barle and down the river until opposite the Station hounds fresh found her, and raced her nearly down to the chemical works and up again by Pixie Copse to Bury where at 3.30 they killed her, thus bringing to a close a very fine run which had given hounds a chance of showing what they could do, and the field a chance of galloping until their horses had had enough it for one day.

Jan 25th 1902

Sir John Amory's Staghounds met at Fairby Lodge to try for a hind that had made Mr Unwin's coverts her home. The hind was quickly found just above Fairby. Ran the whole length of the covert towards Cove, then turned up over the hill as if going for Van Post and the Huntsham coverts. Keeping, however, to the right, she led hounds past Allens Down on by Chevithorne Barton, and across the Lowman valley to Sellake, where she was viewed by Mr Mackenzie, and, taking to the road, looked as if she were going through Halberton, but with a left hand turn she led hounds to Rock House, where she crossed the canal and made away to Tiverton Junction. Keeping to the left of the railway she got as far as Sampford siding, when a short check occurred, but the driver of a passing goods train viewed her going into Pounds Copse (Burlescombe), and the news being quickly conveyed to Mr Amory, and hounds were soon again on the line of the deer. Close to the light railway leading to the quarries, she had laid up, and just as hounds fresh found her, she got right on the main line of the G. W. R. as an express train was coming. The quickness of the first whip Mr A. de Las Casas, and the promptness of the driver in stopping the train, averted what must have otherwise been a serious accident. The hind then ran to within a mile of the town of Wellington, and coming round left handed, passed Langford, Heathfield Common, and Spring Grove, nearly into Wilveliscombe and onto Croford Mills, where this gallant deer was taken at 4.30, having kept going for nearly five hours. Among the field who were in at the finish were the Master Mr Ian Amory, the two whips Messrs Las Casas, Mr and Miss Renton, Capt. Amory, Mr L. Amory, Mr C. Carew, M.H., Mr Corbett, Mr Boles, Mr F. Dunsford, Mr L. Unwin, M.F.H., Misses Chichester (2), Miss Mackenzie- Ashton, Messrs Yandle, Hayton (2), Pring, and Pethick.

Feb 1st 1902

These hounds had another big run on Friday last from their meet at Gibbet Moor. The pack was kennelled at Horestone Farm (Mr Boundy's), and tufters were taken on to Cruwys Morchard coverts, where a small deer had been for some time. Hounds were not long in finding her in Merryfieldhayes and two deer went away at once through Looselands, across Witheridge Moor, through Hill Town coverts, right over Tidderson Moor, away over Rackenford Moor, Sydeham Hill, Bickham Moors; then bearing to the left, on as if for East Anstey. Keeping by the side of the line, however, the deer did not cross the railway until Brushford was nearly reached, whence she led hounds through Coombe and on to Dulverton, where she was viewed passing close to the town. This good deer then went on through Burridge and North Moor and right on to the Barle Valley, past Hawkridge and Three Waters, over Ashway Side, Winsford Hill and Allotments. Here there were a great many deer about, but Mr Amory found the hunted one, raced her back over Winsford Hill and Ashway Side to the Barle Valley, down by Castle Bridge, up the Danes Brook, over Anstey Common, and back to the Barle again. One portion of the pack ran down by Mounsey Castle to Marsh Bridge and over Court Down, this gallant deer was taken in Exe Park at about 5 o'clock. If a straight line were drawn across the map from the find to the kill of this run the distance would be found to be over 14 miles, but as hounds ran it was as far again, It was one of the biggest runs of the season, and amongst those out to enjoy it were Mr Ian Amory the Master, Messrs, Las Casas, Mr Boles, Miss Amory, Mr Dunsford, Miss Seymour, Mr Hill, Misses Chichester, Messrs Beedell, Chave, Zelley, Webber, Harris, and others.

March 28th 1902

These hounds met at the Royal Oak, Gibbett Moor, on Saturday, the pack was kennelled at Spurway, and it soon became evident that the deer had been disturbed, for it was some time before Mr Amory found. In Little Waspleigh, however, three deer were discovered, and ran thence to Rifton Blatchworthy Wood, and nearly to Sidderson Moor, where the pack was laid on. The chase now lay by way of Willycrop Moor to Bickham, over Bickham Moors to Estworthy, and on as if for East Anstey, but a left hand turn brought hounds back to Swineham Hill and Rackenford Moor, down by Sydham and straight down the valley to Chain Bridge, then up over the hill towards Wonham. With another left hand turn the deer ran nearly into Bampton Town, but came round again to Coombeland, on past Wonham, and down in sight of Exebridge. Then she made her way down to the Exe, over Highleigh, as if for Red Deer, back over the hill and down to the

Exe again by Exebridge. Passing the chemical works she pointed for Haddon, but keeping by the railway line, she passed Morebath village, and was taken close to the railway at Morebath Junction, at the same spot where a stag was taken last August. From find to finish this run was just over four hours.

March 29th 1902

Fridays meet was at Chipstable Cross, there was a fairly big field out, including many from the Wiveliscombe country. Mr Ian Amory had charge of the pack. The company included Captain Amory, Messrs de Las Casas (3), Pugsley, Froude, Ernest and Frank Hancock, Dunsford, Mr J. Renton, and others. The pack was kennelled at Haddon, and the tufters taken on to Chipstable Cross. A good lot of deer were found in Chipstable and in running them round, one of the herd, a young hind, stunned herself and was killed. The tufters were laid on to the rest of the deer, which ran, by way of the Bittiscombe Covers and Skilgate Common, to the deer park at Haddon. Thence down as far as Bury, back through Birchen and Haddon Woods, up to Harford Mill, and the deer park again. Coming down the valley to Harford Cleeve tufters fresh found one of the number – a stag – and, after running up and down for a short time, he was taken in the river close to Harford Mill. The pack were now sent for, and laid on the line of another deer under Haddon Woods. Hounds were led to the deer park, down the river, and up and down the Haddon Coverts for a good while, and, finally, they killed their quarry close to Clamon.

April 12th 1902

A VISITING CORRESPONDENT DESCRIBES A DAY OUT WITH SIR JOHN AMORY'S STAGHOUNDS

It was with feelings of the greatest pleasure that on Tuesday I found it possible to have a glimpse of Sir John Amory's Staghounds, I have read a good about, when they met at the Fox and Hounds, Eggesford. Unfortunately, being an absolute stranger to this part of the country, I felt somewhat handicapped, but, through the kindness of one who was there, I may be able to correctly supplement what I actually saw myself. The hounds had been kennelled over night at Eggesford, and the Master and others drove over in the morning from Tiverton. This pack is the only one in the kingdom that is entirely hunted by amateurs, and right well do they fulfil their various offices. With two such good sportsmen as the brothers Las Casas as whips it would be astonishing indeed if everything was not done as it should be, and I could not help observing how quietly and methodically every necessary duty was done. The morning was fine, with a decided touch of east in the wind, and I was told a fair field put in an appearance to meet them, which included the Master, Mr Ian Amory, his brother, Mr Harry Amory, Miss Amory, Lord Portsmouth, Hon. J. Wallop, Major and Mrs Dunning, Mr A. Severn, Mr and Mrs A. Cruwys, Rev. Paramore, Messrs Cuxton (2) Bowden, Smyth, Gardner, Smyth-Osborne, Northey, Littleworth, Harris, Webber, Miller (2), Selley, Hampton, Webber (2), Bethune (2), Callard, Rippin, Wynne, Prettyjohns, Tripe, Auber, Mortimer &co. On the appearance of the hounds the scene was an animated one, and for few minutes before they were re-kennelled one had a chance of looking at them. Good hard condition they all appeared to be in, and fit to do anything. They always run, these hounds do, remarked a certain gentleman to me, and certainly their looks did not belie his words. After re-kennelling, three or four couple were chosen as tufters and a move was made. A little later the body of the pack were taken on towards Chawleigh. Opinions were rife that we should not be long in finding, while the tufters were taken up to Lammacleave. One of Lord Portsmouth's numerous coverts, from here they came into Olden Clump. From the main road, where all the carriages were stationed, a fine view was obtained. Southcott Wood, just beyond on the same slope of the hill, was their next essay, and hardly had the tufters disappeared in covert when two stags were disturbed, and could be distinctly seen running in company up the wood. They both faced the open together, and ran up over the grass field in full view. Before they reached the top, however, they separated, one going left, the other right handed. The hounds settled to the one who bore right handed, and followed him over the hill into Foxes Covert, a large extent of woodland. Driving him out from here they ran up the valley for about a mile and a half. As the body of the pack were being brought down to be laid on, it is surmised that they came on to the line of the deer, and ran heel line to Foxes Covert. In the meantime their stag had been seen to cross the Tiverton road with one tufter in attendance, and when the body of the pack came back their quarry must have been a long way ahead. Running down the valley by East Cheldon they went up to Affeton, and ran on by Sutworthy, to Week, Gidley Arms, Trishcombe, and up to Ash Moor Gate, where a check occurred. The last I heard of them was that they were running slowly to Chain Bridge. "Roadster."

Oct 16th 1902

"BLOODING" A YEARLING

What is described as "an interesting incident" took place after a kill by Sir John Amory's Staghounds on Saturday not far distance from Lythe Court, on the road from Tiverton to Bampton. Capt. Harry Amory was observed to cross the railway line and make his way to the road. In a short time he returned accompanied by his wife, and nurse, carrying their twelve months old son. With befitting ceremony the boy was "blooded", a small red patch being put on his left cheek. Mr Ian Amory the Master, and a few others witnessed the interesting proceeding which was also "snapped" by a fair camera holder.

Jan 17th 1903

Owing to the Rivers Barle and Exe being so high, the meet of this pack had to be changed from Winsford Hill to Haddon on Tuesday. The pack were kennelled at Goss's, and the tufters were taken into the Deer Park. There hinds were run by tufters over Skilgate Common, where they parted company. The pack were laid on to a hind above Biddiscombe, and drove her back into Haddon and down the valley to Bury. Here she led hounds over the hill and on to Morebath Junction, thence by the railway to the chemical works and on to the River Exe. Hounds did not cross the river, and getting a full view of the hind, she was shortly afterwards killed in the road under Pixey Copse. Going back to the Deer Park, another deer was found, which showed hounds down the valley to Birchen Wood, across Haddel stream, in Swines Cleeve, through Storridge, and nearly to Kings Brompton. Coming back under Haddon, they killed her just before five o'clock two hinds, were, therefore accounted for.

Saturday's meet was at Worlington, they found at Cottonhayes, and the pack were laid on under Winswood Moor. The deer ran through Stone Moor, back to the Cheldon Valley, across the Chawleigh road, and through the Lapford Covers, and made her way round into the Cheldon Valley again. Here she led the hounds through Cottonhayes on nearly to the Gidley Arms, and coming down through the Wick Covers she raced away by

Ernest Bawden, Huntsman of the Devon & Somerset Staghounds taking out the tufters from farm buildings – this would have been a similar situation when Sir John Amory's Staghounds were hunting.

The Yandle family who were keen supporters of Sir John Amory's Staghounds.

Bycott, Huntacott, and down to Cheldon Bridge. Thence over Chawleigh roads into Lapford Covers once more, and hounds were stopped when they were nearing Eggesford when it was getting dark

Jan 31st 1903

This pack met at Cove on Wednesday. Finding their deer under Stuckeridge House, they ran down the valley nearly to Bolham. Their hind took them back through Washfield, Stoodleigh, and Oakford, to Knowstone Wood, where hounds were called off after a long and trying run. A good field was out, but by no means all were able to get to the end.

The hounds met at the Gidley Arms, Meshaw, on Saturday. Among those out were Messrs Ian and Harry Heathcoat-Amory, de Las Casas(2), and several other gentlemen from Tiverton; J. F. Wilkin (Roseash), German, Bird, and Fewings (South Molton), A. G. Hannaford (Brighton), Savage (Croydon), T. Elphick (London), Hulland (Kingsnympton) Mr and Mrs Green (Chittlehamholt), G. Selley (Witheridge), J. Tripe (Parsonage). R. S. Bragg, Frank Webber (Chulmleigh), W. Webber (Morchard Bishop), J. Cobley (Shobrooke), W. Cole (Meshaw), Boundy (Riddlecombe), &co. A regular drizzle maintained all through the day, and tufters were drawn into Week Plantation soon rousing a big stag, and it at once made away for Wixon and on to Bycott. Then it turned round and passed back near Wixon Farm and on towards Sheepsbyre, and reached Stone Moor. Here it crossed the highway to Winswood Farm, Cheldon, and then, veering to the right, came down the valley to the little Dart, passing Stone Bridge, Chawleigh. Here the tufters were taken off and the pack laid on, the stag going right through Chawleigh Barton Wood and passing near the volunteer rifle range. Keeping straight down the valley, it passed opposite Park Mill Farmhouse, through the Cleaves, and crossing the road, reached Rodgments Wood, just opposite the town of Chulmleigh, several of whose inhabitants turned out to see the sport. It next passed Chawleigh Week Wood, on near Chawleigh Week Farmhouse, and when opposite Dartridge Farm crossed the Little Dart and made away up over the hill on the opposite side, passing by Leigh Reservoir. Crossing the main road not far from Chulmleigh Town, it went along Colleton Barton ground, close by Colleton House, and thence down over to Lakehead Moor, and crossed the valley. Then it made up over the hill on the opposite side to Elstone, and went straight on through Newnam Brake. Then it ran over Hill Head Wood, and crossing the River Mole, went through the orchard at Head Mill, close to the water mill. Keeping to the right, it went through Head Woodland, getting on the main road from South Molton Road Station to South Molton, ran along it for nearly a mile. At length it turned up over Snydles Farm, Chittlehamholt, and when just below Whitmore turned down over the hill again, and was lost near the Warkleigh Hotel. Although every effort was made the hounds could not pick up the scent again. Thus a splendid day's sport ended without a kill.

Feb 7th 1903

Sir John Amory's Staghounds met at Stoodleigh, New Bridge on Saturday. There was a large field out, amongst whom we noticed besides Mr Amory (huntsman) and Mr de Las Casas and Captain Amory (whips), Miss Chichester, Mr Renton, Mr Dunsford, Mr Boles, Mr Baily, Mr Pethick, Mr Butt, Mr Hill, Mr M de Las Casas, Mr Down, Mr Blackmore, Messrs Yandle (3), Mr Bater, Mr and Mrs Pugsley, Mr Haydon & c. Mr Amory drew the tufters out at Mr Oxenham's farm and sent the pack on to Cove. Miller had harboured several hinds to Emmerford cover, and hounds soon found them and drove three towards Beer Hill and round by Stoodleigh Park. Here they separated and the tufters settled on to one of the finest of them and ran her by Steart Cover to the Ironwater Mill Stream, up this valley past Spurway Mill to Bickham Cover. Captain Amory had before this gone back for the pack and had lost no time in bringing them on. They were laid on the line of our hind in Sydenham Wood, and ran her at a great pace across Rackenford Moors and Harestone Moor to Backstone Cover, where a check took place. After some patient work on the part of the hounds both up and down the water the hind was fresh found in a deep gully and getting away upon good terms with her the hounds ran faster than ever over the country beyond Thorne Brake and on towards Bradford. Then they swung left handed and we found ourselves galloping for all we were worth past Hilltown and the rough moors fringing Witheridge Moor. It was now a question whether horses could go fast enough to live with the flying pack and it was found that they were not many who did see what hounds were doing about this time. We made the best speed we could, however, past the Royal Oak, Gibbet Moor, or rather some of us passed that house with its sign board without drawing rein – whilst others… but no doubt they were hungry after such a long ride. Any how hounds didn't stop, and many of us didn't see either them or Mr Amory till we found them together casting down the water by Halfpenny Bridge. How they got there is not known to many. Here there was a check and things began to look rather bad when hounds first feathered, then challenged up a small side stream towards Duvale House, and then out of this stream bounded our hind, across one field and into the Exe, where after trying to head away up stream for a bit, she turned down stream, and was quickly killed so ended a real good run.

Feb 14th 1903

On Wednesday last these hounds added another to the many good runs they have lately experienced. The meet was at Mr Dunning's Bridge over the Exe. The tufters were picked out at Oxenhams Farm, and the pack was sent on to Mr Cole's kennel at Spurway Mill. Miller had harboured several hinds in Parhouse Wood – a steep hanging cover facing the road – so the field had a splendid view of the tufters drawing for the deer and of the find. Several hinds were found, but Mr Amory managed to settle all the tufters on to the line of one of the finest of them, and they raced her away by Easterlands and across Mr Dunning's fine park, leaving the court on their right, to Rifton Wood. Here they turned right handed and went down by Spurway Mill, the scene of so many staghound meets, and on through Waspley Wood into Sydeham, where the tufters were stopped and the pack laid on. It was soon evident that there was a very good scent, for hounds drove along over Rackenford, Harestone, and Knowstone Moors at such a pace that horses could barely live with them. The hind evidently felt that it was necessary for her to lose no time either, for she led us straight away from her old haunts and across the big boggy moors by Ditchet Farm, and we made up her minds that we were in for a gallop to Worlington, but the line lay to the left, and when she reached Bradford her courage evidently failed her, and she turned up the valley and back by Creacombe to Rackenford Moor, where after a check of some length she was fresh found in a gorse brake, and rattled down through all the Stoodleigh coverts to Chain Bridge, and down the Exe nearly to Cove Bridge, where she was killed. She proved to be a very large hind, and was pronounced by a good judge of such matters to be either six or seven years old. "Bamptonian."

Feb 21st 1903

On Wednesday last these hounds met at Haddon. The pack was kennelled at Goss' house, and Mr Amory took the tufters on to draw Mr Capel's coverts at Bulland about five miles further on. Goss had harboured six hinds in Huish Cleave, and tufters were no sooner into covert than they found them. They settled on to a splendid hind and raced her back by Sir John Ferguson Davie's covert at Bittiscombe to Haddon. The pack were quickly on her line, and drove her back down to Bury. There. Unfortunately, she turned back and ran into a herd of 13 stags in Haddon Wood, and we were never able to make much of her line afterwards. Mr Amory decided, therefore to draw for a fresh deer, and hounds were taken to West Hill, where they found several hinds, and after running one of them for about an hour up and down and backwards through the great Haddon coverts, they drove her away over Skilgate Common and back by the fish ponds and Lowtrow Cross to Haddon; down the Haddeo to Bury, back again and up the Kingsbrompton water to within half a mile of the village. Here they fresh found her, and almost coursed her all the way from there back to Haddon and down the valley to Bury, where at five o'clock she was killed. She proved to be a very fine hind – about five years old.

On Saturday these hounds met at Kipscott Barton, Mr Pearce's farm, a meet that is looked forward to by many staghunters, and which has been the starting point of two wonderfully good runs already this season. Hounds and horses were taken to Molland Station by special hunting train, and were met by a large field of local sportsmen. Mr Pearce most hospitably entertained all comers to breakfast. Hounds were kennelled in his buildings, and with only two couple of tufters the hind was soon found. No time was lost in laying on the pack, and it was at once apparent that scent was very good. The country round here is an ideal one for hunting over – a succession of great wild moors, carrying a very good scent, enable hounds to work out the line by themselves, and there is nothing but the chance of an occasional bog to prevent everyone seeing what hounds are doing all the time. The hind left us over the best of the country, and it was a pleasure to see the hounds doing all the work without asking for any help from the huntsman. We ran by Bullaford and Cross Moors to Wadham, and on by Luckett Moor to Whitefield, then left handed by Western Moor to Bommerton and Hall Wood. Here we got on to a very good terms with our hind, and raced her past Molland Station and down to the River Yeo down stream for half a mile, and away by Whitechapel and Rawstone, over the Gortonhill Moors to South Molton, within half a mile of which we fresh found her, and ran her back over much the same country, and away as if for East Anstey. Onto Bottreaux Mill and heading back to Molland she was quickly killed. This run lasted just two and half hours, and from beginning to end there was no check except as much as was caused by hounds being cast down the water.

March 21st 1903

At Gidley Arms, Meshaw, on Saturday, a good number of horsemen out included Messrs, Ian Amory, Harry Amory, Las Casas, Butt (Tiverton), Snow (Knowstone), Bird, German (South Molton) Lieut R. Preston Whyte (Leigh House), J. Mothersdale (South Molton), G. H. Selley, Dr Mead (Witheridge), Frank Webber, Jnr. Tripe (Chulmleigh), W. Cobley (Bealey Court), S. H. Vicary, J. Webber (Cheldon), F. Ford (Chawleigh), and others. The Harbourer (Miller) reported that deer were in Cottonhay Plantation, and on the tufters being put in there, three were soon roused; these immediately came into the open, and a fine view was obtained of them by the hunters. The three at once made away across Yelland Moor, and from thence to Winswood Moor. Crossing the Moor they made away for Mounticombe, and on reaching Mounticombe Moor they divided, and the tufters went after a fine stag which now led away to Stone Moor and into the plantations at Hunticott. Then turning around it made away near Hunticott Farm, and down over

Stone Ground and crossed the river (Little Dart) into Chawleigh Barton Wood. On emerging from the wood it passed along near the Chulmleigh Volunteer Rifle Range, through the cleaves, and going up over the hill reached Upcott. From there it made away to Southcott Farm, and passing over Hilltown Farm came to Chenson. Here it turned back over to the left, and made away for Chawleigh Leigh, and getting down into the valley again crossed the river. On reaching Cheldon Bridge the pack were laid on, and the stag made away across East Leigh Farm to West Leigh, and through the wood. Then, crossing the main road, it went through Chawleigh Barton Wood and down the valley, keeping near the river and passing near Park Mill Farm. He next turned up over the hill crossing the Cleaves, and passed along near the cottages at Chulmleigh Bridge. A large number of the townspeople of Chulmleigh turned out to view the sport, and across the valley obtained a fine view of the stag as it cleared the hedge into the main road, and over the hedge on the other side to Chawleigh Week Farm, where hounds were within a few yards of their quarry. On getting into Chawleigh Week Farm it put on a spurt and hounds were soon left some distance behind. It went right along the centre path in the wood, and the watchers had a splendid view for upwards of three quarters of a mile. The stag leaving the wood, passed near the farm buildings at Week, and crossing the road reached Scamp's Piece. Shortly after, and when just below Dartridge Farm, it crossed the river. Coming up over the hill the stag crossed near Leigh House, and on to Colleton Barton, passing near Colleton House. On passing Colleton Mill it took to the water, and after going some distance down the stream was taken in the River Taw, just above South Molton Road Station it proved to be a fine five year old stag

March 28th 1903

BARNSTAPLE STAGHOUNDS INVITATION MEET

The Barnstaple Staghounds had an invitation meet from Ian Amory on Tuesday, meeting at Chawleigh. Miller the Harbourer reported a single deer in the Cheldon Valley, and at 10 minutes to 12 o'clock the pack were laid on near Stone Mill. Having beat the coverts to the south bank of the Little Dart, the deer ran to Wixon, and on to Waterloo. After crossing the Romansleigh road and going through Balls Plantation he came back over Meshaw Moor to Mouseberry. As he passed Ash Moor the leading hounds were racing him in view. Having traversed Rackenford and Willicroft Moors he went down by Broadmead to the Iron Mill Stream. Up to this point from the lay on hounds had probably ran 19 miles, and every one was ready for the brief spell which resulted. At length he was viewed as he soiled, and hounds ran him up through the covert towards Steart and down again to water above Chain Bridge. Later it was found that hounds had taken their deer to water again near Cove. Under Stanterton he took to the river once more and swam down till he reached Bolham Weir. Here he made his land stand. The current was so strong that the hounds were all but swept away by the stream. The stag was taken just above Worth House the run had lasted about five hours.

April 18th 1903

Considerable excitement was caused at Dulverton on Saturday afternoon, shortly before three o'clock, by the appearance in the high street of a fine stag, closely followed by hounds and horsemen of the Devon and Somerset Staghounds. This was the finale of a fine run, in the course of which a wide stretch of country was covered. The meet that morning was at Veniford Cross, near Minehead, a point about twelve miles due north of

Dulverton. A stag was found in a covert close by, and hunted through Dunster, Slowley, Luxborough, Withiel Florey, Kingsbrompton, and Barons Down, across the Exe, and then by Hollam into Dulverton. Taking refuge in the stream close to the workhouse, the stag was killed in the presence of a large concourse. It is very rare occurrence for a deer from the Minehead district to find its way to Dulverton. While the above run was in progress the followers of Sir John Amory's Staghounds were enjoying excellent sport in the Devon and Somerset country. They met at 10.30 at the Carnarvon Arms near Dulverton where the hounds were kennelled. There was a large field no less than 30 horses being brought from Tiverton by train. The tufters being taken to Knutsford soon found a hind, which ran away past Wilway and over Northmoor Hill to Hynham, thence to the Barle and Slade, and across Ashway Side towards Winsford Hill, skirting the Punchbowl, where she doubled to the Allotments. After a brief check hounds followed the line to the Exe above Broford, and then up the valley past the former site of the chemical works, then circling to the right, they came down the Exe valley to Hele Bridge and Haddon. After some time spent in beating up and down. The hind was taken in the water about half past one, after a two hour run hard galloping in a most delightful country.

May 9th 1903

On Friday Sir John Amory's Staghounds met at Haddon, a large field turning out to meet them. The pack was kennelled at Goss's house and Mr Amory took five couple of tufters on to draw Mr Capel's coverts at Chipstable. The tufters were no sooner in covert than they found the deer, and without a moments waste of time every hound came away with a good hind only just in front of them. They ran her to Sir John Davie's coverts at Bittescombe, up to Skilgate Common, and then away left handed by Ranscombe, and across the railway by Venn Cross to Hayne Moors. Here the tufters were stopped and the pack laid on. Scent was not very good, but hounds worked the line with great patience by Morebath Junction to Bampton, where after a considerable check, owing to the receipt of totally erroneous information, the deer was fresh found and quickly killed. This finished the season probably the hardest and certainly the best in the history of these Staghounds. The year 1902-1903 will be famous for a serious of wonderful runs, as well as for even a larger number than usual of days hunting in which those who have been out with these hounds have been given a day's sport far above the average. The number of deer accounted for amounts to a total of 41, 14 in the home country south of the Devon and Somerset railway and 27 in the Devon and Somerset country, north of the railway. Altogether these hounds since they began work seven years ago, have killed 233 deer. Within the last few weeks two runs have fallen to their lot either of which is worthy to be permanently recorded in the history of Staghunting, and neither of which is likely to be forgotten by those who took part in them. On March 20th the meet was at Stoodleigh (Newbridge), a hind was found at once near Emmerford and was run by Spurway Mill to Rackenford, then back to Chain Bridge and away by Wonham to Haddon and was not taken till she had led hounds to Monksilver, on the Bristol Channel, a distance from Rackenford to Monksilver 20 miles in a straight line.

Sketch by Terry Gable

On April 27th, a hind was found near Hawkridge and was run nearly to Dulverton, then back to Winsford Hill, Withypool Common, Landacre Bridge, Honeymead, Exmoor Forest, on to Larkbarrow and into the Culbone Woods, again looking down on the Bristol Channel. Here hounds were stopped and it was a long trot of 18 miles back to Dulverton, which was reached about 9 o'clock, and hounds got into kennel just as the clocks were striking 11.

This pack hunted, by Mr Sanders invitation from Mounsey Hill Gate on Friday, and added three good hinds to the satisfactory list of deer taken from the Winsford Hill district during the past week. This should go far to lessen the destruction of crops, which a superabundant herd have affected throughout the winter all round the vicinity of Sir Thomas Acland's beautiful stretch of heather that lies between Redcleave and Comer's Gate. Kennelling at Stags Head, Mr Ian Amory drew Cripple Cleave, which covert, true to its designation, held a crippled hind, as well as sixteen other deer. This hind was speedily taken at Miltons Rocks, and the tufters resumed work at Edbrooke Wood. Running by way of Bradleyham, the pack divided, and after a circuit of Withypool Common and Molland Moor, a second hind was taken under Wellswood, and the third below Withypool.

Sept 26th 1903

Like many others who have, no doubt, been looking forward to the opening meet with pleasure, I felt, I must confess, somewhat disappointed to learn that instead of the function taking place as usual at Stoodleigh Court, the venue had been changed to Chawleigh for Saturday last. The very sudden death of General Spurway made it impossible to hunt this side of the country so soon after the sad event, so the boundless hospitality of the genial Squire of Stoodleigh Court could not be taken advantage of, and Chawleigh was the meet fixed on. It is a long ride out from Tiverton, but on arrival there we found Mr and Mrs Baker, of Chawleigh Barton, ready with a warm welcome and a bounteous spread of good things, to which we did ample justice. Then, accompanied by a keen field of local sportsmen, we wended our way to Cheldon Farm, where the pack was kennelled and tufters drawn. Miller, owing to the previous week of bright, dry weather, had found harbouring somewhat difficult, but had made sure that Wixson Wood held a good stag, as well as several young deer. These latter were soon on foot and away, but it was not till 12.45 that our huntsman was able to rouse the big deer. After a turn round the covert he broke with tufters close behind, ran to Ball Covert on to Wick Coverts, across the Chulmleigh road to Lutworthy, where tufters were stopped and the pack sent for. Capt Amory had over three miles to get back to Cheldon, but it seemed no time till his return, and at 1.50 the pack was laid on, and the stag fresh found in Lutworthy. The field up to this had been speculating on a run to the Exe, but the stag turned, making his way through Cuddenhayes, through Affeton Plantation, across Mounticombe Moor, on to Stone Moor, then keeping to the left to Stone Wood, and across the Dart into Chawleigh Barton Wood. He then went out over the Chulmleigh road, through Moortown, through Nethercott, and on to Southcott. Here hounds were at fault for some time, and nothing could be made of the line. Our huntsman, with a happy inspiration decided to beat the thick covert near where hounds had last owed the line, as the brambles and thorns were here in such a mat that hounds could not force a way through them. At the huntsman call a keen band of beaters were soon formed into the line and almost directly the stag jumped up in front of Captain Amory and was away. He ran to Fox's Covert, on past Chenson to Chenson Wood, out on to Hensford nearly to Lapford Forches. Keeping to the left across Chawleigh road into Pouncers, past Cheldon, down the water to Stone Mill, on nearly to Chulmleigh and then back up the river, and was taken under Chawleigh Wood at 6.55pm. This end was only achieved by the indomitable perseverance of our huntsman and grand hound work by the pack, for scent was very indifferent all day. He was a good bodied deer with rather a peculiar head, having all his rights and two on top one side, with only brow and a long upright on the other.

Nov 7th 1903

Finding some deer under Easterlands on Wednesday, these hounds ran one by way of Chain Bridge, up the Iron Mill Stream to Aldridge Mill, on to Bickham, and away across Rackenford Moor. From here hounds were led to Baxton Wood, where they fresh found. It was, however, of little avail. On following their quarry back over Rackenford Moor hounds got on the track of fresh deer, and were stopped.

The atmospheric condition on Saturday were against a large field for the first day's hind hunting, but a good number assembled at Ash Cross to greet the Master. Among these were Capt H. Heathcoat-Amory, Messrs A., C., and M. de Las Casas, Miss Chichester, Miss Renton, Mr Renton, Mr Corbet, and Mr Hill. The pack was kennelled at Spurway Mills. Two hinds were found in Big Waspley, and were run down the valley to Aldridge Mills, where they divided. One part of the pack run up to Bickham and the other half went down the valley with the Master. Near the Chain Bridge the pack drew together and ran their hind over Stuckeridge and down by Hangmans Hill nearly to Stoodleigh. Passing by Steart she went down to Cove siding, where she crossed the river into Mr Unwin's coverts. From here hounds followed a cold scent to Van Post. Coming back to Knighshayes coverts, they ran out of scent near the Waterworks. It rained hard from start to finish and it was surprising that the sodden ground carried as much scent as it did.

Dec 5th 1903

Meeting by invitation at the Carnarvon Arms, Dulverton, on Wednesday morning, these hounds had an excellent day's sport. After running a hind from Ellers Wood to White Rocks, two more were viewed in the valley that leads down to Tarr Steps, and Captain Amory who was hunting the hounds at once laid on the pack. The deer at first made for Winsford Hill, but were turned by a steam roller and ran back to the Barle. Here the deer divided, and one hind to which the pack stuck crossed the river, and went straight up the other slope in full view of the field. There was not time to stop on Hawkridge, for hounds ran across the top and down into the Danesbrook, crossing which, by the well known gate in the water, we went up the steep slope to Whiterocks. From here without a check hounds fairly raced across Anstey and Molland Commons, with only Captain Amory and three others in attendance, and horses had to gallop their best to live with them. On Molland Common, near Combe Woods, hounds were stopped for a few minutes to allow the straggling field to get up. Then on again and right handed to Willingford, where hounds checked at the water. Hitting it off on the other side, away they went again as fast as ever, and, leaving Sandyway on the left, came to Sherdon Water. Here the deer had evidently got in the stream and gone up to it, and after a check of about five minutes hounds found the line higher up, and after galloping over some big rough moorland enclosures, where the going was somewhat heavy, the field found themselves at Emmetts Grange, and here, with hounds still running as though they meant to go all day, many had perforce to cry "Enough". The hind went on to Barcombe, where gradually turning left handed, hounds swept on without a check to Whitefield

Down and Hole Water. Here our hind had been seen in the water, and after a slight check Fred Goss the Harbourer viewed her. From thence hounds ran her almost in view to High Bray and Brayford, near which latter place operations had to be closed by reason of the gathering darkness. Thus ended one of the greatest of moorland gallops. The line could hardly have been better if chosen beforehand. Hounds ran well together all the way, and the pace was fast enough for the veriest glutton. Hounds and horses were taken home from South Molton Station.

Dec 12th 1903

These hounds were unable to hunt last Wednesday owing to the frost and it was at first feared that Saturday would have to be a blank day. After a short delay in the vicinity of Hele Bridge things improved, however, and a good run was enjoyed. The tufters roused two hinds in Bury Castle and raced them over Peterspiece through Barllynch Wood and up the valley to Chilly Bridge. Hounds which had been kennelled at Hele Bridge, were here laid on, and crossing the river into Stockham they ran back into Exe Cleeve and came up the river again to Broford and into Southhill, through Southhill Plantation to the Allotments. There were now several deer on foot. Hounds settled on one which came back through Redcleeve into Winslade Wood and turned into Haddon, where a considerable time was spent. Ultimately the hind came back over Baron's Down and went into the river near Hele Bridge. Emerging the hind ran up the valley as far as Chilly Bridge, near where she was killed.

Jan 16th 1904

These hounds met at Spurway Mills on Saturday morning, and a fairly big field turned up, which increased as the morning wore on. Amongst those present were the Master Mr Ian Amory, and the two whips (Capt. Amory and Mr M. de Las Casas), Messrs Corbet, Renton, Dunsford, L. Amory, A. and L. de Las Casas, Jarvis-Baily, Yendell (2), Yandle, J. Zelly, Heal, and a lot of others. Hounds began by drawing Rifton, where two hinds were, at once found. Running through Blatchworthy, they turned up over by Whitnole and on to Williscroft Moor, near which one of the hinds failed to get over a fence quick enough and was killed by Capt. Amory. Meanwhile the Master had gone back for the pack, and taken it up the valley to the Rackenford road, where it was laid on to the single hind, which, instead of going to the coverts, had turned left handed and ran nearly to the road. A halloa soon put matters right, and turned back across the moor, hounds raced her to Bickham, where she beat up and down, in the hope of putting up fresh deer. None being there, she was forced to fly down the valley of the Iron Mill Stream to the Chain Bridge, and through Bryants Copse to Halfpenny Bridge. Fresh finding her, hounds coursed her back to Chain Bridge. Not finding anymore deer here she went out over the top into Steart and then down the valley past Emmerford. Hereabouts four or five deer crossed the same field as hounds, but fortunately in the opposite direction, and the pack swung on at a good pace after the hunted hind. Going down the valley hounds passed New Bridge, and went on through Hatherland to Pilemoor, where they turned left handed again and came through Standerton Wood and on to Courtney. From here the hind went to Lurley, and then to Loxbeare, where there was a short check. Hounds being soon put right, however, they crossed the road and passed close to Sidborough, and on nearly to the blackksmith's shop at Templeton. Running down the Templeton Bottom they went away to Witheridge Moor and Hilltown Coverts, turning upwards to Tiderston Moor and back nearly to Rackenford Mill. Fresh finding, hounds pressed their hind to

Rackenford, past the Rectory, and on as if for the coverts at Rackenford. Here strength was however, failing, and she was killed close to the village. The run was one of the best this season. Hounds were running continuously from the find at 11 till a few minutes past 4 o'clock.

Jan 30th 1904

These hounds met at Worlington on Wednesday in fine weather, and a fairly big field was out to meet them. The tufters were drawn at the meeting place and the pack was sent on to kennel at Bealey Court. As soon as the tufters were thrown into Coton Hayes, seven hinds fled out singly, the last of which the Master decided to hunt. Laying the pack on just outside the cover, they first ran down into Affeton Old Plantation, and waiting there for the hounds, the deer came back again straight through Coton Hayes over Lutworthy Moorlands, the Chulmleigh road, into Week Wood, where the deer was headed by some men at work. Turning back towards the Gidley Arms the deer crossed the South Molton road and straight on to Creacombe and on into Baxton Wood, where there were three deer in front of hounds, but sticking to the hunted one they drove across Harestone Moor into Great Down on across Rackenford Moor to the Bickham Covers straight down the valley past Spurway Mills, and right down to Chain Bridge, turning up the Exe Valley from there the deer crossed the river at Stuckeridge Bridge into the Wonham Coverts, running there right up to Highleigh where the deer was fresh found in the young cover. Racing back through the covers, the deer came to the water again above Chain Bridge and was taken soon after close to Duvale. The time from laying on at Coton Hayes till hounds got to Chain Bridge the first time, a point of 13 miles, was about hour and a half.

It was so frosty Saturday morning that there seemed little hope of hunting, but after waiting half-an-hour, Mr Amory decided to make a start, though the ground was very slippery and was really never rideable all day. The pack was kennelled on Dry Hill, and moving off from New Bridge, where hounds met, Mr Dunning's coverts at Steart were drawn. Three hinds were found here, and after running them up round the Stoodleigh coverts and past Mr Daniel's house at Stuckeridge, the pack was laid on down by the Exe, between Stuckeridge and Wonham. Hounds ran the hind up through the Wonham coverts towards Exebridge and back over the top of the hill by Bampton to Duvale. She then crossed the Exe to Emmerford and taking to the water went down stream for more than a mile before she landed, thus causing a long check. Hounds were eventually laid on again near Bolham, ran close to the town of Tiverton, crossed the race course, the river and the leat, and passed close to Waratah, the residence of that well known stag hunter Mr Corbett. The hind then continued up over Prescott and away by the Hensleigh kennels to the valley of the Little Dart, where hounds were stopped in the dark at 5.15, after what may be considered a much better day's sport than there was any right to anticipate, considering the hard frost and the state of the ground.

Feb 20th 1904

Following a largely attended lawn meet at Mr Macadam Smith's residence at Wiveliscombe on Wednesday, hounds were taken on to Mr A. Capel's coverts at Bulland. Fred Goss the Harbourer reported that all the hinds had left and only two young stags were there. Mr Amory drew with the pack, and one of these, roused in Middle Hill, came out and went straight to Bittiscombe coverts and up over the hill to Skilgate Common. Going the whole length of this he came into Haddon Hill close to Frogwell Lodge, and running straight over the moor to Wynne Corner, he came down to the Haddeo by way of Clanmer, crossing into Storridge, he went across Lyncombe Lakes and away over Barons Down to the Exe. Turning downwards he passed Hele Bridge and then over the top into Pixton Park, where he joined the herd of Fallow deer, and not finding a way out, the pack drove him around the park. Finally jumping the palings, he crossed the Barle into Allers Wood running through here, he kept up past Brushford and on past Coombe, coming down again by Nightcott. He then crossed the railway about a mile from Anstey Station. Here we thought his point must be the Rackenford coverts, but always bending to the left he came down behind Highleigh to the Exe, and hounds brought him to bay at Oakford Bridge and killed him at Halfpenny Bridge.

On Saturday the meet was at Chawleigh, and hounds put in another good run to their credit. Miller reporting that two deer had been taking a walk during the night around the Rectory Lawn. Mr Amory drew with the pack for them, and hounds came up to them in Foxes Covert. After a turn or two around this big covert, he came away over the Eggesford Ford and on into Chawleigh Week Covert. Thence the line lay down the valley past Chulmleigh, where a lot of the field were thrown out, and upward by Kings Nympton and across the park. He was ultimately killed below South Molton Road Station at Kingsbridge, and hounds at once trotted off on their 25 miles journey home.

Feb 26th 1904

Whenever it may please the worthy Master to bring his splendid pack of hounds into the Chawleigh district he is assured of a successful day's hunt. Notwithstanding the boisterous wind and frequent storms, a good number of riders and pedestrians presented themselves in the centre of the village on Saturday to witness the "Meet" and to enjoy the chase. Deer are known to be numerous in the woods surrounding this parish adjoining the Little Dart and Taw. Harbourer Miller, assisted by the keepers on the estate, spotted no less than five deer in Chawleigh Barton Wood on Friday evening; but before daylight next morning two fine animals had shifted across to "Olden Clump Plantation" on Southcott. Mr Ian Amory, Captain H. Amory, the Messrs de Las Casas, and other gentlemen arrived from Tiverton about 10am, and after a short pause at the Barton, decided to go in quest of the two deer that had left their previous hiding. A move was made with the whole pack. Within ten minutes of leaving the village the hounds cracked off, having caught scent near the Rectory. Riders and hounds pushed on rapidly to Foxes Covert driving both stags in front. Separating, a fine five year old gentleman doubled back and was followed through Southcott Woods, Upcott ditto, Chawleigh Week, across the dart to Chulmleigh, thence to Kingsnympton. At 2pm, being hard pressed he took to the deep waters of the River Mole, just a mile from Head Mills and was quickly dispatched. Among those present at the death were Mr Ian Amory, Capt. H. Amory, Messrs de Las Casas, W. Littleworth, G. Pope, R. Parkhouse, and Miller. Just before his death the animal furiously attacked one of the leading hounds, "Sportsman", and the dog had to be shot. The deer was carted back to the Portsmouth Hotel, where, by Mr Amory's order, the carcase was dressed and quartered by Mr W. Ware, who soon distributed the joints as destined by the genial Master.

The meet on Tuesday was at the Carnarvon Arms. Hounds found at once in Steart Woods, ran up the valley as far as Heal Bridge, and away across the Exe into Bury Castle. From here she ran past Bury Village into Swinescleave and Storridge, and on to Harford Cleave and to the Deer Park. In the meantime the pack was being brought on from the Carnarvon Arms, and it was laid on at Skilgate Common. Running down into Sir John

Ferguson Davie's allotments, she came down close to Upton and through Bittescombe Coverts, nearly to Chipstable. Turning left handed, she ran across the moors to Clatworthy Wood, where there was a slight check. Hounds getting away again ran away across the Brendon Hills, and had to be stopped some miles further on, as it was found they had got on to the track of a male deer. Mr Amory went back to Clatworthy Wood again, but could not get on terms with the hunted hind.

March 5th 1904

Meeting at the Carnarvon Arms on Wednesday, the pack was kennelled at the hotel and tufters found a lot of deer at once on the top of Steart. Going away to the Exe by way of Hele Bridge the deer took a turn around Hele Ball, and thus away out over the top across Court Down. Fresh finding their deer in Ball Neck they raced her by way of Higher Combe to Southhill and away to the Allotments on Winsford Hill, where she tried the usual way of putting up fresh deer, but Captain Amory had viewed her away into Burrow Wood, and the pack was soon on her line. Driving her through the Punch Bowl, she went on past Comer's Gate, which she left to the right, and hounds drove her as if for Exford, but turning upwards she crossed the road again and came down the Barle by Landacre Bridge. Thence the line lay across Withypool Common and through Lords Plantation. She came down to the Barle again at Hindspool, from here she beat down the river to Tarr Steps and into Ashway Hat and on down past Three Waters, and onto Castle Bridge where she was killed. It being early, and Mr Amory having news of a crippled hind being seen in Burridge Wood, he drew for her. She was found and was soon caught near Dulverton.

Meeting on Saturday at the Royal Oak, Gibbet, hounds put in another rare day's sport with a fairly big field to enjoy it. The tufters went on to Knowstone to draw for the herd that has been making that district their headquarters and finding at once she came back. It was seen that scent was good, as they drove her over Beaples Hill to Branscombe, and on to the Rackenford Coverts, across the moor where one or two found a bog that was covered with the snow. The hounds were racing their deer as she came down through Bickham and on past Spurway Mills to Coleford Water. She went through Wheatland and crossing the road close to Ford Farm ran down to the front of Stoodleigh Court. Hounds ran her to Parkhouse Water and thence to the Exe at Washfield Weir. Turning back through Washfield the deer had waited for hounds and now running harder than ever she came back over Dry Hill through the Steart Coverts and down and across the river at Half Penny Bridge. Going on up over the hill she brought us close to Bampton and running not far from the railway she passed to Morebath Junction and came down to the Exe again at the chemical works. Hounds were now close to her and she was given no rest as she went over Riphay and then on across the railway above Brushford, where she was killed. Finding this good hind soon after eleven she stood up till nearly three, and it is the best day that hounds have had in the Stoodleigh country. Among those out during the last week were the Master Mr Heathcoat-Amory, Capt. Harry Heathcoat-Amory, Mr, Mrs, and Miss Manderson, Messrs L. Amory, Corbett, Boles, Dunsford, J. Jarvis-Baily, Yandle (3), Selly, Butt, Pring, Pethick, and many others.

March 19th 1904

A fairly big hind hunting field turned out in a beautiful weather at Spurway Mills on Wednesday, to great the Deputy-Master (Capt. H. Amory), Mr Ian Heathcoat-Amory having been unavoidably called away. Beginning operations in Town Wood, several deer went away down the valley with the tufters in close attendance. At Barels Cottage they turned over the top and went away through Steart, on past Emmerford, and into Parkhouse Water, and back again over Stoodleigh Moor. The pack, which were waiting in the road, were at once laid on, and ran her into Wormsworthy. Racing her up the valley she beat up the Coleford Water and went into Rifton, and hounds been close behind drove her nearly to Gibbet and on Wooliscroft Moor. Thence the line lay for Sydenham, then through Waspeyhayes, and down the valley of the Iron Mill Stream to Chain Bridge, hounds bringing a three hours gallop to a close with a kill near Oakford Bridge.

There was another good field out on Saturday at the Carnarvon Arms near Dulverton. In the forenoon scent was a missing quantity, but at about one o'clock the pack was laid on to some deer going into Haddon Wood. After running up and down the valley of the Haddeo for some time a good hind was seen going away through Harford Cleave with two hounds close behind. Driving her up through the Deer Park and back over Haddon Hill, the pack was brought into play at Pixey Copse. They ran their hind down the river, past the Chemical Works, and fresh found her in Ellars Wood. Having taken a turn or two round the wood she went away over the top on to Combe, and keeping left handed came up to Anstey Station. Bearing to the right she entered Armour Wood, and was soon on Anstey Common. Instead of going on into the big coverts at Hawkridge, where so many deer have saved their lives, she came down to the Danes Brook as far as Lyshall Wood, and on nearly to Molland Moor Gate. Fresh finding her on the moor, not far from Slade Bridge, hounds drove her sometimes in and sometimes out of the water down the Danes Brook to Bury Bridge, where she was taken about six o'clock under Dippers Copse. Among those out during the week, in addition to the Deputy Master (Captain H. Heathcoat-Amory), were Mr E. A. V. Stanley, M. S. H., Mr L. Amory, Miss Amory, Mrs L. Mackenzie, the Misses Chichester, Messrs W. Renton, F. Dunsford, H. M. Crosby, Archer, J. Jarvis-Baily, Corbet, Boles, Webber, and a lot of sporting farmers.

Mr E A V Stanley, Master of the Quantock Staghounds who was present at the Meet

March 26th 1904

The meet on Saturday was at Spurway Mill and a large field turned out to greet the Deputy-Master (Captain H. Heathcoat Amory), including Major Chichester, Mr L. Unwin (M.F.H), Mr. C. Carew (M. H.), Miss Amory, Miss Archer, Messrs M. and A., de Las Casas, J. Javis-Baily, G. Archer, F. J. Boles, W. Renton, Corbett, J. Butt, S. Webber, J. Zelly, W. Hayton, Snow (Knowstone), J.Blake, and a lot of sporting farmers. Tufters were laid on to some deer on Rackenford Moor at about 11 o'clock, and eventually ran a hind back to Spurway Mill, where the pack were kennelled. Hounds ran to Aldridge Mill and on into Southercott, where there were a lot of fresh deer up, and hounds divided. One lot ran their deer back to Rackenford, and the others came down to Chain Bridge and away to Steart and into Emmerford Coverts. Fresh finding in the river at New Bridge, she ran through Washfield Wood and on to Standerton, through Courtenay, and on to Pitt, close to the farmhouse, where she waited for hounds. Hounds racing her now took her close to the Rose and Crown over the hill to Combe Butler and on to Combeshead. Crossing on to Ditchets Farm she came to the Long Drag close to the Master's residence. Running down the drag she came up to Prescott and right down the meadows past Mr

Winton's house and to the river at Head Wear. Hounds now got a view of her and ran her by Sir John Amory's electric works and across the railway close to Bolham. Passing close to the Master of Foxhound's house at Hayne she came down to the Fish Ponds, and up through Mr Unwin's coverts at Fairby, and eventually came down to the water at New Bridge, where she was killed.

Oct 1st 1904

There was a large field to greet the Master Mr Ian Heathcoat-Amory at the opening meet of this noted pack at Chain Bridge on Saturday. Among those out were Sir David Wilson, Captain H. Heathcoat-Amory. Major and the Misses Chichester, Messrs A. and J. C. de Las Casas, L. A. Corbett, F. J. Coleridge, Boles, Mrs Pugsley, Messrs Williams, Cresswell, Pearce, Chapman, Major (2), Mr and Miss Lawrence (on wheels), Mr and Miss Renton, Mr Hancock, Mr March-Phillips, Dr Payne, Messrs Bevan, Heard, Tarr, Vearnicombe, Pring, Yendell (3), Haydon (2), Poole (2), Frisby, Chanin, Mr and Miss Macalister, Miss Boles, Mr and Mrs Tarr and party (wheels), Mrs Henson and party (wheels) Miss Babbage (wheels), Mr Holmes, Misses Campbell, Mr Yates, Misses Yendell, Mr Adams, Messrs Perry (2), and several from the Dulverton country. Ernest, riding in scarlet, brought the pack from the Hensleigh Kennels looking in the pink of condition. After the usual preliminaries the pack was taken back and kennelled at Duvale. Four and a half couple of tufters were here selected, and the Master trotted off to Wormsworthy, where two good stags had been harboured. A turn was taken round the covert and one of the stags ran away by Barle Cottage, over Hamslade. The tufters were stopped and the pack laid on near Oakford Village. Hounds ran down to Spurway Mill, into the big Waspleigh Wood, and on into Bickham. Complications arose hereabouts through a number of hinds getting up. Eventually the hunted stag was fresh found in Bickham and ran down as far as Aldridge Mills, only to get into a herd of hinds. Nothing more was done, and late in the afternoon hounds were taken home.

Oct 15th 1904

A good number of the supporters of this well known pack kept tryst (Latin *trista* 'an appointed place in hunting') at Chain Bridge on Saturday. The pack was as usual kennelled at Duvale and the tufters went on to Stuckeridge North. The deer had, however, shifted from here, and tufters were taken on to Wormsworthy, where they found at once. They got well away with their deer and ran by way of Waspleigh, to Sideham and Bickham. Crossing Rackenford Moor, the stag went to Great Down, and after a turn or two up and down the coverts, he came back again over the moor. In the meantime one of the whips went back to Duvale for the pack, which was laid on at Aldridge Mills. Hounds ran hard down the Iron Mill Stream, fresh found in the water close to the Keeper's Cottage, and forcing their quarry down to Chain Bridge went up over Bryant Copse and away to the Steart Coverts. Turning back to the Exe at Halfpenny Bridge, the stag crossed over, breasted the hill, and ran on nearly to Bampton, but keeping to the left to Coombshead and down to the water at Highley Weir. Continuing his line up the valley he turned near the railway not far from the chemical works at Exebridge, and keeping to the railway, passed Morebath Junction and across the line close to the village. Hounds got a view of him soon after and was killed in a field half a mile the other side of Morebath Village. He was a good bodied stag with brow, tray, and two on top.

Oct 22nd 1904

The meet on Tuesday was at the Carnarvon Arms near Dulverton and hounds were kennelled at Bury. Tufters roused a stag in the Deer Park at Haddon and raced him over Haddon Hill and across Skilgate Common. The pack was laid on close to the Bittiscombe coverts, whence the line lay across the valley as if for Chipstable. Some young deer being found ahead, hounds were brought back to Sir John Ferguson Davie's allotments. A big stag was soon roused, and ran back through Westhill, into Haddon and on to Hartford Cleave, and Clammer, away out of Baron's Down and to the Exe at Hele Bridge. Thence the line lay up the valley through Exe Cleeve and Exe Park to the water at Stockham and on down the valley past Ware to the river, close to Dulverton Station. Passing through Ellars Wood the stag got down to the water at New Bridge and was killed about 4.30. He was a big stag with all his rights, five atop one side and three on the other.

Following the meet at Duvale on Saturday, there was a find in Stuckeridge and the pack was laid on near Nethercott. Hounds ran past Oakford to the Red Deer across nearly to Anstey. Coming down the valley close to Brushford the stag crossed the railway by the chemical works and ran past Shillingford and Morebath Station and on to the Bittiscombe Coverts where the hunt was stopped owing to fresh deer getting up.

Oct 29th 1904

Following the meet at Worlington on Wednesday tufters found at once in Affeton Plantation. The pack was laid on going into Cottonhayes and ran on towards Mouseberry, across the Gidley Arms Road into Wick Coverts, down through Ball Covert, and on to Waterloo. Turning left handed they came back to Stone Moor and entered the water under Chawleigh Barton, where hounds ran up to their deer. Breaking away again he ran through the wood on to Upcott, through Sethercott, and down to the river by Eggesford Station. He was bayed, but breaking away again he ran up the bottom towards the Rectory grounds at Chawleigh and down to the water above Stone Mill, where he was taken after a run of about three hours. A good stag with three and two on top.

Another fine deer was added to the list of slain on Saturday. The fixture was at Rackenford, the starting place of many a good day's sport; the day reminded one of summer more than it did of autumn, and there was a large field to greet the Master. Operations commenced in the coverts behind Cruwyshayes House, tufters driving their deer across Rackenford Moor, through Bickham to Spurway Mill, where the pack was laid on going into Wormsworthy. Running down the valley nearly to Barle Cottage he turned over towards Oakford and came down nearly to Oakford Bridge. Thence the line lay up the valley to Highleigh and on to Riphay. Running on nearly to Brushford, he kept by the railway and up the valley close to Anstey before coming back to All Ways End. The end came near by. A good stag with all his rights and three atop both sides.

Nov 5th 1904

A novel expedient was adopted on Wednesday to get the hounds to the fixture at Chawleigh. In the past the pack has always been taken by road, a distance of seventeen miles, the journey by rail being out of the question, as it would involve a long detour round Exeter. On this occasion a light van wired at each end was brought into use. It was taken just before 7 o'clock in the morning to a heap of stones on the Long Drag, where a wire door was opened for the hounds to enter. Accustomed as the hounds are to go into fresh places no difficulty was experienced in getting them to mount the heap and enter the van. A steam motor known as the "Little Giant" was requisitioned to draw the van, and so well did the scheme work that in three hours time the pack were safely at Chawleigh. The field was a large one. Miller had harboured a single deer in Leigh Wood and the Master decided to draw with the pack. Hounds found at once and ran their deer straight away to Worlington, on through Pedley Wood and straight to Thelbridge Cross. Crossing the road hereabouts he continued his course down the valley and away to Washford Pyne and on close to Puddington and Pennymoor. Scent was never better, and hounds followed their deer at a rare pace back through Merryfieldhayes and on to Witheridge Moor. Passing through Hilltown hounds raced through Northcombe and across the Rackenford road not far from Gibbet. Thence the line lay into Rifton, through Wheatland and down by Coleford Water nearly to Halridge Mill; then down the Iron Mill Stream to Chain Bridge. After running through Bryants Copse hounds fresh found their deer in Steart Coverts, and brought him to water at Duvale. Breaking away again he went through the Wonham Coverts to Stuckeridge, and turning up over Stuckeridge North he came down to the Iron Mill Stream under Down Wood where he was killed. The furthest point was sixteen miles, and the pace was so fast all through this fine run that many well mounted followers got left behind.

Following a meet at the Carnarvon Arms on Saturday, the day was spent between Anstey Common and Winsford Hill, several deer being up.

Nov 19th 1904

In wild and windy weather on Wednesday some deer were found in Rackenford Wood. One of them was run over the moor and down by Bickham to Stoodleigh, and through the Stoodleigh Coverts, over Stuckeridge and down the valley to the river, where hounds were stopped. The rain was now driving heavily, and everyone must have been glad to hear the order for home.

The meet was at Spurway Mill on Saturday. Tufters roused several hinds in Summerclose Covert, and ran them by Stanterton and Stoodleigh Park, Rifton Covert and back to Aldridge Mill, where the pack was laid on. A real good run of three and a half hours ensued. Hounds ran their hind through Town Wood to Oakford, and over the Oakford road pointing for Anstey, but turning left handed they came back into the Iron Mill Stream up to Champles Farm and down through the Stoodleigh Coverts to the Exe, away by East Stoodleigh to Emmelford and Bere Hill and on down the valley nearly to Worth. We next ran right handed by Washfield and back by Pilemoor to the Stoodleigh Coverts again and down the Exe by New Bridge, where she was lost.

Nov 26th 1904

The meet on Wednesday was at the Carnarvon Arms near Dulverton, and some deer were found in Bury Castle. Hounds ran them through Exe Cleave and Stockham to Broford, whence they brought a deer back through Exe Park to Barons Down and on into Haddon. Having run the whole length of Haddon hounds had to be stopped owing to fog.

A large field greeted the Master at Bampton Down on Saturday. Operations commenced in Cudmore Brake, a deer going away to Zeal Ball. Thence the line lay through Priestland Covert, and then away straight for Cove, through Mrs North Row's Coverts, and on through Bickleigh Covert and Fairby, where she was headed by some beaters. She was fresh found above Gogwell, and ran away through Palfreys, and into the top end of Allen's Down, away down over Chevithorne Barton to Fordlands, and on past Bradford, where she was fresh found in a stream. Running back through Craze Lowman to Gornhay, she crossed the road not far from Mr Glendinning's, and ran on past West Manley. She crossed the road again near Black Bridge, and she was killed in the canal not far from Tidcombe House.

Dec 10th 1904

The meet was at Bury Village on Saturday and the pack was taken to Frogwell Lodge to kennel. Tufters drew the Deer Park and found a deer at once. Two hinds went away over the hill to Skilgate Common nearly to the Allotments, where the two hinds turned back to the Deer Park. The one selected ran down the bottom and around Westhill, past Steart, through Harford Cleeve and Haddon Wood and down the valley to Bury, away by Pixey Copse and across the river and on to close by the Carnarvon Arms. Thence the line lay to the Chemical Works and away over the top of the hill as if for Morebath. Turning short back she came down the valley again, and turned into Haddon by Birchin Wood. Here she ran the water up past Clammer and on nearly to Harford Mills, where hounds fresh found her in the water and drove her all down the valley to below Bury. The end came just below the village at about 2.30.

Dec 17th 1904

A big field met Sir John Amory's Staghounds at Newbridge on Wednesday. The pack was kennelled at Dryhill, and the tufters were taken to Willeycleave. Finding several deer at once, after a turn round the coverts we ran back across the Stoodleigh drive into the Emmerford Coverts. Meanwhile one of the whips had got the pack out, and meeting the Master in the lane, the pack was laid on going into Steart. Running across into Highwood we ran her up the valley through Champlesclift to Wormsworthy. Turning back across Nethercott we went over Stuckeridge and down to the river at Chain Bridge.

Hounds fresh found her in the water, and she ran up through the wood, coming down into the Steart Coverts again. On through the Emmerford Coverts she ran, and down to the water to Newbridge. Driven on, she went down the water past Hatherland and Worth and she was killed near Sir John Amory's Lodge below Head Weir. It was a sharp run, lasting from 11o'clock till 2.

A good hind hunting field kept tryst at the Keeper's Cottage, Winsford Hill, on Wednesday last. On the Allotments being drawn three deer went away at once through the Punch Bowl and on to Comers Gate. Turning through to Comers Cross and down across the moors to the Exford road, just below Stone Cross, we came to the vicinity of Stone, where hounds had to be stopped. Going back again to the Allotments we got on the line of a deer, and went away to Comer's Gate again, on to Bradley Ham, and down the Barle Valley by way of Tarr Steps. The pack were waiting at Ashway Side, and were put on the line of a hind and calf, which went into Ashway Hat. Fresh finding them here they ran across Ashway Side to Southhill, from there to Redcleave, and into the Exe Valley by Broford and Stockham, over Barons Down into Storridge. Running the valley we came to Hartford Mill, whence hounds drove their deer down to Clammer, then over Barons Down again to the Exe, in the Water at Barlynch. Driving her up the Exe Valley again hounds fresh found her in the water under Redcleave, and drove her up over the covert to Southhill once more and on to Southill Plantation where unfortunately, we had a herd of deer in front of us. It was now getting dark, and hounds had to be whipped off.

Spurway Mills was the venue on Saturday. We found at Rifton and ran by Blatchworthy to Willicroft and the iron mill stream by way of Throwcombe and Waspleigh. Thence the line lay to Chain Bridge and over the top of Steart. Scent was bad and early in the afternoon the order was given for home.

Dec 24th 1904

Good days seem to be the rule with this pack this year, but Saturday's run will not soon be forgotten by those who rode through it. The meet was at Aldridge Mills and by reason of the fact that the Tiverton Foxhounds met at Hensleigh to draw Mr Amory's Coverts the field was not a large one. It included only those who prefer a day with the Staghounds to the rival attraction of a days fox hunting. Among those who were out in addition to the Master, I noticed Mr A.de Las Casas, Col Masefield, Mr J. F. Pugsley, Major McNeile, Messrs Meade, Pring, E. Yandle, B. Yandle, M. Haydon (Stoodleigh), W. Haydon and C. Haydon (Prescott), Channing and Coles (Rifton), and M. Haydon (Castle Barton). The pack was kennelled at Spurway Mills and Mr Amory drew Wormsworthy and Nethercott coverts blank; but in Down Wood tufters soon found a young stag and as the time was getting late the pack was laid on and away they went with a dash which showed that scent was right. This young stag began by taking quite an unusual line, going away over the hill as if for Anstey was his point. Soon changing his mind, however, he swung around right handed and came back by Oakford, making for Stuckeridge and the Exe near Chain Bridge; then right handed again by Bryants Copse and Highwood Plain down through the scrub across the railway and the river, then up by Cove and Marwood to Van Post and the Cobbacombe Coverts; then right handed to Plushhayes, where on his own farm we picked up Mr Blackmore, jun., who to judge by the way in which he rode through the remainder of this run bids fair to rival his father as a good guide to follow over the roughest part of any country. Away by Huntsham Wood and Bere Down to Ashbrittle, Appley Village, Greenham, and Hollacombe we reached White Ball, over which hounds ran as if they meant to go to Wellington Monument, but the stag was evidently turned by a man who was ploughing and bearing right handed we found ourselves in the neighbourhood of the Burlescombe Quarries. The stag soiled in the canal near here and then apparently made up his mind to make his original point, for he bore away sharply left handed across the main Great Western line by Burlescombe Station and led hounds straight through the big coverts by Maidendown and over the Down itself; then down the valley by Prescott to Culmstock. Here hounds fairly ran up to him and catching a view raced him over the vale and to the river where he was killed. The pack was laid on at 11.20 and ran with scarcely any check until 3 o'clock. The extent of the country covered must have been great. The distance from the point where the stag was found to the point where he was killed measured straight across the map is 14 miles, but if a measurement could be taken of the line hounds ran it would certainly be found not to be less than double the distance. It must surely be many years ago since the Staghounds were seen in Culmstock Village.

Jan 7th 1905

"Cinqfoil" has an interesting account in *The Field* of the doings of this pack after the recent meet at Highercombe. It looked hopeless at first, he says, but as the fog was clearer in some of the valleys Mr Amory was not to be deterred. After describing the tufting operations, which started in the Allotments and came to an end near Spire Cross, "Cinqfoil" proceeds: The Master disappeared into the fog to turn up a moment or two later with the pack, which had been brought on along the road. Hounds ran merrily along the southern side of Winsford Hill, but divided near the corner of Knaplock Bog, one section, with which the writer cast in his lot, turning back to Tarr Steps and downward to Hawkridge, the other section heading for the upper part of the Barle. These again divided, and one section ran to the river under Bradley while others crossed the hill to Ash, and among the intricate combes and enclosures which lie between Exe and Barle, disappeared into the fog to be found no more. It was a case of every man for himself, the little bands of riders being scattered all over the country. They were undoubtedly fresh deer which went down below Tarr Steps, so a small party of two sought the high fields above Hawkridge Rectory, and hearing some hounds running under Bradley, went thither, but only found two couples hunting in Greystones Wood. Hopelessly at fault, we were joined subsequently by Mr Amory and a few others, collected about five or six couples, and made good the valley up to Withypool, but in vain. Joining forces with the whippers-in, who had stopped hounds in the lower valley above Ashway, we made a wide circuit in search of the pack, but only picked up a few couples, the main body, it subsequently transpired, having run, totally unaccompanied, a grand line across the Barle, and away to Molland Common, subsequently swinging round into the Barle Valley low down. Scent had been first rate all the time, and hounds ran their hardest. The Barle Valley country is not an easy one to live with hounds in at the best of times, but when it is alive with deer, and an impenetrable mist prevents one seeing more than a hundred or two hundred yards, anyone may be excused for losing touch with the pack.

On Tuesday hounds were at the Carnarvon Arms at 9.30, and trotted off to Bury Village, where the pack were kennelled; then jogged up the Haddeo Valley to the Deer Park to draw, and on the way counted a fine herd of sixteen stags standing on the heather above Hartford Cleeve. A herd of hinds with a few male deer were found at once, and away we went at best pace over the heather for Skilgate Common. The herd scattered, and some, including a heavy stag, came back; but the rest went on, and we enjoyed a cherry gallop by way of Haddon End to Sir John Ferguson Davie's coverts, about a mile below the fishponds. The deer crossed the deep combe without hesitation and headed away over the enclosures beyond, a friendly lane helping us to keep touch with hounds till we reached the heathery downs above Huish. Here many fresh deer were on foot, both stags and hinds, and tufters separated, but the main body stuck to the line of a hind, which, after running right through the Bulland coverts, and headed as though minded to seek the far off shelter of Maiden Down, doubled short back and gave a gallop as hard as ever we could go to Haddon. We viewed her, accompanied by her calf, as she crossed Hartford Cleeve, and again in the water by Clammer, but fresh deer caused delay. Tufters were soon on the right line, and ran hard in Surnes Cleeve and away to Lincombe. Across the rough inclosures above Storridge they ran hard, brought the line back to Clammer and up to Higher Lodge, Baron's Down. They next ran a hind out from the lower corner of Barlinch Wood to Bury Castle, but opinions differed as to whether it was a fresh deer or not. The pack were now brought on from Bury and this gave a respite to horses, which those who had been all the way with tufters sorely needed. Bury Castle and Pixie Copse were alive with deer, but hounds ran the line over the Exe and skirted Pixton Park to Jury and Hele Ball. So fast did they run through the coverts of Exe Cleeve and Stockham that they nearly slipped us altogether, and would have done so but for a friendly holloa on the hill. By riding hard over Court Down and through Loosehall Wood to the Barle we caught them again as they ran up the valley under Draydon Farm. Below Mounsey hounds turned, climbed the hill to Summerhouse and went on by way of Hinam to the Hawkridge Coverts, where there were a number of fresh deer on foot, and it was impossible to recover the line of the hunted hind. It was now close on four o'clock, and if it was the same hind we began running just after ten she must have had quite enough, for we had covered many miles of very rough ground.

Jan 14th 1905

These hounds met at Highercombe on Tuesday, and when the pack had been kennelled here the tufters were taken on to draw Southhill Plantation. Finding at once a herd of seven hinds it was soon seen that there was a scent, as the hounds drove them over the heather to Red Cleave. Here hounds divided, most of them turning back over the hill as if for the Allotments in chase of a good hind, but, changing her mind, she turned short back to the Exe, coming down to the water just below Bridgetown. Going on down the valley she passed at the back of Milton Rocks, through Winslade Wood, Exe Park, and right on to the end of the covers, above Hele Bridge, doubling back through the woods she came down to the river close to Barlinch, where the leading hounds came up to her; then, having been driven through Exe Cleeve, she came down again to the water close to Hele Bridge, and up through the Barons Down Woods to Louisa Gate, and on into Haddon. Running through Swinescleeve and coming down to the Haddeo, above Clammer, she ran up the water nearly to Hartford Cleeve, but, turning into Haddon Wood, she shook off her pursuers by joining a herd of stags. Meanwhile, Mr A. de Las Casas, who was hunting the hounds in the unavoidable absence of the Master, was running another hind with two and a half couple of hounds down the Exe Valley by Broford, then through Stockham and on to Hele Bridge, and then on over Haddon Hill, keeping the south side of the hill, then on over Skilgate Common to the Bittiscombe Covers, where he got up to them. With the pack some six or seven miles away, and no one to send back, he reluctantly decided to go on. Running her around Ramscombe hounds carried the line on to Petton Cross, and ran the meadows close to the line as far as the viaduct at Waterrow; then turning out over they ran her out nearly to Kittisford, where she was killed. It was a splendid performance of both huntsman and hounds, being close on a twelve mile point with only five hounds, one of which was lost before the finish.

On Saturday the meet was at Bury, and a large field was out as the day wore on. Kennelling the pack here, the tufters had a long trot before them. As a herd of deer had been doing a lot of damage at Chipstable. Mr Amory (whom everbody was glad to see out again) decided to give those covers a rattling. Finding several deer at once in Middlehill they broke out, going through the Huish Covers and away back to the Bittiscombe Covers and on to the top close to Skilgate Common, where one of the hinds left and went on into the Allotments and down into the Deer Park, the tufters now driving her along, they drove her quickly through West Hill and past Steart and then on into Storridge down as far as Syncombe. Crossing into Haddon Wood she went up the water to Harford Cleeve, when she turned back into Haddon Wood. The pack was now laid on pushing her along, we soon ran down to Bury and then down to the river by "Weir" then up through Pixton nearly into Dulverton. Turning up over the hill as if for Hollam, but keeping left handed hounds brought her to water at Marsh Bridge, then up through Northmoor to water at the Keeper's House, then up through the Summerhouse cover and down to the water under Hinam where she was killed.

Jan 21st 1905

There was a fairly big field at the Carnarvon Arms on Wednesday. The pack was kennelled at the hotel, and a strong lot of tufters taken out to draw Pixie Copse. Finding no deer here, information was given the Master that there was an injured stag in Sir John Davie's Allotments on Skilgate Common. Taking hounds on there the tufters drew the Allotments but could not find the injured stag. They were then laid on to four deer that was standing on the moor. Running the deer back across Skilgate Common, tufters ran into the Deer Park and straight down into Hartford Cleeve and into Haddon Wood, where the deer divided. The tufters came back over Haddon Hill with a hind and yearling, across Skilgate Common to the Bittiscombe Coverts. Here hounds were stopped while Mr Frank Dunsford kindly went back to Bury Village for the pack, which had been taken on there. Laying the pack on in Ramscombe they ran through the Deer Park round Ramscombe to Petton Cross. Bearing to the left they next ran back over the hill to Raddington; thence straight on to Chipstable Village. Then, turning up over the hill, they came into the Chipstable Coverts at Middlehill, Fresh finding their deer here they took a turn over the moors towards Huish, and finally killed close to Middlehill.

The meet on Saturday was at Worlington, a representative field being out. The pack was kennelled at Bealy Court and tufters were taken on to Ball Covert to draw. Finding there immediately they ran by way of Waterloo to the Stone Moor Coverts, where the pack was laid on. Running through the Stone Moor Coverts he came down under Sydeham and into the Chawleigh Barton Wood. Going on as if he were making for the Eggesford Coverts, but taking a short turn to the left, he came down through the wood to Stone Mill. Then, running through Leigh Wood, he came up over Pouncers and across the road as if going to Lapford Woods again, but keeping up the valley he came across to

Thelbridge Cross and right on to the Merrifieldhayes Coverts. Here he took a short turn right handed and ran right away to Cheriton Fitzpaine and about a mile further on was safely taken at Mr Mildons at Upcott Barton.

Jan 28th 1905

These hounds on Wednesday were advertised to meet at Bury Village in the Dulverton Country, but a sharp frost overnight, and some sleet that had fallen made the roads too slippery for horses to travel on. After waiting till the last moment it was decided to abandon all thoughts of getting to Dulverton. About 10.30 the sun having driven a lot of the frost away Mr Amory thought it would be a good time to go and disturb a herd of deer that had been doing Mr Selley at Rhyll a lot of damage, so it was a very small field that met the Master about 11.30, but they increased during the day to about a score, including the Master, Mr Ian Amory, Messrs A. and C. de Las Casas, Mr F. Dunsford, Mr J. C. Yandle and his four sons Messrs Haydon, Pring, Poole, Headon and a few others. The deer having left the Rhyll Coverts the tufters drew Wormsworthy, Little Waspley, Big Waspley and when Bickham was reached they found a herd of five or six which, having taken a turn around the cover, went away for Rackenford Moor. One of them turning short back the tufters were soon driving her along fast as she was making her way back to Bickham. She was met on the top of Sydeham by the pack that had been brought on from Spurway Mill, where they had been kennelled. Now driving her along it was soon seen that there was a first rate scent. Running down the valley, Waspley, Nethercott, and Town Wood were quickly run through; and when nearly down to Chain Bridge the hounds ran up to their deer, which had been waited for them in the Iron Mill Stream. Breaking away with the pack in close attendance through Stuckeridge and North Stuckeridge Wood and down to the River Exe under Wonham, she crossed and ran the whole length of the Wonham covers to Highleigh, where she came to water. Again crossing, she ran up through the wood, then right handed as if for Riphay and Brushford; but, bearing left handed, she ran up the valley nearly to Anstey. Then turning up over the hill, she brought us back to Red Deer; then she bore away for Bickham Moor, and then crossed on to Rackenford Moor, where, instead of going to the big covers where there were fresh deer, she ran right down the valley to the turnpike road under Rackenford. Rearing left handed she soon brought us back to Whitnole and on through Blatchworthy and Rifton to Coleford Water, then on through Wheatland, past Aldridge Mill through Wormsworthy and down the Iron Mill Stream nearly to Chain Bridge, where she turned up through Stuckeridge and down to the Exe at Stuckeridge Bridge. Having run up the water nearly to Oakford Bridge, she entered the Wonham Covers again, which she ran up as far as Highleigh, and then down to the water again and into the wood, where she doubled about in the hope of putting up fresh deer. Not finding any she was viewed coming down the water under Highleigh, and a friendly holloa soon had the Master and pack there. Hounds now got a view of her, and it was soon all over, Mr Percy Yandle cleverly headroping her. Scent was very good specially during the first part of the run which lasted five hours without practically a check. Finding her just before one o'clock she was killed about ten minutes to six.

Feb 4th 1905

These hounds met at Bury on Wednesday. There was not a very big field out in the earlier part of the day. The pack being kennelled at Bury, a strong draft of tufters were taken out to draw West Hill, the Harbourer reporting a lot of deer there. While going up the valley news of a crippled stag was brought to the Master as being lying down in the heather not far from Upton Lodge. Not finding him there, hounds were taken into the Deer Park. They had hardly been thrown in before the stag was viewed in company with another coming out of Upton Wood. The hounds were soon on his line, and after a turn around he came back by Upton Farm and into Westhill, where hounds changed on to a hind, driving her past Steart, through Huscombe Wood and across Hartford Cleeve. She joined a herd of stags but hounds sticking to her she was driven through Haddon Wood and to the water above Clammer; crossing into Storridge she went straight up over the hill nearly into Kingsbrompton, and then bearing away left handed she came back to the Exe Valley by way of Exe Park and into the water, where hounds bayed her. Breaking away, she soon came to the water again close to Barlynch, where after a little difficulty she was killed. It being quite early a fresh lot of tufters was drawn, and a herd of deer were soon moving in Bury Castle. After a turn around they went across the Exe at "Weir" and into Pixton Park, around which they drove their deer, going back on the line they had just come they divided in Rookwood; one hind with four couple coming up the meadows by Hele Bridge, while another with two or three hounds in pursuit made a point high up on Hele Ball. Sticking to the one that went up by Hele Bridge, they ran her hard up the valley through Exe Cleeve and to the water under Stockham, across and then through Winslade Wood, and up the valley till we came to Red Cleeve. Then on to the open moor on Southill, straight through Southhill Plantation and on to the Allotments and the Punchbowl, where she turned back into Burrough Wood and joined a herd of deer, so saving herself. As it was getting on in the afternoon it was thought inadvisable going on after them. As hounds were going down the valley another hind was viewed in the water with two hounds hunting her; the rest were soon laid on and running hard through Exe Cleeve into Stockham, where hounds unfortunate divided, the hunted one going on through Broford into Red Cleeve, Southill, and then across Ashway Side to the Barle, then through Ashway Hat to Three Waters, when as the light was beginning to fall the hounds had to be called off. Among those out during the day I noticed Messrs A. and J. C. de Las Casas, Mr E. Hancock, Messrs Yandle (3) Messrs Woodbury, Goss and several others.

Feb 11th 1905

That the present season has been the very best there has been since the pack was started in 1896 will be readily admitted by those whose good fortune it has been to participate in the brilliant sport that has been provided. Scent has been extremely good and some of the runs have lasted between five and six hours, the end having come more than once in entirely new country. One day the deer was killed in the canal at Tiverton; on another occasion an excellent run came to an end at Culmstock; only a few weeks ago a deer was dispatched at Cheriton Fitzpaine, while on Saturday we ended for the day near Cullompton eleven miles from the scene of the meet but as hounds ran quite double that distance. Wednesday's meet was at Chawleigh, and among the field were Mr Ian Amory (Master), Messrs Las Casas, Dunsford, Renton (3) (Tiverton), Miller (Wembworthy), R. Woollacott (Ashreigney), Partridge (Chawleigh), F. Webber and B. Cobley (Chulmleigh). The Harbourer reported several stags in Bycott Plantation, and on the tufters being put in, no less than ten stags were roused. One of these were singled out, and immediately made for "Waterloo", and from there onto Wixon Farm. Then it made across Week Farm and up over the hill to Broads Moor, where the pack was laid on. The stag then turned away to the right towards Affeton, West Worlington, and thence across Burridge Farm. Then it made away to East Leigh, Chawleigh, also crossing West Leigh, and then making its way to Chawleigh Barton. Continuing its journey at a racing pace, the stag went down the valley through the Cleaves and then up the hill to Roughments. Here it turned again to the right, and then going down over the steep fields at Chawleigh Week, crossed the Little Dart river, and made up over the hill on the other side through Leigh Barton, Chulmleigh. It next crossed the Barnstaple Turnpike Road near the old Toll-House at Leigh Cross, and then went down the valley close to the railway line under Colleton House, but directly before reaching Colleton Mill it veered round to the right and crossed the road again, passing near Colleton Farmhouse, and on through Station Wood to Elstone. Thence it crossed to Hill Head Farm, and at last took water at Head Mill Weir Pool, where it was captured. It had given a splendid run of one and a half hours without a check, and horses had a hard gallop, only a small number being present at the death. The head has been given to Mr John Tripe, who has hunted with the Staghounds for several years, but is now unable to do so being nearly blind as a result of an accident two or three months ago.

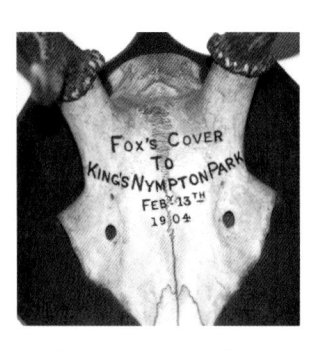

Fox's Cover to King's Nympton Park on February 13th 1905.

The advertised fixture for Saturday was at New Bridge, but as the hinds had changed their quarters the meet was at Spurway Mills instead. Despite the inclemency of the weather there was a large field out including Miss Amory, Miss Chichester, Col Macefield (on wheels), Major Campbell, Mr. L. Unwin, M.F. H., Messrs. A.and J. C. de Las Casas, Mrs Pring (on wheels), Messrs F. Dunsford, W. A. L. Corbet, Meade, T., J., B., and F. Yandle, J. Selley (Hilltown), Courtenay, Haydon, W. Haydon, J. Jarvis-Baily, J. F. Pugsley, H. March Phillipps, Snow (Knowstone), Beedell (Sydham), Headon and Frisby (Stoodleigh), A. Pring, J. Blake, Osmant, J. Blake, J. W. Goddard, Down (Bampton), J. C. Hill, H. M. Crosby, G. Archer, Mogford (Storridge), and A. Heal (Washfield). Five couple of tufters were taken to the Cruwys-hayes coverts and soon roused a hind and yearling. Hounds brought them back through the Rackenford coverts and drove them across the moor through Bickham and down the valley past Spurway Mills, and the pack was laid on going into Little Waspleigh. Going on down the valley through Wormsworthy and Champles Cliff we came to Chain Bridge, and having run through Stuckeridge came to the Exe again just below Stuckeridge House. Thence the line lay through Duvale Wood and out over the top as if going for Bampton; but turning right handed she came to the Exe again just below Halfpenny Bridge; then up over Highwood and across Highwood Plain into the Steart Coverts. Getting no rest here she was driven downward through Emmelford and Hatherland right on through Washfield Wood and then to the Exe close to Sir John Amory's electric light works. Crossing the railway near Bolham she passed close to the kennels of the Tiverton Foxhounds then she took a turn round Knightshayes Court, the residence of the Master, and running across the park came out near Chettiscombe. We crossed the Lowman at Gornhay and kept upwards as far as Crazelowman; then crossing the Halberton road we were soon running our deer past Brithembottom and close by Warnicombe House as if for Bickleigh, but keeping left handed she took us round under the Hillersdon Coverts, where hounds got a view of her and raced her for a mile across country where she was not long taken at 11.30.

Feb 25th 1905

It was a representative field which assembled at West Worlington on 18th inst., and an excellent run which followed. In Cottonhay Plantation a fine four year old stag was roused. Breaking covert he at once made away for Broads Moor, and thence by way of Week, Chulmleigh, and Ball Covert to Waterloo. Turning left handed by Bycott he went back over to Wixon Farm, and getting down into the valley crossed the river, reaching Kempland Farm. Making his way up over the hill to Stone Moor, he crossed the highway to Stone Barton and forded the Little Dart. Then he skirted Chawleigh Barton, and going down the valley passed near the Volunteer Shooting Range, and came across the Cleaves, passing opposite Park Mill Farm. Then he went up over the hill to Rodgments, and thence to Upcott. Turning to the right and crossing James's Week he came down close to the railway by the New Lodge, and then turning back through James's Week and Upcott he ran over Nethercott and Southcott Farm, into Foxes Covert, where he doubled about for some considerable time. Being at length evicted he made away to Chenson Farm, and up over Toneyfield to Hansford. Crossing the highway he passed through Duckham Farm, and on to East Leigh, thence across Burridge Farm and down into the valley, and being closely pursued got into the Little Dart just under East Cheldon where he was taken after a run extending over three and a quarter hours. Among those in at the death were the Master, Messrs S. Webber, Worth, Selley, F. Webber, W. Parkhouse, and a few others.

March 4th 1905

In fine and bright weather hounds put in another good day in the Dulverton country on Wednesday, accounting for two more deer. The meet was at Bury, and the pack was kennelled there while a strong draft of tufters was taken on to Mr. A. Capel's covers at Chipstaple, where the deer had been doing some damage. Not being long in finding in Middle Hill, tufters were soon running over the heather and through Huish Cleave with a hind and yearling. Sinking the valley they ran down past Sir John Ferguson Davie's house at Bittiscombe and on to the Allotments on Skilgate Common at best pace. Then, running sharp down the valley, past West Hill and King's Wood they took a turn out nearly to Kingsbrompton and back by way of Lyncombe. The pack was laid on to the hind at Barlynch. Passing here at best pace through Exe Cleave she went out over Court Down to the Barle Valley by way of Loosehall Wood, then up past Draydon, Mounsey Castle, Dipper Copse, and on to Three Waters, where she turned up over Hawkridge into the Danesbrook. In these strongholds she might easily have beaten hounds had not the pace told its tale. Hounds followed the line up the Danesbrook as far as Slade Bridge, where they came up with their deer. Racing her back to Castle Bridge and into the Barle, she was taken in the meadows under Mounsey Castle. The Master having heard that two or three hounds were racing another deer, hurried back with the pack, and a second deer was taken close to Weir.

The meet was at Worlington again on Saturday, a fairly big field being out. The Harbourer having two deer in Cotonhayes the pack was taken on to draw and they were laid on the one that left the bottom end of the covert and crossed into Affeton Old Plantation. Instead of turning down the Cheldon Valley along the line usually taken he went away across Winsford Moor to Kempland and on into the Stone Moor Coverts, across the Chulmleigh road and away past Stone Mill over the Chawleigh road and into the big coverts that overhang the River Taw. He was pushed through Chenson Wood and crossing the valley not far from Nymett Bridge turned over the top nearly to Coldridge, but bearing away left handed he came back to the coverts above Eggesford House; then, turning again, he crossed the Hayne Valley and went straight on to Winkleigh, passing close by the church and making up the valley at a good pace to Broadwood Kelly. All the villagers turned out to see the sight. Running on to Monk Okehampton and then down to the valley, hounds fresh found him and he was killed in the Ockment about a mile above the village. It was a great hunt lasting over three hours without a check, hounds at times running hard. Being 30 miles from kennels, hounds and horses started for home without delay, getting back about 10 o'clock.

March 11th 1905

Following the meet at Highercombe on Wednesday a draft of seven tufters were taken to the well known Allotment enclosure on Winsford Hill. A herd of upwards of fifty hinds have held possession of this cover for several weeks past, and some ten minutes enquiry with the tufters proved sufficient to set them all in motion. Scattering into contingents of a dozen or more each the deer soon went away over the open by way of Devil's Punchbowl and Ashcombe, towards Comer's Gate. Two warrantable stags were viewed in company with the hinds, and presently an old hind and a smaller one stole away to Bradley Rookery, where Mr Amory laid on his tufters afresh, and, after a scurry over the grassy slopes of Bradley Ham, facing Withypool Village, hounds returned at a great pace over the heather to the Allotments and Draydon Knap. Four miles and more had already been covered at best pace, and the big hind, a particularly fine one, was repeatedly viewed in front of hounds as she bore away down the wooded valley of the Exe. The pack were now brought into play, and drove their hind for another five miles from covert to covert until the Exebridge Chemical Works were almost reached, where, after a check, she was fresh found, and soon gave evidence of her strength and fleetness. Topping one fence after another in her stride, she did another three miles with hounds straining after her on a burning scent, with heads up and sterns down, leaving Bury Village and Hartford Bottom behind her and climbing the steep ascent of Storridge. The pack were barely three minutes behind as she twisted through the oaken coppice and bore away for Quarkhill Combe, whence she was bustled out at all speed, and made another dart of two miles down the course of the Haddeo to England's Woods. Outside this hounds checked, but presently Mr. Amory fresh found her in the corner of a field near Bury, and all she could do was to race down the streamside meadows to the junction of the Exe and Haddeo, where she was captured in deep water at 2.30, nearly three hours and a half after she was roused in the Allotments, the pace having been excellent throughout. While the closing scenes of this fine hunt were being enacted, a stray couple had brought another hind to water at Barlynch Weir, and Mr Amory lost no time in trotting hounds to the spot. She ran for a mile to Pezzlecombe Ford and was there speedily taken.

April 8th 1905

The meet on Wednesday last was in the Worlington country again. The pack was kennelled at Bealey Court and tufters finding at once in Bycott drove their deer back through Ball Covert on into the Week Coverts and over the Chulmleigh road, where the pack was laid on. Running through Cottonhayes and into Affeton Young Plantation our deer came away in the company of four others. He was, however, soon singled out and ran down the Cheldon Valley as far as Stone Mill and then out over the road to Chawleigh. Thence the line lay down into Eggesford Coverts at Chenson, through Foxes Covert and Southcott, Upcott and Chawleigh Barton Wood. Running next over Stone Moor we went away to Wixon. Here fresh finding in the stream he was quickly taken about 3 o'clock near Week School.

Following the meet at Hele on Saturday tufters found a deer in Pixie Copse and the pack was eventually laid on to three deer which had gone down the water and across the railway into the Stoodleigh Country. Hounds came up to them in the river close to Mr Tracey's fish hatcheries and, dividing, the body of the pack ran parallel with the railway to Morebath Siding, where they crossed the railway. Re-crossing close to Morebath Station they turned up over the hill into Haddon. Fresh finding in Hartfield hounds raced their deer down the valley to Bury, where she turned over the top again as if she were going to make the same round again, but keeping left handed she nearly reached Morebath House, and half a mile lower down the valley she was killed.

April 15th 1905

The meet on Tuesday was at the Carnarvon Arms, and the pack was taken to Bury to kennel. Tufters drew West Hill, where there were a lot of deer up, and the whole day was spent running one deer or another between the Deer Park and Wynne Corner, hounds having to go home without any Venison.

On Wednesday there was a bye day at Bealy Court in the Worlington Country. A young stag was roused at once in Ball Covert, and went away with tufters close behind him. Hounds drove him across the rough pastures to the Week Coverts, through the whole length of these coverts, past Mouseberry, and on to the South Molton road. Tufters were here stopped, and the pack was laid on near the Gidley Arms. After running across the fields parallel with the road for about a mile they went away to the right to Creacombe, at which point the deer was not far in front of them. Still pushing him they ran down past Ramscombe and on across Hazen Moor. Next they forced him through the Rackenford Coverts and on across Rackenford Moor, down through Bickham and Sydham to the big Coverts of Warbrightsley, and on down the Iron Mill Stream past Hangmans Hill. A curious thing happened here. The Devon and Somerset Staghounds made their appearance by the Oakford Side with a hunted hind, and the two packs at once joined. Fresh finding the Devon and Somerset hind in the water, it was soon all over with her. Then, after separating the hounds at Barle Cottage, we went on after the stag which had crossed the Exe close to Bampton. Running out over Birchdown he came down close to the railway not far from Morebath and keeping parallel with the railway nearly to the Chemical Works crossed the metals, and went down through Pixey Copse and across the meadows to Bury Village. He entered Haddon by way of Swine's Cleave, and keeping left handed came down to the Exe under Barons Down; then running up the valley past Barlynch he was taken close to Chilly Bridge, where the Devon and Somerset Staghounds met in the morning. It was a great run; the points from Ball Cover to Bampton and from Bampton to Chilly Bridge would be quite 25 miles.

Saturday's meet was at Hele Bridge. Finding at once we rattled a deer up the valley past Chilly Bridge, Broford, and across Winslade Wood, out over the hill past Mr Everard's house at Milton Rocks, then turning short came back to Redcleave, and across the river into Winslade Wood again. The pack was in waiting at Southill, and ran her through Southill Plantation, across the moor to Contest. Then bearing right handed, they went to the Punchbowl and up to Coombe, where she doubled back again and came across the road. Leaving Bradley Bog, she came down by Bradley Farm to the Barle, and after keeping down the river for a time, she went over the hill by Tarr Steps and sank to the water again under Hawkridge. Hounds fresh found her under Dippers Copse, and ran her up over the hill by Mounsey Castle. Where complications were set up by fresh deer. The hunted deer went away to Southill on to Redcleave, and sank to the Exe not from Kents Weir, where she was taken about four o'clock in the afternoon.

April 29th 1905

Recent runs with this well known pack have furnished a brilliant sequel to the good sport enjoyed earlier in the season. The meet on Tuesday was at Bury and the pack was kennelled at Hele Bridge while tufters drew Swines Cleave, where three hinds were soon on the go. It was, however, not until an hour later that the pack was brought into play, being laid on under Barons Down to a single hind that that had come away from Storridge and ran through Hele Ball and out over the top to Court Down, through Loosehall Wood and across into the Barle Valley by way of Ball Neck and Marsh Wood. She was fresh found up the valley at Castle Bridge, and ran up over Ashwick to Mounsey-hill and away across Winsford Hill, over Bradley Moor to the Barle under Westwater. Then down to Honspool, and over the top to Hawkridge, Danesbrook, Anstey Common, and Molland Moor, and then through Cloggs to Lords Plantation. Going down the Barle again she was fresh found at Hindspool and taken not far from Three Waters.

May 6th 1905

The meet on Wednesday was at the Carnarvon Arms Hotel, and the pack was kennelled at Coombe House. Tufters found near Coombe House and a deer went by way of the Summer-House and on up the Barle Valley past Higher Coombe to Mounsey Hill Gate and on to Winsford Hill. Here she joined a herd, but being cut off ran on by Bradley Bog and back to the Barle again, the pack being ultimately laid on at the top of West Barton Wood. Running across Lythall Wood she turned up the valley and ran to Molland Moor Gate. Thence the line lay backwards towards Anstey Common to the Barle again by way of Hinam, where she was fresh found. Hounds raced her up through Marsh Wood, then down to Marsh Bridge, Warcleeve, and across Ford Down to the Exe, by way of Stockham. Here she turned through Exe Park, but instead of coming down to the Exe again she kept away left handed. Passing Kingsbrompton on the right she went on as if for Slowley, but hounds fresh finding her and she was eventually killed close to Armour Farm, about four o'clock.

On Saturday the meet was at Higher Coombe. A lot of deer were found in Red Cleave, and the pack was laid on to one on Southill. Running hard she turned away down Ashway Side, soon bringing us to the Barle by way of Ashwick. Then she turned on Hawkridge into the Danesbrook, and up over to White Rock, where she was fresh found. Hounds raced her past Slade Bridge and on across Anstey Common, Molland Moor, and close to West Molland. Then turning upwards she brought us back by way of Cuzzicombe Post and Willingford Water to the Barle again. We had a long check near South Barton Wood, but, getting news the pack was laid on at Castle Bridge; and after a turn as far as Three Waters, she then came over into the Danesbrook. Hounds fresh finding her, drove her upwards and eventually she was killed under Hawkridge about 5.30. Laying the hounds on again in the Barle Valley, they kept another deer on the move, with the result that she was killed about 7.30 above Hindspool.

May 13th 1905

Mr Ian Amory brought a field of close upon thirty pursuers to Highercombe on 30th ult., of whom the greater part came by train from Tiverton, says a writer in *The Field*. Trotting out to the meet the Harbourer on South Hill, with his tufters at heel, he was met with the intelligence that Winsford Hill was bare of deer, but that a small herd of hinds had pastured overnight in the Mousehanger Meadows, and had moved off into Redcleave. Tufting failed to rouse them here, and Hollam Wood in turn was drawn blank, but Wick Wood produced two long legged members of the herd, and these at once made their way through the very coverts just drawn to South Hill, where the waiting pack were by

this time in readiness in
charge of the kennel huntsman, and
all was in train for a lay on. Most opportunely,
the two hinds separated, and the best of them
headed boldly away over the open, closely pressed by a
couple and a half of tufters. Some newly burnt heath steadied the
pace from moderate to slow on Varle Hill, where three hares sprung from
their forms right amongst the feathering pack. The hinds foil, however, was
soon struck in good fashion, and away went the hunt down Ashway Side, driving
merrily against the wind, but just short of Hat Wood something had blanched the hind,
and a cast back, a very unusual thing in deer hunting, proved the true solution. By the
Ashway inclosures the line led down to Slade Copse and the deep and muddy going of
the Barle Valley at its wettest. Uphill through the coppice in Buckminster Wood, the hunt
went uphill to the open on to Whiterocks Down, with hounds driving and straining and
racing for place, when out sprang the hind on the summit, in bad case indeed unless she
could speedily find some fresh deer to share her troubles. Two stags strode away on one
side, but the pace was too great, and hounds were too close to her haunches for the hind
to reach them; so away she went leaving the woodlands behind her, and dashing right
away for the wide moor-lands of Anstey and Molland Commons. For mile after mile the
pack drove straight against the wind, and the pace tailed them out not a little, but Mr
Albert de Las Casas checked the leading two couples at Anstey Gulley, and Mr Amory
promptly up several more to the front. Driving on through the tall heath of the southern
front of Molland Common, hounds looked like a white thread upon the dull brown
carpet of sombre moor; then winding across the conbes, climbing the steep ascents, but,
pushing on and upwards at a round pace all the time, they presently followed their hind
to the boundary of Cuzzicombe Down, when she swung back through the ranks of the
field to Moorhouse Ridge and Lower Willingford. The cooling stream of the Willingford
water must have tempted her sorely, but she dashed straight through and bore away
over the fields for a mile and a half past Cloggs Down, then struck down Hunter Combe.
Another mile at a steady, tireless gallop bringing hounds through Rowdown to the Barle
at Ashway Ham, and it seemed as if now this good straight necked hind must die at
once, but a long cast down the river side failed to find her, so there was nothing for it but
to cast again, and the pack, presently striking a line in Rowdown, had a herd afoot.
Among them was the hunted hind, and, when at last hounds settled to her foil, she just
managed to cross the well known ridge, and was taken in the Danesbrook under
Hawkridge. Another was subsequently pursued, and, after a long and wearying hunt
taken at Bradley Ham later on in the day.

A twenty four hour's rainfall stopped just in time for the concluding meet at Hele Bridge
on Monday. The first gallop of the day was straight and fast enough to satisfy the most
exacting, for half an hour's tufting in Bury Castle resulted in the departure of two hinds
by way of Jury Hill and the sleeping pastures of Hele Ball. The pack opened on the

double foil with a will, and although scent subsequently proved catchy they were at once on terms with a hind, and drove her for mile after mile in a style which made one wonder if these could really be the same hounds which had been so late afield only two days before. For the first two miles it was a straight rush through covert to Stockham Park, where the hind broke to the view of the field only just clear of the few leading couples. She raced along the first few fields taking the high bush covered banks as though they were but sheep hurdles. Then she made through the Broford Woods and away to the heather of South Hill with the field tailing out behind. The miry paths were too soft to gallop in, but the heather, though full of water, afforded a better foothold, and consequently hounds had only just arrived at the Allotments, five miles from their starting point, when Mr Amory was with them, the leading section of the field bearing in view over the contour of Draydon Knap. A cast forward to Burrow Wood immediately produced two fresh deer, one of which led hounds all the way back to the very point from which they had started an hour and a half before. Much to and fro hunting ensued, and eventually a well beaten hind was hunted to Higher Willingford. Mr Amory had finally given her up, when at 6.45 a single hound struck her foil afresh, and in a few minutes more she was taken. One of the hounds on his way home to kennel was run over by a train on the Devon and Somerset railway, near Exebridge, early the following morning.

Sept 23rd 1905

There was a large field out on Thursday when these hounds met at Haddon for their first bye meet this season and there were a lot more waiting at Chipstable when the tufters were taken to disturb the deer which had made their home in Mr Capel's coverts. Goss had harboured eight or ten deer, among which there were at least four good stags, and it took a good bit of time before one was persuaded to go. It was soon seen that scent was bad, as hounds could not push their deer along. Running into Huish they drove their deer round the bottom and away past Bulland Lodge nearly to Waterrow, where he turned up over the hill as if for Wiveliscombe. It was here found that hounds were running a young stag. So the tufters were stopped and taken back again to Middle Hill. A good stag was soon set going and directly hounds were out of covert it was seen that scent had improved. They drove their stag back to Haddon by way of the Bittiscombe coverts, across Skilgate Common and then into Haddon Hill, where the pack was brought into work, running him straight down to Huscombe Wood. Here he tried the old dodge of turning up a young stag to let him bear the brunt of the chase. Capt. Amory soon stopped the hounds and bringing them back they were cast round the wood without getting a touch. He then kennelled the pack at Hartford Mill and drew the wood, the stag being fresh found in the heather, where he stood and bayed the hounds for some seconds. Then, coming back through Hartford Cleeve hounds drove him down through Haddon Wood nearly to Bury village, where he again stood at bay, but the pack being brought down the water by one of the whips he was soon forced to fly again. Coming down to the water by Clammer he was driven up the valley for a good two miles, sometimes in the water and sometimes out. Then, breaking away, he went through the corner of Storridge and down to the stream that leads away to Kingsbrompton. He next made a rush through Kingswood to Huscombe with hounds close to his haunches and made a final dart to the water at Steart. Not being done yet he took refuge in a garden, where he defied everyone for a considerable time but was at last cleverly lassoed by Mr Froude Hancock. He was a good stag with all his rights and two very long points on both sides.

September 30th 1905

The opening meet of this well known pack of hounds attracted sportsmen and sportswomen from a wide area to Chain Bridge on Saturday morning. It was a sight that was worth going a long way to see, the densely wooded hills rising up from the Exe forming a pleasing setting to a scene that was animated as it was picturesque. The Master Mr Ian. Heathcoat-Amory was supported by Capt. H. Amory and Mr Ludovic Amory wearing scarlet. Among others present were Mr W. C. L. Unwin (M. F. H.), Mr Frank Dunsford, Mr J. C. de Las Casas, Mr M. de Las Casas, Mr F. J. Coleridge Boles, Mr W. A. Corbet, Capt. Langdon, Mr and Mrs L. Mackenzie, Mr March-Phillipps, Mr J. C. Hill, Mr J. Jarvis Baily, Mr and Mrs Pugsley, Major Chichester and the Misses Chichester, Miss Amory, Mr R. S. Pethick, Mr E. Creswell (Exebridge), Mr H. M. Crosby, Mr J. W. Goddard, Mr Courtenay Haydon, Mr Woodville Haydon, Mr T. C. Yandle, Mr J. Yandle, Mr P. Yandle, Mr C. W. Nelder, Mr J. A. Marshall, Mr S. Webber (Palmerston Hotel), Mr S. Webber (Seven Crosses), Mr A. Pring, Mr J. Farrant, Mr F. Webber (Diptford), Mr Heywood (Ash Farm), Mr J. Blackmore (Plushhayes), Mr Mogford, Mr W. Burnett, the Misses Hancock (Stagg Mills), Misses Burnett, Mr P. E. and Miss Marrack, Misses Frost, Mr and Mrs Frisby, Messrs C. Davey, F. T. Townsend, R. S. Webber, F. Adams, F. Knight, and Sergt-Instructor Jones, of Bampton. Those on wheels were almost as numerous. These included Mrs de Las Casas, Mrs Nicholetts, Mrs W. H. White, Mrs S.H. Fisher, Mrs and Miss Luxton, Mrs Jarvis Baily, Mrs and the Misses Ford, Miss Yandle, Mrs Pethick, Mr and Mrs Gibbons, Mr Ashplant, &c. A stag was found in the little covert by the side of Aldridge Mill, and after a turn or two up and down, he went away to Town Wood, where the pack was laid on at a quarter to one. Running right through the wood he lead the hounds straight down to the Chain Bridge. Thence the line lay through Highwood and nearly into Steart; but turning short back the deer came to the water not far from Duvale, afterwards running through Duvale Wood and on close to Wonham, through Coombehead, and down to the railway near Morebath Junction. Then he ran down the valley not from Exebridge, and beating up the water turned up over Highleigh and on past the Red Deer to within a couple of miles of Anstey Station. Turning left handed he came back past the Bickham Coverts, and keeping still to the left he got to Rackenford Moor, and crossing it went on as if for Creacombe. But turning short again he passed to the keeper's house and came down to the stream which runs under Rackenford Moor, and after beating down the water was finally taken close to the village. It was a four hours run but despite the fact Master Ivor Pethick, who is only seven years of age, managed to be in at the death. There were an extraordinary large number of cyclists and pedestrians out, but though none of them were anywhere about when the morte was sounded some of them had several glimpses of the stag in the early stages of the run.

Oct 21st 1905

These hounds put in an enjoyable day's sport in the Stoodleigh country on Wednesday, 11th inst. The day's business started with the tufters drawing Rhyll, but the deer having shifted their quarters they were taken to Nethercott Wood, where they roused a heavy and strong stag in company with several hinds, which led most of the tufters astray. They were, however, soon stopped and brought back, and the stag having in the meantime laid down in a gorse brake, the pack was soon laid on. After being fresh found, the stag came back, crossing the Iron Mill Stream into Wormsworthy and then running down the valley to Chain Bridge. Here he crossed into the Wonham Coverts, and going out over the top ran down to the town of Bampton. Turning left handed, he now ran

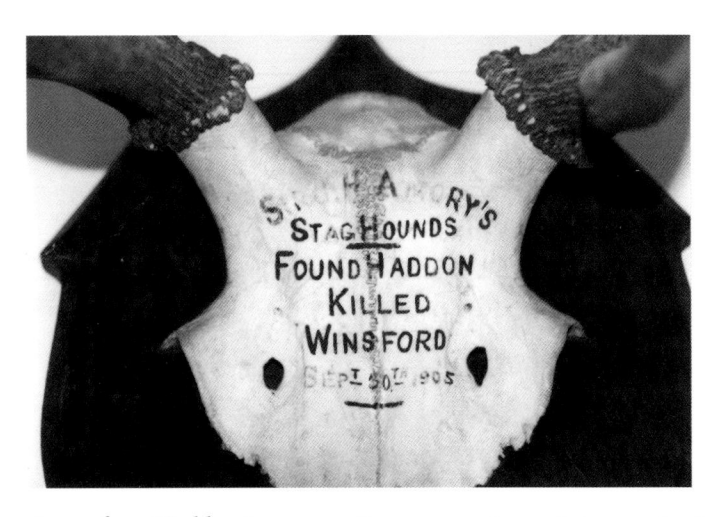

A run from Haddon to Winsford Sept 30th 1905.

away to Coombehead, and then down to Morebath Junction. Thence the line lay by the railway to the Chemical Works; then crossing the Exe he made his way past Exebridge and Riphay on to Brushford, where there was a short check, but picking up the line hounds hunted him away past Allways End and Blackerton. Running on past Anstey, we soon reached Yeo Mill, and went on to Hipscott and through the coverts there, past Molland Station, and then out left handed to the South Molton road and on nearly to Bish Mill. In the water near here he was fresh found, and after a turn or two up and down he was soon taken – a fine stag with all his rights and three atop on each side.

It was a real good day and a hard one for both horses and hounds. Among those in at the finish besides Capt. H. Heathcoat-Amory, were Messrs F. Dunsford, T. C. Yandle and his three sons, Headon (Ford), Mogford (Pilemoor), A. Pring (Tiverton), Selley (Hilltown), Brown (Rackenford), and several others. The time occupied by the run was three hours. From the lay on to Morebath was a five and a half point, and from Morebath to where we killed fourteen and a half miles, and hounds must have run much further. Saturday's fixture was given up owing to the Earl Fortescue's funeral.

Oct 28th 1905

There was a large field out at Rackenford on Saturday. The Master decided to draw with the pack and several deer were soon on foot not far from where we killed on Wednesday. One went one way and one another, but the pack stuck to the best of them, which ran away by Great Down and on to Rackenford Moor. After running down the valley he turned back to the coverts, whence the line lay on past Cruwyshayes nearly to Bradford Ponds, turning away to Ditchitts, then on to Creacombe and to the Gidley Arms and Cotonhayes. So far the stag had run the same line as the one taken three days previously; but he now went on by way of Affeton to the River Dart at Cheldon Bridge, then straight out over the top, crossing the Chawleigh road, on to Lapford Wood, past Chenson through Foxes Covert, and Southercott and Upcott and down the river by Rashleigh, where he crossed the railway and went up the valley to Leigh Cross and Hollowcombe. Gradually turning he came back under the Eggesford foxhound kennels at Wembworthy and after a final rush he was killed in Rashleigh Bottom. A good stag with all his rights and three on top one side and brow, tray and two on the other. The field on Saturday was a large one, including a number of hunting farmers. Among those out were Miss Amory, Mr F. Dunsford, Mr A. de Las Casas, Miss March-Phillipps, Miss Maisie March-Phillipps, Capt. Hollond, Miss Chichester, Miss Blanche Chichester, Major Chichester, Mr Soames, Miss Soames, Mr W. Renton, Mr Froude Hancock, Mr Corbet, Dr Meade, Mr March-Phillipps, Mr Cobb, Messrs S. Webber, A. Pring, Goddard, Marshall, Farrant, W. Haydon, M. Haydon, J. Butt, J. Yandle, P. Yandle, Gurney, Brown, Heal, Mogford, Matthews, Ayre, Vesey, Loosemore, Pethick, and S. Vicary.

Nov 11th 1905

A good run followed the meet at Spurway Mill on Saturday. Tufting began at Rifton, and hounds soon had a hind on the move. The pack was laid on going into Wormsworthy, and ran right down the valley of the Iron Mill Stream to Chain Bridge, then down nearly to Halfpenny Bridge, where the deer turned out over the top into Highwood. Thence the line lay through Steart, under East Stoodleigh, and out over Dry Hill into the Emmerford Coverts. Finding no deer here hounds pushed her up the valley past Pile Moor, and on under Stoodleigh Court to Rhyll and into the Rifton Coverts again. Hounds next drove her down the Coleford Water to Aldridge Mills and down the Iron Mill Stream again. She now crossed into the Stuckeridge Coverts and came down to the Exe not far from Stuckeridge Bridge, and turned up through the Wonham Coverts and out over the top as if for Morebath; but altering her mind she came down nearly to Bampton, and she was killed about three o'clock in the Batherm, just below Sir Edwin Dunning's slate quarries.

Nov 18th 1905

Although it was wet there was a big field out to meet the Master at the Gidley Arms on Saturday. The pack was sent on to Bullacourt whilst the Master went on with the tufters to Waterloo. Finding several deer there the tufters ran back with one by way of Stone Moor to the water under Chawleigh Barton Wood and the pack was soon laid on and ran down the valley across the river not far from Chulmleigh Bridge, then away through Upcott and across the railway into the Eggesford Coverts. Coming back again, however, the deer crossed the line into Southcott not far from the Fox and Hounds Hotel at Eggesford. Thence the line lay up the valley, through Foxes Covert and Chenson Wood, and on into Lapford Wood, where some time was spent. Unfortunately hounds divided, one part running their deer back through Lapford Wood and Chenson, down to the water not far from Eggesford Station. Here the deer crossed the railway again and went up by way of Hayne Valley through the Eggesford Coverts, on nearly to the foxhound kennels at Wembworthy, then up the valley past Staple Green, and was ultimately taken at Orrey Mill. Meanwhile the other part of the pack ran up through Lapford Wood to Chawleigh Wood and down to Cheldon Bridge, away through Affeton Old Plantation to Winswood Moor. Then crossing by Week the deer ran away to Waterloo and Bycott away across Horridge Moor and down not far from Chulmleigh and was eventually lost not far from the rifle range under Sydenham.

Nov 31st 1905

In wild and showery weather these hounds met at Knowstone on Saturday last. There was a fairly big field, composed mostly of farmers, some of the members of the hunt having thrown in their lot with the Tiverton Foxhounds, who had a bye meet at Cove. The pack was kennelled at Mr Vesey's, at Bransford, and five and a half couples were taken on to draw the big woods, where several deer were soon on the move. A young stag was the first to bear the brunt of the chase, but on Baple's Hill hounds were stopped and taken back, and it was not long before the tufters had several hinds in front of them with their attendant calves. After a turn or two round the coverts a hind and calf came away on Baple's Hill and ran down close by where the pack was kennelled. Hounds were let go on the foil on Hazen Moor, and running hard soon reached the Rackenford Coverts, when they crossed the moor and ran down through Bickham and the Iron Mill Stream to the River Exe. Having turned out for Highwood and entered Steart and the deer was now driven through Emmerford and nearly to New Bridge, where the Foxhounds could be heard quite plainly. She then turned and came down to the river close to Cove Siding, where the smaller deer was left, and turning up over Steart again once more crossed the Iron Mill Stream and entered the Stuckeridge Coverts. Thence she ran over the top into Stuckeridge North and down and across the Exe into the Wonham Coverts, on to Coombeshead, and out across the road as if for Morebath, but turning left handed she came down the valley nearly to Exebridge, passing to the Chemical Works and then over to the River Barle and on past Dulverton Station. Hounds came up to her in the water under Pixton Park, where she was killed. Scent was very bad in the closing portion of the run. Among those out were the Master Mr Ian Heathcoat Amory, Mr A.de Las Casas, Mr and Miss Soames and Mr Thomas (East Anstey), Messrs Thornton and Marshall (Dulverton), Mr Snow (Knowstone), Messrs J. Zelley, T. Yandle, J. Yandle, P. Yandle, A. Heal, F. Mogford, J. Butt, W. Haydon, L. Haydon, & c.

Dec 16th 1905

Good days with this pack have been the rule this year, but the run on Saturday last was not only the run of this season but of many seasons, and those of us who were lucky enough to see it will not forget either it or our ride home after it. The meet was at Chawleigh, and amongst those out we noticed, besides Mr Ian Amory (Huntsman) and Mr Ludovic Amory (whip), Messrs de Las Casas, A. Luxton (Master of the Eggesford Hounds), H. P. Martin, Carter, Tripe, S. Webber (Tiverton), W. Webber (Lapford), Tripe, Littleworth, Baker, Webber (Chulmleigh), S. Vicary, J. Butt, C. Haydon, L. Haydon, W. Haydon, Parkhouse (Chulmleigh), Pope (South Molton Road), Webber, sen. (Hollowtree), etc. The Harbourer reported that there were no hinds in the country within reach of the meet, but that there were two or three herds of stags, and that they were doing a considerable amount of damage to the farmers. Mr Amory therefore decided to draw for a young stag. Hounds were kennelled at Mr Baker's farm, Chawleigh Barton, and four couple of tufters were drawn. Seven stags were soon found in the Stone Moor Coverts. Tufters settled on to the line of two three year olds and got them well away from those coverts. They were duly stopped, and a signal from the huntsman to the kennel huntsman (Ernest Hellard), who was posted on some high ground within easy reach of the farm where the hounds were kennelled, quickly brought the pack. They were laid on at 11.50, and it was at once apparent that scent was first rate, for although the deer had been gone some little while hounds picked up the line and ran it as if they were almost in view, across some rough moors and down into the Wixon Covers, through the length of these and out at the far end; the field emerging only just in time to see them disappearing over the next skyline, on over the great Odam Moor, right handed into Week Cover, and away to Cottonhayes. It was a race between hounds and horses, hounds won and if they hadn't taken another right handed turn out of the Cheldon Valley and over Winswood Moor the number of those who could have seen them again that day would have been very easily counted on the fingers of one hand, and your correspondent would not have been amongst those fortunate few. However hounds did take that right handed turn and most of the field were given another chance of cutting in again on good terms. The deer had by this time separated and hounds had settled on the bigger one of the two, a fine three year old stag. The line now lay by Sheepsbyre and Bycott, a cover in which a fresh herd of deer was known to be lying, a herd which our stag would no doubt have roused, and amongst whom he could no doubt have effaced himself if he had been given time. But Mr Amory and his flying pack were too close, so there was nothing for him but to go straight through the covers at his best pace and on down the deep valley leading to Horridge Moor over which hounds drove along with a head and determination which did credit to their kennel huntsman. The proverbial sheet would almost have covered them, no hounds ahead and no stragglers. From here the deer had evidently determined to seek refreshment in the flooded waters of the Mole, which he reached by Kingsnympton Park, and down which he allowed himself to be carried for half an hour or so; but a quick cast down stream, and hounds hit off his line almost at the junction of the Rivers Mole and Taw, where he had left the water and gone up into the big larch coverts which fringe the Taw for some miles besides its course towards the sea. Hounds hunted the line very prettily through these covers and presently fresh found their deer. By the time he had climbed almost to the top of the ridge dividing the Rivers Taw and Mole, but hounds were bustling too fast through the trees and tangled underwood, so he turned straight down the hill again and swam the Taw, jumped the London and South Western fences, crossed the line, and made away at right angles to the river pointing towards Burrington. There was a ford close to the point where he crossed the river, but the water was too high to make a crossing possible. There was therefore nothing to be done but set to work and ride hard for the nearest bridge, more than a mile away. This we did but as we rode we wondered whether we should ever see the hounds again. Luckily for us some sheep had foiled hounds not far beyond the point where we saw them last when we were on the other side of the river. Some of the hounds must have made a wider cast than others, for when we came up we found about half the pack just setting down to the time which they had then recovered, whilst the other half had no doubt gone on some time before, for there was nothing to be seen or heard of them. Our half pack worked out the line with great determination and with the help of some judicious forward casts we ran the line quite fast enough for horses which had already gone so far and so fast, by Portsmouth Arms Station and Northcote over a delightful country, made up chiefly of succession of wild rolling moors to Roborough. Near here the leading hounds were overtaken and stopped by Mr L. Amory. The delay was but short before the rest of hounds came on and reunited pack led us over several miles of country which was quite new to us all. We passed close to Beaford and in a wooded coombe between that city and Torrington we fresh found our deer and raced him almost in view for another mile or so before he was killed in a small stream three miles from Torrington at five minutes past four. The run lasted four and a quarter hours during which time there had only been two short checks, one in the River Mole and the other towards the end of the run while the leading hounds were kept waiting for the body of the pack. The distance from the place where the stag was found to the place where he was killed measured, in a straight line 16 miles, and hounds and horses had 32 miles back to kennel.

Bembridge Wood Sept. 15th 1906.

Dec 30th 1905

Following a fair sized meet at Bury on Tuesday, a deer was found in Pixie Copse and ran back into Haddon, where two or three hours were spent between Bury and the Deer Park. In the afternoon hounds ran one away over Barons Down to the Exe and by way of Stockham past Chilly Bridge and on by Broford to Red Cleave, Thence the line lay over Southhill and back by way of Broford to the Exe where the deer was taken.

Jan 6th 1906

A holiday field met the Master at the Carnarvon Arms on Wednesday. The pack having been kennelled at Hele Bridge tufters roused a lot of deer in Bury Castle, dispersing them

Mr C. W. Nelder and his daughter – proprietor of the Carnarvon Arms Hotel who were both present at the Meet.

A meet at the Carnarvon Arms Hotel near Dulverton.

in all directions, and the one selected went on straight into Haddon, right up to Harford Mills and back again over Baron's Down to the Exe. She ran on right up the valley by way of Chilly Bridge and Red Cleave to Southill, where Mr Amory stopped tufters to give the pack a chance. No sooner had they been laid on to the foil of this tough hind that they raced away with such a head that showed that scent had wonderfully improved and that the flying pack would take a lot of catching. Just touching Southill hounds streamed away a little to the left as if for Ashway Side, when this good hind strained her head, and ran the whole way over Winsford Hill, over the best galloping ground. Then having turned down to the Barle close to Withypool she was fresh found close to Bradley Ford, a ding dong race ensuing to Tarr Steps, past Three Waters and Castle Bridge to Marsh Bridge. She was not done yet, for she breasted the hill and took us over Court Down and away to the Exe Valley by way of Stockham. Running downwards through Exe Cleeve, Hele Bridge, and on through Brookwood, down past Weir, and through the river ran up to her in the water below Perry Farm. She broke away, however, and went out past Dulverton Station into Allers Wood, but turning short back she was killed quite close to the Carnarvon Arms Hotel.

Jan 20th 1906

The meet on Saturday was at the Gidley Arms and the pack was kennelled at Bealy Court while tufters roused a herd of deer in Wixon, whence they drove one to Bycott and Waterloo and across the road into the Ball Covert and away into Week. Here hounds turned up over the moors and crossed the Gidley Arms road and ran up the valley, leaving Creacombe to the right, and over Ashmoor to Baples Hill. Thence the line lay into the Knowstone Woods and across Hazon Moor; then leaving the Rackenford Coverts to the right hounds ran into Bickham and Sydham and out over Broadmoor into Rifton Coverts, and on through Wheatland and the valley of the Iron Mill Stream to Chain Bridge. The deer now ran out over Highwood into Steart Coverts and after a lot of beating about was taken at Newbridge.

Jan 27th 1906

A fairly large field greeted the Master at Worlington on Saturday. There were ten deer in Cotonhayes and as the tufters were being thrown into covert one of them went across Lutterey Moor, the rest of the herd going on to the Cheldon Valley. Tufters settled on the line of the single deer and after a turn or two round the coverts he went away by Lutterey Moor as if for Gidley Arms, but turning back he was met by the pack, which on being laid on close to him ran through the Wick Coverts and across the big Odam Moors on to Ball Covert. Thence the line lay into Waterloo and down to Wixon; but turning upwards the deer ran across Horridge Moor and nearly into Chulmleigh. Now turning to the right he took us away nearly into Kingsnympton Village, and, coming down to the big waters at South Molton Road, he turned upwards again and came back through Colleton and as if for Chulmleigh. He was nearly beaten when hounds fresh found him and raced him down to Dart Bridge, where he was taken after a run of about three hours.

Feb 3rd 1906

The meet on Saturday was at the Carnarvon Arms. Hounds were taken to Bury to kennel, while tufters drew the Deer Park, dispersing a herd of deer in all directions. Part of the tufters drove one down the valley, through Haddon Wood, and back again several times. A single hind crossed the line at Clammer into Storridge, and ran out over by Barron's Down. The pack was laid on to her foil at Hele Bridge and ran down through Rook Wood, back again and across the fields into Hele Ball; then right up the valley by way of Exe Cleeve and Stockham to Chilly Bridge. Thence the line lay through Broford and down to the river close to Milton Rocks. She then ran back by Winslade Wood on to Exe Park, and hounds ran up to her under Barlynch. Breaking away again, however, she ran up the valley again to Milton Rocks, where she was killed about 1.30. Coming back again to Haddon, we got on the line of a young deer the tufters had run earlier in the day, and hounds after a turn or two up and down the deer was eventually killed. Hounds were afterwards laid on to a good hind and spent some time in running up and down Haddon. She went down by way of Bury Castle into Hele Bridge, and was killed under Rookwood.

Feb 10th 1906

Following the meet at Bury on Wednesday, tufters roused a lot of deer in Haddon, and ran a herd of stags through Storridge before getting on to the line of some hinds. At 2 o'clock the pack were laid on to five hinds, but another hour elapsed before one went away over Haddon Hill into the Deer Park and away across Skilgate Common to the Bittiscombe Coverts and to Ramscombe. There were more deer afoot, but in the end hounds got away with a single hind past Petton Cross and on to Morebath where she was killed.

The meet on Saturday was at Worlington. Tufters roused a lot of deer in Bycott and ran through Waterloo and across the old moors into Ball Covert, then down into Week, and on across Lutworthy to Cotonhayes. The pack was ultimately laid on to a hind at Affeton Young Plantation, and turned down towards the Cheldon Valley below the Keepers house. There was a check here, but hounds were soon on the line of a young stag and ran him down past Stone Mill into Chawleigh Barton Wood, through Chawleigh Week and Upcott and right up through the Lapford Coverts. Coming back on pretty well the same line, they turned out over Southacott in the valley of the Dart again and the stag was finally taken alive close to Chulmleigh Bridge.

Feb 16th 1906

Kennelled overnight at the fox and hounds, 17 couples of these hounds, all looking in the pink of condition, and which have already this season accounted for close on 30 stags, met at Eggesford on Saturday. Up to a very short time ago stags were numerous around Eggesford, and it was only a few days since that 10 stags deserted Mr Vivian's Lapford Wood, having been disturbed there by a rabbiting party. Five stags and a fox also crossed the path in full view of Mr Augustus Luxton while shooting with Mr Martin of Colleton Manor, a short time ago. Thus disturbed, the keepers could give out very little hope of a certain find in the near vicinity. At 10.30am however, Ernest Hellard (Kennel Huntsman) set hounds on the move in response to a wire sent to him by the worthy Master Mr Ian Amory to bring them on to the Chawleigh Village where hounds were held up at the Barton. By this time Harbourer Miller had arrived, having located a stag in the Molland Woods. It was however a most miserable morning, for in addition to the very keen wind blowing, rain and sleet fell heavily at intervals. Notwithstanding this however a fairly large field turned out. On being laid on, tufters set to work at once by rattling over the hills to Rowsley, when they doubled back on to the Ball Covert. From here they turned right handed over to the Coton Hayes. By this time the field found

The Fox & Hounds Hotel, Eggesford – where Sir John Amory's Staghounds were kennelled overnight when hunting in the Chumleigh District.

themselves well into the teeth of a drifting snow storm of sleet and rain and a very thick mist also enveloped both valley and hill, blotting out the view so much so that the tufters became lost. They had vanished but where no one knew. On the pack being brought up to Coton Hayes no tidings of the tufters beyond that they had passed on an hour before, going then in the direction of Stone Moor, could be gleaned. Seeing this the worthy Master thought it best to make a by-cast, the pack being taken from Bealy Court through to Stone Moor to Chawleigh, from there to Eggesford, where they galloped down the turnpike on to Hansford. The cast was made with the chance of hounds hitting the line off, but it proved unsuccessful and at 3.30 at Hansford the pack were held up and the field dispersed for home, leaving both tufters and stag somewhere unknown.

March 3rd 1906

Sir John Amory's Staghounds met in the Dulverton country on Wednesday, in bright but frosty weather. There was not a very large field out to meet the Deputy Master (Mr L. Amory), but among those who turned up were Mr F. Dunsford, Mr A. de Las Casas, Mr Nevill, Mr T. Yandle and three sons, and Mr. Marshall. Laying tufters on to a hind and yearling on Draydon Knap, they ran merrily on nearly to Mounsey Hill Gate, as if to join the herd that was lying in the Allotments on Winsford Hill; but turning short back they made their way down to the River Barle, by way of Three Waters, into the Hawkridge Coverts. Away across Hawkridge Ridge the hind and yearling went, and across Whiterocks to Anstey Common and Molland Moor, nearly to Cuzzicombe Post, where they turned short back across the moor, and the pack being brought on they were laid on to the hind and yearling under Molland Moor Gate. There being now several deer on foot one part of the pack ran their hind back across Molland Moor, while the other part ran the yearling back across Anstey Common, where they were stopped by one of the whips and brought back. The pack being reunited, they ran merrily back to Anstey Barrows, where they divided again, the body of the pack running their deer right handed across Anstey Common down to the Danesbrook and over Hawkridge, and finally taking a good hind after a turn or two up and down the Barle near Castle Bridge. Meanwhile another part of the pack had got on the line of another deer on Molland Moor, and drove her down to the Danesbrook by way of Slade Bridge, through Church Wood nearly down to Castle Bridge, where she crossed in Dipper's Copse. Then through Mounsey Castle and Draydon, on to Ball Neck and through Loose Ball Wood, across Court Down, and into the valley of the Exe by way of Exe Cleeve, coming to water not far from Barlynch. Then down stream past Hele Bridge and New Bridge, hounds coming up to her not far from the chemical works where she was killed.

March 10th 1906

Another good day fell to the followers of this pack on Saturday last, when the meet was at Worlington. Hounds were as usual kennelled at Bealey Court, but they did not have to remain there long before being laid on to a deer which had been roused in Affeton Young Plantation. Running through Affeton Old Plantation, they entered the Cheldon Valley and kept to it until they reached the bridge, where they turned up through Burridge Wood, crossed the Chawleigh road, and sinking to the bottom, ran nearly to Morchard Bishop. Here they began to turn to the right and came back to the Lapford Woods and down to the railway, close to Nymett's Bridge, where they crossed and ran out over the hills and across the bottom to Coldridge Village. After crossing a number of moors unknown by name to most of the field, for they were now in country with which they were not familiar, hounds came up to their deer in the Taw. He was, however, by no means done, and breaking away he ran through Ashridge Wood and nearly into North Tawton, near which place he was taken in the Taw, after four hours. Hounds had a 30 mile trot back to kennel.

March 17th 1906

One of the longest and furthest runs there has been for ten years fell to the lot of those who kept tryst at the Gidley Arms on Wednesday last. Hounds found their deer at 11.30 and ran him for five hours without a check, although at times hunting was rather slow. A great extent of country was covered, the final scenes being enacted in the parish of Yarnscombe, where he was set up in the middle of a field, but not before he had damaged a hound or two. Miller had four deer harboured in the little plantation at Mouseberry, the smallest of which ran away at once for the Lutterey Moors. Tufters were speedily laid on and ran through Cotonhayes and Affeton Young Plantation, where the pack was brought into play and ran on into Affeton Old Plantation. Thence the line lay over Winsford Moor, and across the road into the Stone Moor Coverts, then through Sheepsbyre and up over the other side through Waterloo and Bycott Coverts. Here they began to turn to the left, bringing us over Horridge Moor on to Waddington, and close to Kingsnymnpton, then down the valley to Head Mills, where the deer had soiled some half an hour previously before running through Kingsnympton Park, and down and across the Mole not far from High Bullen. Crossing out over the top of the hill a holloa forward told us he had come down to the Taw about a mile above Portsmouth Arms Station. Keeping close to the river and the railway he ran half a mile below the station before crossing. Happily there was a fording place near by and we were soon running over the top of the hills until we found ourselves close to High Bickington. Hereabouts our deer took a turn to the right nearly bringing us back to Umberleigh, but bearing upwards again he brought us to Atherington and then sank to the mills, where there was a slight check. Hounds hit off the line where the deer left the water and they were soon running merrily again through the larch plantation above us. Climbing the hill we soon passed Yarnscombe on our left and a mile or two further on came to the Stevenstone Coverts near the Hon. Rolle's residence. Hounds fresh found their deer in one of the coverts and raced him back for a mile or two much the same line as they had come till they set him up in a gorse brake. He broke away again, but could only go a field or two before being taken at the back of the farm buildings at Cogworthy. It was a good sixteen mile point, but a great many more as hounds ran, certainly twice the distance and most probably more. We were now 35 miles from Tiverton, and horses and hounds did not get home much before midnight. Among those who took part in this great run were Mr L. Amory (Acting Master), Miss Amory, Miss Chichester, Mr Pethick, Mr J. Tripe (Chulmleigh), Mr W. Webber (Lapford), Mr Webber (Chulmleigh), Mr Vickery (Cheldon), Mr W. Little and son, Mr W. Haydon, Dr Meade, Mr Coles (Rose Ash), and many others.

March 24th 1906

When these hounds met in the Worlington country on Wednesday week, found their deer near the Gidley Arms, and killed after a five hours run near Yarnscombe, no one thought that another such a day was in store for them the next time they were out. But this was so; and many of the followers of these hounds who were present at the meet at Worlington on Saturday had to cry off some time before the finish. The pack was kennelled at Mr. S. Vicary's, at Cheldon Barton, whilst Mr L. Amory trotted the tufters off to draw Burridge Wood. It was not long before the tufters were running merrily up the valley to Affeton Old Plantation, where they turned up through Cotonhayes, across the moors to Broad Moor, then into the Wick Covers, turning up over the big Odam Moors and coming into Ball Cover. Crossing the road into Waterloo, he came down the valley through Wixon, into the Stone Moor Covers, and crossed the Chulmleigh road. Mr. Amory now let the pack go. Coming down to the Dart by the rifle range at Sydenham, hounds ran down the valley past Chulmleigh Bridge, turned out over into the Eggesford Covers by way of Upcott and Southercott, then up the valley nearly to Chenson; on towards Foxes Covert and came back to the River Dart, with two deer in front, which separated in Chawleigh Barton Wood. One went away to the Stone Moor Covers, the other ran down past Stone Mills, where hounds were laid on again. Running up the valley, through Leigh Wood and Burridge, they crossed the road into the Lapford Woods, by way of Pouncers, then down through Chenson Wood, Foxes Cover and Southcott, hounds ran past Eggesford Station to Chawleigh Week. Down to the River Taw, and crossing the railway just by Colleton, our deer began to run short, hounds being almost close to his haunches. Back again, we went into Bourne Wood, around which they scurried him several times. Breaking away at last, he crossed the road, nearly jumping over the head of the Hon. Sec. of the Deer Damage Fund, and then went out over the top. After sinking the valley again, he ran over Bidivin Moor nearly into Ashreigney, through Ash Wood, then across still more enclosed country, he brought us to Burrington Moor. Leaving Burrington on our right, hounds drove along across several rough valleys, nearly to Roborough; then on to High Bickington. After running nearly around the village, hounds turned away right handed. It was now getting dark but hounds were still running hard. Most of the field had cried off, their horses had had enough. From this point there was no one with the hounds except the Master and Ernest Hellard (The Kennel Huntsman). Still running they went on towards Langley Ford, the farthest point hounds ran last Wednesday week. After crossing the stream they came nearly into Yarnscombe, but keeping left handed, crossed the road into the coverts at Cranford Cross. It was now 7.45pm., and hounds could only be followed by the ear. They went on to the Stevenstone Covers, on past High Bullen, a holla forward luckily allowing Ernest to get to their heads as they were just crossing the road into Stevenstone Park where they were stopped. It was now after eight o' clock, and then began a long tramp back to Eggesford, which was not reached until nearly midnight.

28th Aug 1906

Mr Ian Amory as Huntsman

A writer in the *The World* has the following reference to Mr Ian Amory in an article on the Devon and Somerset Staghounds and their history, just now the change of Masters is engaging everyone's attention in the west for the Master of the Devon and Somerset occupies a unique position. Mr R. A. Sanders though not connected with the West Country, except by marriage, had held office both long and successfully. He has been ably aided in Sidney Tucker his huntsman, though he was the first Master to hunt the staghounds himself. Mr Amory, a born huntsman with a rare knack of getting to his hounds in a strange country, now hunts Sir John Amory's Staghounds pack from Tiverton, while Mr E.A.V. Stanley goes straight as a die when hunting the Quantock pack, between these two naturally lay the succession, but though the formers choice would have been universally popular, when he gave away to his younger confrere staghunters congratulated themselves on having such an excellent second string to the bow.

A run from Bembridge Wood September 15th 1906.

Sept 22nd 1906

The bye meet at Haddon on Tuesday last was largely attended, despite the fact that the Devon and Somerset Staghounds were there the previous day. Two fairly good stags were roused in Venn Brake, and one of them went away at Lincombe Lakes by way of the Exe Valley, but when the pack was laid on scent was so bad that they could do little with it. Gradually they worked the line out over Court Down to Higher Combe, where they got mixed up with a lot of hinds. Later on the pack was laid on to some deer on Winsford Hill and came down by way of Ashwick to Three Waters. Nothing was done after that.

There was a big field on Saturday at the bye meet at South Molton Station. Tufters spent some time in Hacche Wood, and eventually the pack was laid on to a two a top stag which ran to Bremridge Wood. They were later changed on to a heavy stag and scent being rather good drove him down to the park at Castle Hill and into the river. The best part of the next two hours was spent in the wood adjoining Castle Hill, and the stag was ultimately taken in the river about half a mile below the mansion. He had all his rights and three and four atop, three on the off and four on the near. It was a good day for foot people, of whom there were a good many out.

Sept 29th 1906

There was a large attendance at the opening meet of these hounds at Rackenford on Saturday last. A stag found on the moor came back through the Stoodleigh country, being visible from the road on many occasions as he made his way down the valley of the Exe.

He was viewed lying down on some fallow ground near the Exeter Inn, and on being roused went up over Highwood Plain. Entering the Exe just above New Bridge, he was not allowed to tarry long, and going up over again, he returned to the water not far from Lythecourt, where he crossed the railway line, but was prevented from crossing the road. Running on down the valley he was taken in the ornamental water of Bolam House, after a run of two hours.

Oct 6th 1906

A fairly large field turned out at Haddon on Tuesday, despite the fact that the Devon and Somerset Staghounds were there the day before. Fred Goss had harboured several good deer in Upton Wood, but some time elapsed before a stag was roused and went away through the Deer Park and across Skilgate Common, the pack being laid on in the middle of the common. Having run to the Allotments he came back over the common into the big Haddon woodlands, and for the next two hours we were continually moving him from one point to the other between Bury Village and Upton Lodge. The stag was eventually taken in a kitchen garden at Clammer.

Following the meet at Chawleigh on Saturday, tufters were laid on the line of three deer which were seen leaving the Barton Wood and going into Leigh. Tufters were not, however, able to make much of it and the pack was brought out, but they found nothing except a small stag which came back through Burrow Wood into Leigh Wood, and through Chawleigh Barton Wood. Crossing the valley by the rifle butts at Sydeham he made for Stone Moor, but crossing the valley by Sheepsbyre he turned right handed through Ball Plantation and on to Wixon. Then he set his neck for the Gidley Arms and ran right down the valley past Ashmoors and Creacombe through Backson, where hounds put up five runnable stags. They kept to the hunted one, however, and crossing Rackenford Moor came down the Iron Mill Stream to Chain Bridge and coursed him up the Exe nearly to Stuckeridge Bridge. Coming back he entered Duvale Wood and crossed the Exe close to Halfpenny Bridge, but came back to the water again by Holmingham and ran down the stream as far as the rifle butts at Cove. He now turned up through Steart and East Stoodleigh and came back close to the Stoodleigh kennels. Hounds were eventually whipped off at dark close to Champles Farm.

Oct 13th 1906

Despite the rain which fell on Saturday morning a large field, including many ladies, attended the meet of Sir John Amory's Staghounds at Knightshayes Court, the stately home of the founder of the pack and of Lady Amory, whose hospitality was thoroughly appreciated. The hounds were paraded in the pink of condition, and with the large field standing around, formed the subject of several good snapshots, with the court as a background. Among those present were the Master (Mr Ian Amory), Mr H. Amory, Miss Amory, Mrs Ian Amory, Mrs H. Amory, Lady Manners, Mr and Mrs L. Unwin, Miss M. March-Phillipps, Mr J. C. de Las Casas, Mr and Mrs L. Mackenzie, the Misses Chichester, Mrs and Miss Manderson, Col. Macefield, Mr E. Hancock, Mr Corbett, Mr Boles, Mr and Mrs Pethick, Mrs S. H. Fisher, the Mayor and Mayoress of Tiverton (Mr and Mrs H. Mudford), Mrs Pugsley, Mr W. Glendinning, Mr Down (Sampford Peverell), Mr R. Briggs, Mr W. H. Quick, Mr and Mrs J. G. Carswell, Miss Babbage, Mr Drake, Mrs and Miss Gameson, Miss Rabjohns, Father Damen, Master Ivor Pethick, Messrs Pearce (Halberton Court), S.Webber, S. Thorne, F. Butt. A. Pring, M. Goodland, H. Pearce,

Rabjohns (2), C. Haydon, W. Haydon, M. Haydon, Ware (Moorstone), Headon (Stoodleigh), J. Farrant, J. Zelly (Rackenford), Heard (Pitt Farm), Brown (Rackenford), B. Heal, H. Pearce (Whitnage), and many others too numerous to mention. On many occasions the Tiverton Foxhounds have owed a good deal to the Master of the Staghounds in providing them with foxes when they were none too plentiful. To day Mr Unwin had an opportunity of returning the compliment and providing a stag for the Master of Staghounds in his covert immediately below Gogwell Farm. The stag was one which has been lying in the vicinity for three years, grazing with the cattle, and occasionally leading young stock astray, Hounds had not been more than a quarter of an hour in covert before the whistle was heard, signifying that a stag was afoot, and although scent, especially in the first half hour, was noticeable by its absence, the smartness of the officials of the hunt made up for a good deal, and hounds pushed their quarry through Brickbats Plantation by Firebeacon, across by the waterworks, through Allers Wood, and away past Pitt and Crocombe and through Allers Down. Turning to the right, we came past Fordlands, and into the Lowman Valley by Onekoo's Nest; then turning westward we reached Mr Peter Were's farm at Bradford, and crossed the Halberton road. The stag crossed the canal at three different points, and was set up at bay close to the G. W. R. Viaduct. Being a young deer with some run left in him he broke bay and made away straight for Thorn's Copse, up the hill, and away towards Cullompton. Near Five Bridges all trace of him was lost. Later it was reported that a deer had been seen crossing Bradfield Park, and thither hounds were taken, but too long a time had elapsed since he was seen for hounds to be able to do anything, and so this good deer had to left for another day.

Oct 20th 1906

THE DEVON AND SOMERSET STAGHOUNDS
RUNNING WITHIN FOUR MILES OF TIVERTON

After a long run the above hounds killed a stag at Bradley Down, within four miles of Tiverton on Saturday. This is somewhat unusual line from the moor. There were a large number of spotsmen in at the death, and as some of them were hunting from Porlock, they had 30 miles to go before getting home.

For the first time this season Sir John Amory's Staghounds had splendid scent on Tuesday last. The meet having been at Bury Village, tufters roused in Swinescleave a good stag which, after a turn up the valley as far as Lincombe Lakes, came back through Pixie Copse and on to Bury Castle. The pack were laid on the Minehead road going down to the Exe. Fresh finding him in Pezzlecombe Wood, hounds raced him back to Perry, away through Pixton and down and across the Barle and away through Allen Wood to Coombe. Here our stag turned left handed, and ran down nearly to the railway above Brushford, and kept up the valley nearly to Knutsford, where hounds fresh found him in a gorse brake. Racing him back over much the same line to Coombe and Allers Wood, he came down to the Barle, and ran down its course, past the Carnarvon Arms, to Perry. Thence the line lay through Pixie Copse and nearly into Bury Village, where hounds fresh found him and raced him back through the bottom to Pezzlecombe Wood again and down to the river by Hele Bridge, where he was taken about 1.30, after a fast two hours' gallop. He had brow, tray, and three atop on each side.

Oct 27th 1906

Following the meet at Haddon on Wednesday the tufters were taken to Sir John Ferguson Davie's coverts at Bittiscombe, whence a young stag ultimately went away over Skilgate Common, but came back to the Allotments. The pack was brought into play later in the Deer Park, and drove their stag at top speed away through Uscombe Wood, across Hartford Cleeve and nearly to Wind Corner. Turning short back the stag came back over much the same line to the Deer Park, where he put up a bigger stag. Both stags, went away across Skilgate Common into the Allotments, but hounds kept to the younger one, and running through the Bittiscombe Coverts again as far as Ramscombe fresh found him and drove him back over the common into Haddon and down to Bury Village. Running up the Exe Valley to Hele Bridge the stag now turned, and coming back, took to the water by the Chemical Works; but turning up over the hill ran on nearly into Morebath, where he crossed the railway and led hounds nearly to Combehead. Later he was killed in the water not far from Highley Weirpool.

Oct 27th 1906

THE QUANTOCK STAGHOUNDS HUNTING IN THE TIVERTON COUNTRY

Followers of the above hounds had their run of the season on Saturday. The meet was at Elworthy Cross, under the Brendons, and after a stern chase through their own country hounds brought a fine stag into the heart of the country hunted by Sir John Amory's Staghounds. As the stag came through the Bittiscombe coverts and over into Wonham the chase was joined by several of the sporting farmers of the district, and when the morte was sounded near Duvale at 4.30 in the afternoon Mr Yandle and his sons were, of course, on the spot. Mr C. Spiller, of Tiverton, who happened to be driving along the Exe Valley at the time the stag came to water, says he never saw a more noble beast. The stag made a fine picture as he stood on the weir above Chain Bridge defying hounds, and gave a photographer from Dulverton several other chances to take snapshots as he was bayed by hounds in the river. Our Bampton correspondent writes; After the kill the stag was brought to Bampton in a trap. It had a magnificent head, and many people visited the White Horse Hotel yard to have a look at it while Mr Stanley and other members of the hunt were taking tea. This is the second time this season the Quantock Staghounds have visited Bampton.

Nov 3rd 1906

It was a beautiful morning, more like a May morning than one at the end of October, when these hounds met at the Gidley Arms on Saturday. There was not a large field, many having thrown in their lot for the day with the Silverton Hounds, who were meeting at Worthy Bridge in the Tiverton country, but a good few joined in while hounds were tufting. The tufters were drawn at the Gidley Arms Hotel, and the Master went on to draw Waterloo, where the Harbourer had reported deer lying, the pack being taken on to Stone Moor in charge of one of the whips. It was not long before the deer that was to bear the brunt of the days chase was roused, and from the first it was seen that hounds could run. After a turn or two round Waterloo he went on to Bycott, but was soon driven out of the coverts. The pack was let go at about 12. 30, and ran first as if Kingsnympton and South Molton Road was the point the deer was making, but bearing back left handed he just skirted the top of Horridge Moor, and passing to the left of Chulmleigh came down past Colleton to the Taw by Rashleigh Weir. Here we had to cross the river and the railway, and hounds had a slight check, but they were soon put right by the Master. Running back through the Eggesford Coverts and on past the mansion to the river at Chenson the deer went on as if Coldridge was his point, but he turned right handed and ran on nearly to Winkleigh. Being headed he ran back down the valley to within a mile or so of North Tawton, whence the line lay to Bondleigh. Hounds fresh found him hereabouts, and after a final rush of about a mile he ran down to the water and was taken about half past 3 o'clock at Taw Mills. Among those there at the finish were the Master Mr Ian Heathcoat Amory, Mr L. Amory, Mr H. Tudor Crosthwaite, Mr Lawrence Haydon, Mr S. Vicary, Mr Mortimore (Chittlehampton), Mr Snow (Knowstone) and about half a dozen others. Those from Tiverton had 25 miles to go before they got back home.

Nov 10th 1906

A stag had been seen in the Exe Valley just below Tiverton on several occasions during the last few weeks, so a bye meet was held at the Tiverton Town Hall by special invitation of the Mayor on Friday last in order that he might be hunted. It was the first time that a meet of staghounds had ever taken place in Tiverton, and as a result the event created a considerable amount of interest among the townspeople. Regular followers of the hounds were more interested because the stag they met to hunt was believed to be the one which led a large field such a merry chase after the meet at Knightshayes Court last month. Horsemen and pedestrians began to assemble outside the Town Hall at 12.30, and by 1 o'clock, the hour fixed for the meet, there was almost as big a crowd in Fore Street as there was when the result of the Parliamentary election was made known in January last. The windows of the Town Hall, the Angel Hotel, and all the houses in the locality were thronged with interested spectators, while all the photographers in the neighbourhood were busy taking snap shots of the stirring scenes being enacted in the street below. Sir John and Lady Heathcoat-Amory attended the meet in their carriage; Mrs Ian Heathcoat-Amory

Sketch by Terry Gable

and party came in a motor car. Other members of the Heathcoat-Amory family present were the Master of the staghounds Mr Ian Heathcoat-Amory, Mr Ludovic Amory, and Miss Heathcoat-Amory. The field also included Mr C. Carew, M. H., the Hon. Mrs Lionel Walrond, Messrs J. C.and A. de Las Casas, Mr J. C. Hill, Mr Corbet, Mr Renton, the Misses Chichester, Miss Wynter, Mr and Mrs J. F. Pugsley, Mr J. W. Goddard, Messrs T., W., L. and M. Haydon, Mr R. S. Pethick, Mr J. G. Pedler, Mr H. Pearce, Mr W. Glendinning, Messrs W. Thorne, sen. and jun., Mr S. Webber, Mr A. Pring, Mr W. C. Rowcliffe, Mr J. Farrant, Mr Marshall, Master Ivor Pethick, Mr C. Spiller, Mr J. Goodland, Mr Cuming, Mr P. Chappell, Mr T. A. Chave, Mr S.Thorn, Mr Rowden, Mr J. Butt, Mr G. Takle, Messrs. Rabjohns (2), Veysey (Cullompton), Norrish (Cadleigh), Yandle (3) (Duvale), Williams (Sampford Peverell), Pring (Gornhay), F. Pring (Pitt), Yells (Rembarton), Blackmore (Plushayes), Marks (Halberton), Mogridge (Cadleigh), Pearcey (Chevithorne), and many others too numerous to mention. Among those on foot were the Mayor and Mayoress (Mr and Mrs H. Mudford). Excitement ruled high when the Kennel Huntsman (Mr Ernest Hellard) brought sixteen and a half couples of hounds from the Angel Hotel, where they had been kennelled while the field was assembling. The Master made a brief speech to the foot people, for whose convenience the meet had been held at one o' clock. He mentioned that it was very kind of Mr Pease to allow hounds to go into his coverts within a few days of the holding of a shooting party, and expressed the hope that everyone would do their best not to disturb the game. If the field got a view of the deer he hoped they would not shout all at once or the hounds would not know which way to go. After these few remarks the Master turned his horse into St Andrews Street and the field moved off in the direction of Holwellcombe, where the deer had been lying all the morning. The pack was kennelled at Mr Heard's farm while tufters were thrown into the combe, whence the deer emerged in full view of the foot people, many of whom had never been so near a stag before. A youth named Leonard Harris, of John Street, found himself much too close to be comfortable, the deer jumping clean over his head. After running in a ring round the farm the deer jumped into a turnip field, and made his way in view of a number of foot people who had assembled on Exeter Hill, up the grassy slopes towards the road to Butterleigh. The ease with which he cleared the hedge into the road and the one on the further side was a revelation to those who had not seen a stag hunted before. The pack was laid on with all possible speed, and presented a pleasing picture as they streamed over the road and up the meadow to the left of Gogwell Lane, and thence to Higher Warnicombe. Crossing the road hereabouts the deer lead hounds at a rattling pace into and through Thorn's Copse, and into the valley beyond, leaving Brithembottom on the left and then bearing right handed till he came to Moorstone Barton. Running on towards Cullompton railway station he crossed the railway near Five Bridges, and then took practically the same line as he did when last hunted. Reaching Bradfield Park he tried all sorts of dodges in the hope of shaking off his pursuers, but hounds stuck to him and eventually forced him out at the top end of the woods. Thence the line lay through Kentisbeare to the Blackdown Hills, and over a furze-clad moorland, where there was plenty of grief owing to horses putting their feet into rabbit holes. The field had become smaller by degrees and beautifully less when after galloping over this delightful stretch of country for several miles, hounds began to descend to the lowlands beyond. Of those who were still in the running very few had the slightest knowledge of the country they were riding through, as they raced onwards through the Walford Lodge estate and on between Honiton and Luppitt. The end came just as it was getting dark at Mohuns Ottery, four miles north east of Honiton. Considering the distance traversed there were a fair number in at the death, including Miss Amory, Miss Wynter, Miss Chichester, and Mrs Pugsley. After the morte had been sounded all who had stayed out this remarkable run rode on into Honiton where the arrival of so many horsemen and horsewomen caused no little excitement.

One or two caught a train to Exeter, but the majority, some 40 or 50 in number, came home by road, leaving Honiton at 7 o'clock and arriving at Tiverton from 10 o'clock onwards. It is computed that hounds must have run 30 miles after this deer.

Dec 29th 1906

On Saturday after the meet at Spurway Mill hounds drew several coverts before finding a deer in Wheatland. Pushing across into Little Waspleigh, they fresh found him in Big Waspleigh Wood with two others and ran them through Thowcombe and on by way of Mead Down, across Willicroft and to Blatchworthy, where the deer separated, each being pursued by equal divisions of the pack. One lot of eight or nine couples drove a single deer through Rifton, across Coleford Water, then through Wheatland, Wormsworthy, and Champles Cliff to Chain Bridge and on to the Highwood Plain, where there was a long check. Hearing that the rest of the pack were running another deer farther down, Mr Amory brought hounds down to Rock, where the deer had crossed the river and railway, but the leading hounds had a long start. They ran their deer up through the fishponds, then on to Gogwell and Palfreys, then touching Allens Down they bore away for Huntsham, then swinging around to Zeal Ball they ran him down to the Batherm where he was killed about four o'clock.

Feb 23rd 1907

On Saturday the meet was at Rackenford. Miller had harboured a number of deer on Ditchitts Moor, and the pack was kennelled at the premises of that good staghunter, Mr Brown, to draw the tufters. This done the pack was taken on to Mr Veysey's at Bransford. Tufters soon roused the deer, and ten of them were at once on foot. Separating in all directions, one lot went away towards Bransford and another lot towards Baples Hill and the Knowstone Woods. The hind tufters settled on ran back into Baxton and turned out over into Knowstone Woods. Eventually hounds were laid on to three hinds on Hazon Moor, and ran one of them back at best pace through the Knowstone Woods nearly to Bish Mill. Turning, the deer came back over Baples Hill and down nearly to Creacombe; thence she ran nearly to Branscombe, then just touching the Knowstone Woods she bore away through Knowstone Moor and Hazon Moor into the Rackenford Coverts, where she joined other deer. Hitting the line again, hounds ran through Bickham and Spurway Mills, then through Little Warbrightsley to Rifton Wood, through Blatchworthy and on to Willicroft Brake, then out over close to Tidderson Moor, and the Hilltown Coverts, then across the Witheridge Moor to Looseland, where hounds had three fresh deer in front of them. It was now getting dark, and Mr Amory stopped hounds.

March 9th 1907

A fine day's sport fell to the followers of these hounds on Saturday. The meet was at Worlington, and there was a good field out, including the Master Mr Ian Heathcoat-Amory, Mr Ludovic Amory, Miss Chichester, Messrs W. and L. Haydon, Mr Snow (Knowstone), Mr Brown (Rackenford), Mr Hulland (South Molton), Mr Vickery (Cheldon), Messrs Tripe and Webber (Chulmleigh). Many others joined the hunt as the chase progressed. Miller had harboured several deer in in Cotonhayes, among them a young stag, and tufters drew for some time before the right one went away. After he had taken a turn out across Affeton Moor the pack was laid on to him as he came back into Cotonhayes. Running through the covert he turned left handed and came down through Affeton Old Plantation and away across Winswood Moor to the Stone Moor Coverts. Throwing these behind him he passed through Wixon, skirted the Waterloo Coverts, and crossed the road into Bycott. A rather long check ensued owing to scent being none too good, but hounds eventually picked up the line in the moors at the bottom of the covert and ran their deer by Garland Cross out nearly to Alswear Village, and through Great Heal Barton. Through the outskirts of South Molton the line lay by Honiton Barton and down the river Mole to Meeth Gate, and on past Warkleigh. At Kingsbridge under Kingsnympton Park hounds fresh found their deer quarry, and rattled him out over the top left handed till we came close to Chittlehamholt and down to the Taw at Portsmouth Arms. After running along the bottom for some time he turned out to the right and eventually came down close to Umberleigh Station. Our second check occurred here, but hounds picked up the line again, and we soon found ourselves running close to Chittlehampton. Hounds now got closer to their deer and pressed him hard as he ran through Hudscott and on to Clatworthy Mill. From now to the end they seemed tied to him, and running him down to the water not far from Castle Hill where he was taken. It wanted but a few minutes to five o'clock when the morte was sounded, hounds having been running from 12 o'clock.

March 23rd 1907

There was a large field to greet the Master at Bealy Court on Saturday. Hounds were taken on to Cheldon Barton to kennel, and tufters soon found a couple of deer in the covert beside the Barton. One of these came down towards Cheldon Bridge, where tufters were stopped. A wave of the hand brought the pack to the Master, and on being laid on hounds ran into Burridge, where the hind had waited for hounds. Turning short back she came down the Cheldon Valley through Leigh Wood and into Chawleigh Barton Wood, then turning down under Sydeham she came up over Stone Farm and made away for the Stone Moor Coverts. Through the Wixon Woods and up through Waterloo she came away through Bycott and turned left handed across Kingsnympton road at Garland Cross and kept left handed nearly to Kingsnympton, where there was a check. It was a long time before hounds recovered the line, and when they did complications ensued through a number of deer being up. Hounds carried the line of deer back into Bycott, but nothing more was done.

March 30th 1907

There was a meet on Friday at Rackenford, when hounds got on the line of a travelling deer at Knowstone and after running over some moorland came upon two deer in a covert close to East Anstey Station. Getting on the line of the bigger of the two, they came back by way of Oldways End to Swineham Hill where they crossed Rackenford Moor and came to the Stoodleigh Coverts by way of Bickham, and ran down the valley to Chain Bridge, and out over Highwood Plain. There was a slight check at Steart, but hounds soon picked up the line again and ran down through Emelford, across Hatherland to Standerton, where the deer was fresh found and came down to the water, crossing the Exe and the railway line close to Lythecourt. Thence the line lay through

Croydon and right handed through the Knightshayes Coverts, passing close to the keeper's house, and then down to the waterworks. Out over the top ran the deer as if for Allen's Down, but bearing left handed came nearly to Chettiscombe and then to Chevithorne, and down over the fields close to Peadhill and thence to Pileywell. Next the deer bore away to Poolanthony, crossing the canal and coming down nearly to Tidcombe, then right out over the top nearly to Burrow Corner. Keeping on the top he left Rhode Farm on the right and came down through the lower end of Backswood, where the deer began to run very cunning. Hounds were eventually stopped near Millhayes, close to Bickleigh Station at 7 o'clock. It was a fifteen mile point, but hounds ran more than twice that distance. A fine deer, evidently the one that had been hunted, was seen near Bickleigh on Saturday.

April 6th 1907

A run of 30 miles followed the meet on Tuesday at Higher Combe. Operations began in a gorse brake just below Ball Neck, where tufters came across a herd of hinds, and scattering them in all directions, settled on to the smallest of the lot, which was not, however, desined to bear the burden of the chase. Near Dulverton they were stopped and laid on to a hind and yearling going into Southill, racing then across the Allotments and on across the Punchbowl to Comer's Gate. Here the deer turned as if to run the usual line to the Barle, but instead of doing so they came back by Bradley Bog, where the pack were let go, and ran the deer through Contest Plantation, back through Southill, and down through Red Cleave to the Exe. On ran the hind through Stockham and Exe Cleave to Hele Bridge; then having run down the water to Weir she turned out over to Bury Castle, and having crossed through Pixie Copse turned over the top, passing Morebath Village. About a mile further on she crossed the railway and ran past Shillingford, just skirting Bampton. Bearing now to the left she came nearly to Huntsham and down through Knackers Hill away for the Cove Coverts, passing not far from Cove House. Through Mr Unwin's coverts and Custom Wood lay the line down and across the railway and river near Fairby, on to and through Hatherland Wood nearly to Pilemore. To Courteney and then on across the bottom between the Rose and Crown and Calverleigh Court; then up through the park and down into Combe Butler Bottom, where the deer beat hounds only about half a mile from kennel.

After Saturday's meet at March Bridge, the tufters found several deer in the Summerhouse Covert under Northmoor, and drove them pretty sharp up the valley. After a turn or two round Hawkridge and Three Waters a deer went away through Ashway Hat and on to Ashway Side, and the pack was laid on not far from Tarr Steps. Running out over into Knaplock they passed up the valley by way of Bradley Farm and on to Bradley Ham. Hounds fresh found her in the wood and raced her down to the water at Bradley Ford, where she turned out over the top and ran away over Withypool Common to to Porchester Post. Leaving Lords Plantation to the left she ran on to Cuzzicombe Post and Poulthouse Combe, right round Molland Moor and away back to the Danesbrook by way of Anstey Burrows and the Allotments and down to the water at Castle Bridge. Complications now arose through fresh deer getting up, and after running up and down the bottom for an hour hounds eventually got away with another hind from Mounsey Castle, and ran her up through Ashway Hat and across the Barle close to Tarr Steps. Passing close to the rectory she ran up the Barle and through Westwater, coming down to the water again at Bradley Ford. Having fresh found her in the water hounds bayed her for some minutes below Withypool, but she broke away again and went over the common, running in the same line as the deer that was hunted in the morning by Porchester Post, Cuzzicombe Post, Molland Moor, and Anstey Common. In the Allotments below Anstey Common she waited for hounds, who pushed her down through Whiterocks to the Danesbrook, and was taken in the Barle just below Castle Bridge.

April 13th 1907

On Friday the meet was at Bury. All the early part of the day was spent in Haddon, and it was not until between two and three o'clock that a deer went away over Storridge to Baronsdown, and thense to Barlynch Wood. Crossing the river hounds ran through Execleave and Stockham, mounting to Redcleave, and on to Winsford Hill. Thence the line lay through the Allotments and across the Punchbowl nearly to Comer's Gate, where hounds swung round and fresh found their deer in Bradley Bog. Getting away on good terms with their deer, hounds ran him back over the hill, down through the Allotments, and nearly to Winsford. Hounds fresh found him again in a gorse brake close to Bridgetown and took him in the water about 5 o'clock. While hounds were in Haddon they came into close contact with the Quantock Staghounds who had met at Elworthy Cross and who subsequently killed a deer not far from Dulverton.

Sept 7th 1907

Sir John Amory's Staghounds had a bye meet at South Molton Railway Station on Wednesday. A large field put in an appearance. The weather was fine but dull. Among those present were:- The Countess Pappenheim (Winsford), Messrs Fred Day, F. Yendell (Lords Down), T. E. Dyer (Port), J. Bulled (South Molton), R. Gould, A. Manns, Carey (Court Hall), P. Buckingham, H. Bowden, H. Lethbridge, E. Janes, J. Slader, C. Slader (Marsh), Charles Slader (Hacche), T. Burnell (North Molton), Albert E. Shapland (Church House), F. J. Cosgrave, A. E. Sanders, H. Seage, S. Lock, A. Squire, Jno. Reed (Thorne), J. Bowden (Georgenympton), Wm. Moor, J. Hill, Crang (Cockram), J. Ayre, Cole (Stone), S. Clarke, J. N. Barnes, J. Warner, W. Madge, Buckingham (Landscombe), T. Tucker, H. and P. Couch, G. Smith, Mrs Turner, Rev. E. C. Harries (West Buckland). Conveyances:- Captain Glossop, Whitechapel (3) Messrs F. Cockram (Belgrave), Robert Cock (South Street), Robert Kelland, Ernest Hill (Anchor Hotel), Miss Persse (Alswere), Miss Askew (South Molton). Parties:- Mr Frank Merson, Dr Wigham, Mrs R. S. Crosse, Mr W. H. Hulland (Fursebray), Misses Passmore (Radley, Bishopsnympton), Col and Mrs Abbot. The horsemen numbered upwards of 140; about a score of ladies also being mounted. The hounds were put in the woods in the North Molton Valley, going as far as West Park. There a stag was set on foot and went away towards Bremeridge. After a while there was a turn back to Hacche, breaking cover near the railway station. Going by the railway line the stag crossed the moors and came up by the kennels and on to Woods Moors. Then he made for the Recreation Ground, but turned away a moment later on seeing a number of persons there. His next move was through the Pathfields, where a large number of spectators had assembled, and then by Gunsdown Villas, where he jumped into the station road. Clearing a gate on the opposite side of the road, he ran through Patsams and away down to the shirt and collar factory. Wading through the Mole, he scaled the hill to Bailey-Head, and on at a good pace to Bish Mill. Here he took to the water for a few minutes, but left before the hounds came up. Westmill Cover, leading into Blastridge, was the next point taken by the hounds, but the stag had not gone there. The hunt proceeded round by Bishopsnympton to Ashmill, and afterwards went on to Knowstone and Rackenford. Earlier in the hunt some excitement was caused in South

Molton by the large number of horsemen galloping through North Street and Station Road. In East Street one of the lady riders became unseated through her horse falling.

Sept 28th 1907

It was a perfect morning, the scorching rays of the sun being tempered by a refreshing breeze, when Sir John Amory's Staghounds met on Saturday in Mr F. J. Coleridge Boles picturesque park at Rackenford Manor, for their opening fixture. The field was a large one, and hospitality was extended to all comers, even to the village school children who seemed as interested as anyone in the affairs of the day. Hounds looking as fit as fit could be, were brought to Rackenford by the Kennel Huntsman (Ernest Hellard), the Master Mr Ian Heathcoat-Amory motoring to the meet with Sir John and Lady Heathcoat-Amory and Mr H. Heathcoat-Amory. Others present including Mr, Mrs and Miss Coleridge Boles, Mr Jeffrey Boles, the Hon. Mrs Lesley Butler, Mr L. Heathcoat-Amory, Mr C. Carew, Mr and Mrs L. Mackenzie, Major Chichester, Mr J. and the Misses Chichester, Miss Quick, Mr Newman, Capt. and Mrs Hamilton, Mr L. Corbet, Miss Manderson, Mr H. Cooper, Mr and Mrs J. F. Pugsley, Mr Courtney Haydon, Mr Mark Haydon, Mr W. Haydon, Mr A. Pring, Mr J. Farrant, Mr C. W. Nelder (Dulverton), Mr J. Butt (Washfield), the Rev. E. M. Meadows (Stoodleigh), Mr and Mrs F. Yendell, Mr H. Hippisley, Mr Shellabeer (London), Mr and Mrs Vearncombe (Bickham), Mr R. Frankpitt (Cruwys Morchard), Mr and Mrs F. Matthews (Rackenford), Mr J. Coles (Frankhill), Messrs G. and J. Nott (Rackenford), Mr Veysey (Brushford), Messrs Yandle (Duvale), Mr Brown (Nutcott), Mr Beedell (Sydeham), Messrs J. and F. Zelley (Hilltown), Mr Singerton (Rackenford), Mr Tripe (Parsonage Farm, Chulmleigh). Mr Cox (Heifers, Witheridge), Mr Matthews (Witheridge), Mr Wreford (Radford Barton, Witheridge), Mr Berry (Creacombe Barton), Mr Blackmore (Backstone Moor), Mr Parish (Merryfieldhaies), Messrs Harris (Thelbridge), Mr Blake (Stoodleigh), Mr Selley (Witheridge), Mr Hill (Knowstone), Mr Norman (Washfield), Mr Bucknell (Knowstone), Mr Knapman (Rackenford), and other sporting farmers too numerous to mention from points as far away as Dulverton, Halberton, Bickleigh, Chulmleigh, and South Molton. The pack were kennelled at the lodge, while tufters were taken to draw Haresdown and adjacent coverts. From a point of vantage on Mr Brown's holding the foot people, of whom there was a lot out, were able to catch occasional glimpses of the hounds as they searched for a warrantable stag. As only hinds were found at home, hounds were subsequently thrown into Great Down, a large covert exactly opposite the vantage ground previously spoken of. Hounds had not been in this covert five minutes when a hind bounded away over Haresdown. Presently another hind with a calf in close attendance dashed out of the covert and made off in the opposite direction till they were lost to view in some "vearns", as a farmer friend described the luxuriant growth of ferns intermingled with the heather on Rackenford Moor. It was a fine sight watching Great Down from the opposite hill. The red coats of the huntsmen as they moved about on either side of the wood formed a charming contrast to the sombreness of the adjacent moor, intersected here and there by tall hedges and occasional belts of trees. Suddenly, after a merry burst of music from the pack, the cry went up "There he goes" as a deer bounded away towards Haresdown. But still hounds tarried in the wood, the deer being not one of the required sort. After a comparatively long silence another hind and calf

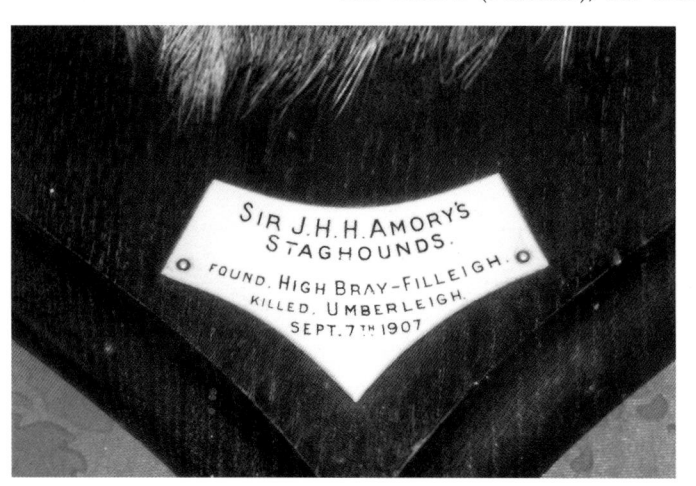

A run from High Bray, Filleigh to Umberleigh in 1907.

made away over the moor, followed not long after by yet another hind, which, however, soon turned and ran back through the enclosure the foot people were in, jumping all the obstacles it found in its way. A remark made to my farmer friend that there seemed to be plenty of deer about elicited the response that there were not nearly so many in Squire Devon's time, when they ate up all the hedges on the moor. He added that last year he had a field of wheat almost entirely spoilt by deer and he supposed he ought to have claimed compensation, but he did not. But for such good sportsmen as these – and there are hundreds of such in the country hunted by Sir John Amory's hounds – there would be very little staghunting. No stag found in Great Down hounds were moved on to the open moor, where they were soon busy searching about in the ferns, which are hereabouts two or three feet high. They speedily roused one of the hinds and calves that had been evicted from Great Down, and back the graceful creatures raced to their former sanctuary. Stags being still conspicuous by their absence, the Master sent back for the pack, with which he drew the Lodge Plantation. Here again there seemed to be plenty of hinds but no stags. As a timid looking hind broke away a little girl at my elbow remarked that that was the seventh deer she had seen, and she never saw one before that day. Suddenly a number of hounds came out of the wood and took exactly the same line as the hind had been observed to take, but they were soon whipped off. It was now about 3.30, and as it was now quite clear that there were no male deer in the neighbourhood the field moved off with the hounds over the moor in the direction of Sydeham and Bickham. Whether hounds got on to the line of a stag or not I do not know; all I know is that Saturday's proceedings left pleasant memories for those who followed the chase on wheel or on foot. Mr Amory drew with the whole pack the coverts on both sides of the valley down to Chain Bridge and to Cove Bridge, but no stag could be found, and at 5 o'clock the order was given for home.

Oct 5th 1907

From the fixture at Chawleigh on Saturday those who were out had another good day's hunt. As it was the first time this season the staghounds had met in this part of the country, there was a big field out to meet the Master. Hounds had been brought on the night before and kennelled at the Fox and Hounds at Eggesford. A big stag having been harboured in Bycott, the tufters were hardly in covert before he was on his legs, and hounds were very quickly on his line. From here he crossed the Romansleigh road into Waterloo and ran down the valley through Wixon where he turned up through the Stone Moor Coverts. Having crossed the road on to and over Winswood Moor, he went through Affeton Old Plantation and down the bottom to the keeper's cottage. Here he turned left handed and came up again and through the Young Covert to Coton Hayes, where he was viewed stealing away back to Affeton Old Plantation again. Hounds were soon pressing him down to the Dart, and through the Cheldon Valley, till he came down through Leigh Wood and Stone Mill. Down the valley he went, past the rifle butts at Sydeham, and just short of Chulmleigh Bridge he turned out over for the Eggesford Coverts. Hounds were stopped for a few minutes on the top of Upcott, but it was not long before they were bustling their stag through Nethercott and Foxes Covert and up past Chenson, where he was viewed. Turning up the valley he met the Master and the pack, and hounds drove him across the road into Lapford Wood and out at the far end. He made his last stand not far from Lapford Station, and after a turn up and down the water he was taken. He had a splendid head, with all his rights and three atop on both sides – the eighth of the season.

From the Sporting and Dramatic News *5 October 1907, This drawing by Lionel Edwards illustrates the incident described below.*

Oct 12th 1907

This well known pack of Sir John Amory's Staghounds has of late been receiving a good deal of attention in the illustrated and sporting papers. In the *Illustrated Sporting and Dramatic News* is a drawing by Lionel Edwards of an incident which occurred in the neighbourhood of Lynmouth. Entitled "A mutal surprise", it depicts a party of hunting men and women meeting a stag face to face in a wood, to the alarm of the horses, underneath the picture is written: Sir John Amory's Staghounds were established in 1896 at the suggestion of a Master of the Devon and Somerset Staghounds for the purpose of hunting that country over which the deer were spreading in ever increasing numbers. The incident depicted above took place in the long woods which lie on either side of the beautiful Lyn. A hunted stag, after giving a good gallop over Exmoor, "soiled" in the Lyn. Refreshed by his bath, he climbed once more into the woods cantering back along the path by which he had come. Turning a corner, he suddenly came face to face with some of the field. The surprise was mutual. The horses snorted and plunged, and the crowd hastened to give his antlered lordship the right of road. A stag, indeed, could give a man or horse a terrible wound with his sharp brow antlers, and such accidents, according to local gossip, have actually taken place. Horses seem to have a natural antipathy to deer. A tired hunter, or even the quietest old crock, will shy and plunge at the sudden appearance of a stag. In the present case, after surveying the crowd for a few seconds, the deer turned sharply to the left, and crashed downwards through the woods to the river again, where some twenty minutes later he was killed. An excellent photograph of the recent meet at Chawleigh is reproduced in *The County Gentleman*. The Master Mr Ian Heathcoat-Amory, Mr L. Amory, and the Kennel Huntsman Ernest Hellard show up conspicuously. In *Lloyds Weekly Newspaper* there appears a photograph of a little girl on a pony of whom is written: "One of the most enthusiastic followers of Sir John Amory's Staghounds is little Miss Joy St Hill who has frequently joined her father in pleasant runs. She rides in unconventional style, barelegged, astride, and without the aid of stirrups."

Oct 19th 1907

Opposite: A photo gallery of a meet at Chawleigh in 1907.

In the *Illustrated Sporting and Dramatic News* of last week appeared a series of interesting pictures of a recent meet of Sir John Amory's Staghounds at Chawleigh. There are nine

117

illustrations occupying the entire page. No 1- The Meet; 2- A bit of difficult Devon; 3- Mr. and Miss W. Hill; 4- An obdurate gate; 5- Halt; 6- Early arrivals on wheels; 7- The Huntsman brings up a straggler; 8-Mr Amory, the acting Master (an excellent picture); 9- Greeting the Master.

Nov 23rd 1907

The meet at Worlington on Wednesday was not a large one owing to its being Eggesford market, but those who were out are not likely to soon forget the sport which followed. Hounds were taken to Affeton Castle to kennel while tufters drew the young plantation. A hind and her calf were left at once, and tufters were stopped and the pack was let go within a few minutes. The deer led in the first place through the larch plantation, then down through Affeton Old Pantation nearly to the keeper's cottage. Thence she bore left handed till she came up over Winswood Moor and after a ring round came back not far from Bealy Court and back into Cotonhayes. Through Lutworthy she led, and on across Lutworthy Moor nearly to the Chulmleigh road, where she turned back on much the same line through Cotonhayes, round Affeton Moor, and back into Cotonhayes pursued by a few couple of hounds. When the body of the pack had joined them they pushed her through Lutworthy, across the moors, and on past Gidley Arms, then right on by Ashmoor and Creacombe through Baxton and Haydon Moor to the Rackenford Coverts. Crossing Rackenford Moor to Bickham she followed the Iron Mill Stream down to Chain Bridge, till she ran up over the top and came down to the river by Duvale, where she was viewed. Hounds were soon pushing her through Highwood, and she came down again and crossed the Exe at Holmingham, but instead of turning into Duvale Wood she followed the railway nearly into Bampton. Thence the line lay back nearly to Wonham, when she turned left handed and came up past Coombehead and nearly down to the river at Exebridge. Turning up over the top she ran parallel to the railway nearly to Morebath Junction, then turning back into the Batherm not far from Bampton she ran up past the blacksmith's shop at Morebath and on to Shillingford, where she was fresh found. Still running upwards she crossed the railway not far from Petton Cross, and hounds came up to her in a little covert, but she broke away again and came back over the railway, but it was her final effort, and she was soon taken close to Petton Cross at about 3.30, after four and a half hours without an apparent check. Only a few were in at the finish of this remarkable hunt, including Lord Ebrington, Mr L. Amory, Mr R. S. Pethick, Mr Yandle (Duvale), Mr W. Haydon, and Ernest. It was a nineteen mile point as the crow flies, but hounds ran much more than this distance.

Dec 7th 1907

Among a large field who rode to these hounds from the meet at Rackenford on Saturday were the Master Mr Ian Heathcoat-Amory. Mr L. Amory, Lord Ebrington, Miss Chichester, Capt. Churchill (from West Africa), Messrs A. and M. de Las Casas, Dr Brown (Witheridge), Mr F. J. Coleridge, Boles, Messrs Haydon (2), Mr Snow (Knowstone), Messrs S. Webber, A. Pring, J. Butt, J. Zelly and G. Zelly. Creacombe was first drawn and we had a sharp split around Baples Hill and back to Knowstone. From here hounds ran back to Rackenford Moor and Warbrightsley and right down to Spurway Mill. The deer was fresh found under Down Wood and passed by Chain Bridge and Halfpenny Bridge to Dryhill, and she was ultimately killed at Combeland.

Above and below: *A meet at the Gidley Arms Inn near Meshaw 1907.*

Dec 28th 1907

After the meet at Chawleigh on Saturday tufting operations began in Chawleigh Barton Wood, but the deer had shifted, and it was not before we reached Bycott that we found. Rousing a single hind with the tufters she beat to and fro for more than half an hour, and then crossed into the Waterloo Coverts, where the pack were let go on her foil about 1 o'clock. It was soon seen that scent was very good, and hounds pressed her hard through the Wixon Coverts and up through Sheepsbyre and on to Stone Moor, leaving the Coverts to the right. Thence the line lay across Winswood Moor into Affeton Old Plantation and down to the valley of the Dart. Running down through Burridge Wood and on into Leigh Wood we soon got to Stone Mill, where a cyclist unfortunately headed her, and she ran back over much the same line to the keeper's cottage at Worlington. Turning up through the Young Plantation she ran through Cotonhayes and on across Lutworthy Moors and on nearly to the Gidley Arms. Then, just touching the Gidley Arms end of the Wick Coverts she bore away nearly to Meshaw, where she turned left handed, and we were soon running not far from Alswear, and on across a lot of moors till we came to Romansleigh, running as if for Kingsnympton. Still keeping left handed, however, she came back through the Bycott Coverts, where she was originally found. Skirting the bottom of Horridge Moor she ran up through the Stone Moor Coverts, and keeping on towards the Dart she came down to Stone Wood and down to the Dart under Chawleigh Barton Wood. A halloa from Mr L. Amory brought hounds down to the rifle butts at Sydeham, and after a few minutes up and down the water another good hind was added to the list under Park Mills, Chulmleigh. The run lasted three hours and three quarters with practically no check.

Feb 8th 1908

A big field joined in the chase on Saturday following the meet at Knowstone. Shooting in the district had caused the deer to move, and it was not till the Stuckeridge Coverts were reached that a couple of deer were found. Hounds raced one of these across the Iron Mill Stream, up through Champles and Wormsworthy, nearly to Spurway Mill, and then left handed to Ash Cross. Fresh finding their deer in a young plantation hounds ran back over much the same line to Chain Bridge, then out over Highwood and through Steart and the Emmelford Coverts to the river and across the railway. Thence the line lay through Mr Unwin's Coverts and right away left handed nearly to the Knightshayes Coverts, passing close to Palfreys and on across the road to Allens Down. A left handed turn brought us at length to the Huntsham Coverts, and as we passed Huntsham Court Mr H. L. Acland Troyte joined in the hunt. After hounds had run over Bampton Down and Hayne Moor the end came two miles further on under Clayhanger.

Feb 15th 1908

On Saturday a large field met hounds at Bullacourt, the home of the Misses Cobley, who provided all sorts of good things for everyone. Among those out were the Master Mr Ian Heathcoat-Amory, Mr L. Amory, Mr A. W. Luxton, Master of the Eggesford Foxhounds (on wheels owing to a kick from a horse), Messrs J. Tripe, and Parkhouse (Chulmleigh), Mr J. Zelley, Mr Brown (Rackenford), Mr Pope (Head Mills, Chittlehamholt), Mr J. W. Goddard (Tiverton), and a large party from Exeter. The meet having been at 10 o'clock tufters were drawn about a quarter to 11, and hounds soon found a hind under Winswood Moor, and were racing her over the moor when she was headed short back by some foot people shouting in her face, and turned up through the large plantations to within a field of Cotonhayes, where the pack was let go on her foil. Instead of rushing into Cotonhayes, where there were a lot of fresh deer, she crossed the road through Lutworthy and over Lutworthy Moor and the Chulmleigh road into the Wick Coverts. Running through these coverts her next point was Wixon, and on into Bycott Coverts, where there were two or more deer in front of hounds. Sticking to the hunted hind the body of the pack pushed her through Wixon to Stone Moor, and then down to the River Dart at Stone Mill, where hounds ran up to her, and gave her such a fright as may account for the extraordinarily fine hunt which followed over a line of country that has never been traversed by staghounds for a great many years. Pushing her through Leigh Wood she ran through Burridge Wood and across Burridge Moor, and then across the Chawleigh road and on nearly into Lapford. From here most of the deer run towards the River Taw, through Lapford Wood, and then down to the Eggesford Coverts. This deer, however, broke fresh ground entirely, and by turning left handed threw out most of the field. Hounds now raced past Forches Cross, and then over an enclosed country to Eastington, touching Middlecott, and then straight on to Stonecross. Thence the line lay to West Sandford, and then to Sandford, hounds passing close to the village, while most of the field went through. Skirting Creedy Park we soon entered Shobrooke Park, the residence of Sir John Shelley. Hounds raced her into the big pond, where the end came within sight and sound of about 100 park deer, who did not, however, betray any interest in the proceedings. I believe I am right in saying that this was the first deer ever killed in this park in anyone's memory. Sir John Shelley kindly invited those who remained of the field into his residence, and dispensed hospitality to them before they began their long ride home. The point from the most distant places touched would be about 14 miles, but hounds must have run double that distance, and the hunt owe a debt of gratitude to the sporting farmers and landowners, who provide such strong deer. The field was very select at the finish, numbering not more than five including Mr Ian Amory, Mr L. Amory, and Mr Tripe (Chulmleigh). Meanwhile the second of the two hinds that were before hounds in Bycott had been pursued by a few couples back through Ball and the Wick Woods to the Gidley Arms and straight for Ashmoor and Creacombe. From here they ran through Baxton to the Rackenford Coverts, and across the moor to Sir Edwin Dunning's Stoodleigh Coverts and down to Chain Bridge, where she was taken by Messrs Yandle late in the afternoon.

Feb 29th 1908

It was blowing hard when the meet took place at Eggesford on Saturday. Hounds found five deer in the small larch plantation on the other side of Fox's Covert, and ran them up the valley as far as Chenson. Here one of the five broke back, and the pack was let go as she was going into Fox's Covert. Hounds then ran down the valley by way of Nethercott and close to the Station at Eggesford. The deer then turned out over through Upcott and on out over the hill into Chawleigh Barton Wood, then through Stone Wood and on to Stone Moor, and right handed on to Winswood Moor and down into the Affeton Old Plantation. Here our deer began to run down to the Dart, which she reached not far from the keeper's house, and then down the river to Cheldon Bridge, where hounds ran up to her in the water. Breaking away she ran back through Burridge Wood, on to Leigh, and back to Stone Mill. Hounds fresh found her again in the water near the rifle ranges at Sydeham, and she ran over much the same line as she had done an hour previously up to Stone Moor, but bearing away left handed she came down to the Dart again, and was taken at Park Mill under Chulmleigh.

March 28th 1908

Owing to the death of the son of a respected member of the hunt, Fridays meet at Wiveliscombe was altered to the Carnarvon Arms. Fred Goss reported that there were only a few deer in the Exe Valley owing to the rattling they had had during the past few days, and Mr Amory decided to draw with the pack. Hounds were put in at Hele Ball and found three or four deer in Execleave, running them up the Exe Valley through Stockham, Broford, and Execleave, to Winsford Hill. On Southhill it was found that hounds had a young stag in front of them, and they were thereupon stopped. The pack was taken back and kennelled at Broford while the tufters drew the adjacent woods, and about one o'clock a herd was found in Winslade Wood. Tufters ran the deer round Milton Rocks, away nearly to the Kingsbrompton road, and back into Winslade Wood again. Here a single hind went up the valley past Chilly Bridge, and one of the whips who was on the opposite side brought on the pack. The chase began in Exe Park and continued up the valley towards Dulverton. Through Barlynch Wood they pushed their deer into Swinescleave, and she ran up through Haddon faster than a deer has been seen to go before.

April 11th 1908

On Saturday, the first day of the spring staghunting brought out the biggest field that had been seen since Christmas, and although there were heavy hail storms and the wind was high, hounds ran as they rarely do from the meet at Molland Moor Gate, Fred Goss had a bunch of young stags lying in Longstone Coombe, but just before the meet they were joined by a herd of hinds, so Mr Amory decided to go to Lords Plantation, where there were four young stags. Hardly waiting for the hounds they left at once, and the Master had the tufters stopped while he galloped back to Willingford Bridge for the pack. Let go on to the foil of the four, hounds first ran out over as if for Sherdon. On the common the deer began to back it, three of them to Lords Plantation while the other one turned up over the hill and around Withypool Common. Passing close to the village, he came down to the Barle at Bradley Ham, but he had no time to linger here as scent was too good and hounds were close behind. Coming up over the hill past Comer's Gate on to Winsford Hill, there he ran past Wambarrows on to Mounsey Hill Gate and then down over Southhill and thence through Red Cleeve to the valley of the Exe, past Broford and Chilly Bridge, through Stockham and Exe Cleeve till Barlynch was reached. Here he came down to the river, but hounds were close behind him and soon found him down to Hele Bridge where hounds bayed him. Breaking away, however, he kept for a time close to the river. Rising to the Minehead road, he entered Bury Castle and continued upward as if he was going into Haddon, but a turn or two was all he could manage, and hounds, running him down to the Haddeo below Bury, he was taken shortly after two o'clock.

Sept 5th 1908

Charley Slader had a deer harboured at North Molton on Saturday last in about half an acre of scrub that it was not necessary to kennel the pack. It was a good stag, with three on top on both sides. After a turn round a few fields the stag entered Whitechapel Wood, where the hounds raised a number of deer who went down the valley into Sindercombe, while hounds were in the covert one of the whips viewed the big stag going out over the top of Cuzzicombe Down. Through this a good part of the field were thrown out and did not see hounds for the rest of the day. Menwhile the body of the pack were busy with a stag of the same size who went down past Molland Station and followed the line down to Bottreaux Mill and thence to Yeo Mill and Anstey Station and it took the acting Master Capt. Amory all his time to catch them at Anstey Barrows. They were switched on to the other stag in Coome Wood, whence they ran into Allers Wood and down to the Barle. Rising to Pixton Park our stag decended to the Exe on the other side and hounds had to be finally whipped at Hele Bridge.

An extraordinary good run from Haddon on Tuesday resulted in a stag being killed at Cutcombe.

Charley Slader who harboured for Sir John Amory's Staghounds when in the South Molton District – he is seen here with his wife Ellen and the South Molton Staghounds who followed on from Captain Harry Amory.

Run from Westhill, Haddon – taken at Hagley Bridge below Waterow Sept 29th 1908.

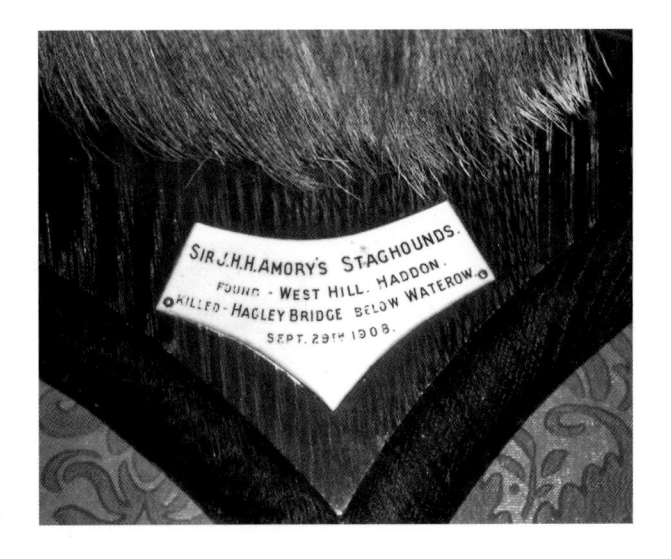

Sept 12th 1908

For the second time this season there was a bye meet of these hounds at South Molton Station on Saturday last. A stag was soon found in a small piece of ornamental furze on Clatworthy, and on being put on the move got into Whitechapel Covert, bearing away to South Aller, where the tufters were stopped and the pack laid on. Hounds hunted the deer towards Kingsland, through Stone, "Honiton", and Georgenympton Rectory, right down the valley below Meethe, where he soiled. Being fresh found he made off to Satterleigh Wood, turning to the left down the valley, and thence to the right through Snapdown, and from there to Warkleigh Barton. Turning again to the right at Shortridge he made for the River Taw, where he again soiled. After running two miles up the valley he was again fresh found, and bore

Meet at South Molton Station.

A sketch of Castle Hill, Filleigh – not far from where Sir John Amory's Staghounds took their stag.

Castlehill North Devon.

Viscount Ebrington M.P.

through the woods for about another two miles, finally taking to the Iron Bridge by the L.& S. W. Railway, where he was taken. Nearly 50 horsemen were present at the death of this fine stag.

Sept 26th 1908

The meet on Saturday was at South Molton, and hounds were taken on to Whitehills to draw. There was a rouse in the Castle Hill Coverts, and it was not long before the pack were laid on to a deer which ran through Bremridge Wood and on into the Brayford Coverts. Thence the line lay up through the old water nearly to Yarde Down as if he was going to the Forest; but he did not leave the big woods and came back on much the same line to Stoney Bridge and out over the hill past Filiton Barton. After making another turn as if he were going to the Forest, he ran up to Barcombe Heath, where hounds ran up to him again. Then he ran right into North Molton village, where hounds set him up in a garden, and through the village with the villagers in pursuit down to the Mole, where he was taken. He had all his rights and two long points on top.

Oct 3rd 1908

From the meet at Chawleigh on Saturday hounds were taken to Bycott and kennelled at Waterloo. The tufters found at once, and after a turn up and down the covert a stag went away to Wixon, where the pack was let go. Running down the valley he crossed to the Wick Coverts. From there he crossed the Chulmleigh road and ran on through Lutworthy as it for the Cheldon Valley, but turning to the left he made for the Gidley Arms by way of Mouseberry. Hounds then ran by way of Irishcombe to Ashmoor, past Creacombe and Ditchetts, through Baxton to Hazen Moor, and then up the water till the line turned away for Rackenford Moor, through Sydenham and the Warbrightsley Covert past Spurway and Aldridge Mills. Through Wormsworthy lay the line to Trew Bridge, and he was taken by the ponds under Stuckeridge.

Oct 17th 1908

On Saturday the twelfth stag of the season was taken after a rather short but very nice hunt. The meet was at tht Royal Oak at Gibbet Moor to go to Witheridge Moor, where deer have been doing a lot of damage. It was found, however, that they had shifted their quarters, and hounds were taken to the Knowstone Coverts to hunt a big stag that had lately been noticcable. Tufters were kept busy until 2 o'clock before they could get him away. After a turn or two round the top of the covert he came back over Baples Hill to Hazon Moor and took a right handed turn nearly into Cruwyshayes. Bearing to the left he came back over Rackenford Moor and down through Sydeham and along the Iron Mill Stream to Chain Bridge. Then he turned out over the top to Highwood Plain and ran nearly to the Rifle Butts at Cove, Ascending the hill he came down to the water again just below Halfpenny Bridge, and kept up the stream to Chain Bridge. After a ding dong chase for about a mile he was taken close to Holmingham. He had all his rights on one side with eight on top, and brow, tray, and five atop on the other.

Oct 24th 1908

Following the meet at Bury on the 13th inst, hounds were taken to Bittiscombe to draw. They soon found and ultimately took a stag with all his rights and three and two atop the morte being sounded near Barlynch Abbey.

The meet on Saturday last was at the Gidley Arms. Hounds were taken on to Bycott to draw and the pack were laid on to a big stag who went across into Waterloo and down through Wixon and out over Sheepsbyre. Here he bore left handed as if for the Wick Coverts, but on Winswood Moor he turned to the right and went down to the Dart under Worlington. Down the valley lay the line through Burridge Wood, Cobley, and on to Stone Bridge. From here he ran through Chawleigh Barton Wood to Chawleigh Week and down to the water by Rashleigh Mills, past Colleton Hall, and on to South Molton Road Station. Thence the line lay down to Head Mills just past Kingsnympton Park, where the stag ran the water and the hounds had a long check. Hounds were an hour behind him when they got news of his going down the Taw. They picked the line out right down the valley past Portsmouth Arms, but scent failed just by Umberleigh Station at about 5 o'clock.

Nov 21st 1908

Wednesday week was rather a poor day for the meet at the Carnarvon Arms Hotel. Hounds went on to Marsh Bridge and were kennelled at Northmoor, where tufters were drawn, and the pack taken on to Hineham. Finding at once under the Summerhouse hounds had several deer up at once, but it was nearly one o'clock before the pack was wanted, and they were laid on going down the valley under Hineham. Complications soon arose, and the pack divided, the greater number of hounds going under Whiterock to Anstey Common and Molland Moor. Meanwhile a few couple of hounds had got on a warrantable stag, and it was not before they got near the Carnarvon Arms that they were got up to and the stag was taken alive.

From the meet at the Gidley Arms on Saturday hounds put in another real good day. Hounds were taken on to Bullacourt the Harbourer having harboured deer at Bycott, and Ernest took the pack on to Mr Lake's at Waterloo to kennel. Finding immediately at Bycott in the Dod Yard the tufters roused several deer, and the pack was laid on to one in Waterloo, unfortunately the deer ran back heel and had got a good start before hounds got on the line. Running back through Ball Covert and through the Wick Coverts hounds crossed the Chulmleigh road to Lutworthy and through Cotonhayes to Affeton Old Plantation; then down to the keeper's house to the Dart and down the valley to Cheldon. Here the deer was headed by a party of shooters, and it was some time before hounds picked up the line again. Running through Burridge Wood they came out to the Chulmleigh road and ran parallel with the road to Three Hammers. Here information was brought that the deer was three quarters of an hour ahead. Hounds ran the line to Pedley Farm and over the road and through Yetheridge Farm to some water underneath. The deer ran in and out of the water for some three miles past Penford Mills, where hounds had killed a hind a fortnight ago from Dulverton. She was slotted by the officials of the hunt about a mile further on and was fresh found. Hounds raced her up nearly to Morchard Bishop, then back to Washford Pyne and past Washford Moor and nearly into Puddington. Turning down over the valley to Beira and on through Kennerleigh they fresh found her on the other side of Kennerleigh Wood and raced her back and killed her halfway between Kennerleigh and Sandford.

Dec 12th 1908

Stoodleigh Court was the venue on Saturday last, and Mr H. B. Money-Coutts entertained a large company. Operations began in East Stoodleigh, where there were several deer on foot. A hind and yealing calf ran down by way of Emmelford to the beginning of the Stoodleigh Valley and out over by Ford Farm to Rhyll, where the pack were let go. Bearing away right handed the hind came down to Coleford Water and thence to Aldridge Mills. There was a fresh find in Town Wood, and hounds raced the deer across the Iron Mill Stream into Champles and away above Hangmans Hill to the bathing ponds. Here she turned up through the wood, crossing the drive and up nearly to the little Covert at Ash Cross; then down through Diptford Bottom and over the big fields into Blatchworthy. Thence the line lay across the Gibbet and Rackenford road to Tidderson Moor, on through the Hilltown Coverts and across Witheridge Moor to Looseland. The pace had been very fast up to now, and just short of the Tiverton and Witheridge road, Mr L. Amory, who was hunting hounds, stopped them in the hope that the field, who had unfortunately been thrown out, would turn up. After a wait of half an hour hounds were let go again, and crossed the road into Merryfieldhayes, whence they ran on over an unusual line of country nearly to Puddington, and then down the valley towards Poughill. With a left handed turn they came back into the vicinity of Cheriton Fizpaine, and ultimately ran nearly to the top of Morchard Hill. Another left hand turn brought them back down the valley past Combe and to the Dart at Little Silver. There was a fresh find in a field a little bit lower down, and hounds raced their deer as if for Seven Crosses, but bearing away to the right she entered the Dart close to Bickleigh Bridge. A quarter of a mile further up the Dart she was taken. Hounds were laid on at a quarter to 12 and killed their deer at a quarter past 4 o'clock.

Jan 23rd 1909

Saturday's field was an unusually small one, only eight meeting the Master at Worlington, and there were never more out during the day that could be counted on both hands. Tufting operations began on Lutworthy Moor and four deer were soon disturbed. At first scent seemed bad, and after crossing the Chulmleigh road into the Wick Coverts hounds could make little of it. Eventually hounds pushed one deer away to the left of the Gidley Arms as if for Rose Ash. Here tufters were stopped, and Mr Amory went back to Bullacourt for the pack. From the lay on hounds crossed the Knowstone road into Irishcombe and down the usual line by way of Creacombe and Ditchetts to Hazen Moor and over Rackenford Moor to Chain Bridge. From here they ran up over Highwood and came down to the water at Halfpenny Bridge, and crossing the Exe into Westbrook they turned out nearly into Bampton. Turning left handed they ran to Combe Head and away nearly to Wonham, then up the valley nearly to Exe Bridge, where they turned up, coming down to water again at Highleigh. Here they bore away left handed to Eastops and away to Sowerhill and then on to Blackerton. Running down nearly to Anstey Station they went on nearly to West Barton, on past Rowerton to Capscott, through the covert of that name to within a few hundred yards of Molland Station, where this good deer was killed at about a quarter to 4 o'clock. From the point where the deer was found hounds ran in the shape of the letter V – to Bampton the line was 14 miles, and from Bampton to Molland Station 11 miles, but hounds ran a much greater distance.

Feb 13th 1909

The meet on Saturday was at Worlington. Miller had harboured a hind and yearling in a patch of gorse in the middle of Affeton Moor, and tufters were soon running them over Lutworthy Moor to the plantation, and away to the Chulmleigh road. After a bit they came back through Cotonhayes, and the pack were laid on at Affeton. Running down to the Old Plantation they went over Winswood Moor and across Mounticombe Moor, skirting the Stone Moor Coverts and down the Dart by Sydeham. Then they ran through Chawleigh Barton Wood, and as if for Eggesford, but turning left handed they came through Upcott and Chawleigh Week. Next they turned right handed back to Chulmleigh Bridge, where the yearling was left. Pursuing the hind alone, hounds soon came by South Molton Road Station and on to Head Mills, then right handed to Kingsnympton, where she was fresh found. It now appeared as if she was going back to the Bycott Coverts, but just short of there she turned left handed and came down to to the river at Alswear. A left handed turn nearly brought us to Romansleigh, but bearing away to the right once more she came down the water under Georgenympton, and the morte was soon sounded. Among those in at the end were Mr Robert Harris, who has attained the age of 79. Mr. Harris formerly farmed Burridge, Seven Crosses, Tiverton. He now lives between Sandford and Cheriton Fitzpaine. To get to the meet he had to ride seven miles. He kept near hounds all day, and after the kill he had to cover another 20 miles to get home. In reply to a query he said he felt as fit to day as he did 40 years ago.

April 3rd 1909

These hounds met at Worlington on Saturday, March 27th, and there followed one of the best, and certainly one of the longest and severest runs which have taken place this season. Two hinds were found at Affeton Young Plantation. The pack was immediately laid on to one, and ran by Cotonhayes to Winswood Moor, Stone Moor, the Wixon Valley, Ball, Week, and so back to Cottonhayes. Although never apparently off the line, it seems probable that hounds must have here changed deer, as it does not seem possible that the hunted deer could have covered the extent of country over which hounds afterwards ran. At any rate, from this point hounds ran round Affeton Moor, and down to Bealey Court, then back to Lutworthy Moor, and by Week and Waterloo Covers to Bycott. Here they turned, and ran the length of the Romansleigh Valley to Alswear. Then right handed till the Gidley Arms were reached, and across the road to Bradford Ponds. Here there was a long check, followed by slow hunting, until our hind was fresh found half a mile below Baxton. From this point hounds raced back to Creacombe, then left handed to Rackenford Moor, and down to Bickham, where this tough hind was at last caught. Out of the field of 20 or 25 riders who started the day, only three riders managed to reach the end, several well known members of the hunt having seen during the evening leading their weary horses homewards. From the time hounds were laid on until the end was reached below Bickham, was five and three quarter hours, and during this time there was only one check of about twenty minutes. At the meet, in addition to Captain Amory, and Mr L. H. Amory were the Hon. J. Wallop, Messrs Tripe, Smith, Zelley, Webber, J. Yandle, Pring, S. Webber, etc.

April 10th 1909

The meet on Saturday was at Dulverton, and there was a large field out. Goss had nothing harboured nearer than Lords Plantation, and on hounds being taken there three young stags were soon on foot. They ran back over Cloggs to Molland Moor, and after a turn round the moor passed over Anstey Common to Slade Bridge, down the Danes Brook, through Church Wood, and over Hawkridge to Three Waters, where the chase came to a end.

Sept 18th 1909

Favoured by brilliant weather, the meet of Sir John Amory's Staghounds was at South Molton Station on Saturday, when the Master was met by 100 horsemen and a large number on foot. A start was made for Oldridge Wood where a deer was quickly roused, and hounds put on, there was a fine gallop to Brayford and back by Lee and Hacche where for a time the hounds were at fault. It was not long before they were running to Bicknor and Radley, and thence down stream to Alswear, where the stag was killed in the water shortly before six o'clock.

Oct 9th 1909

After a run of bad luck in the Eggesford country these hounds brought off a good hunt on Saturday. There was a fairly big field to meet the Master Mr Ian Amory at Worlington, and hounds were kennelled at Affeton Barton while the tufters were taken on to draw Cottonhayes. The deer had shifted, but in Wick Plantation hounds soon found the stag which the deputy Master (Capt. H. Amory) lost at Bycott about a fortnight before. Hounds ran him at great pace through the Wick Coverts into Ball Plantation, and from there through the Wixon and Waterloo Coverts on into Bycott. Here there were complcations for a short time, but hounds fresh found their stag and drove him down to the bottom through the Dodyard and on over Horridge Moor. The tufters were stopped at the bottom of Huntacott, while the Master went back for the pack which was

Meet at South Molton Station.

A run from Holdridge, North Molton – to Alswear Sept 14th 1909.

waiting at the top of Stone Moor. On the pack being laid on, they ran through Stone Wood and across the River Dart, and through Chawleigh Barton Wood, where they fresh found their stag and sent him across the Chulmleigh road into Chawleigh Wick. Then the line lay up the valley through Upcott and Southacott to Chenson, where the stag turned short back and came down to the road not far from Eggesford Station. Then, turning up over the parks as if he intended going back to the River Dart he ran through Upcott, making a sharp turn to the right, and coming back close to the farm at Southacott and down by the laundry. After running up the water he was taken in the river about a mile from Eggesford Station, where the morte was sounded. He had all his rights and two long points on each side. Among those who took part in the run were the Master Mr Ian Amory, Capt. Amory, Mr L. Amory, the Hon. Mrs Butler, Dr Brown, Messrs Harrison (2), Tripe, W. Haydon, J. Selly, Vickery, and Lee (Sandford). The hope was expressed that Mr Amory would hunt in the Eggesford Country as often as he could.

Oct 16th 1909

Sir John Amory's Staghounds met at Knowstone on Wednesday, and the Harbourer reported a warrantable stag in Knowstone Wood. Mr Amory, with the tufters, soon corroborated, and the stag breaking on to Knowstone Moor he was able to enlarge the pack on the heels of the quarry. Thus bustled the stag ran down through the Bickham Coverts and Waspleigh to the wooded valley of the Exe. At Halfpenny Bridge he left the water and trotted up into the woods above, when he probably lay down to rest. Capt. Amory arriving soon after with a few of the hounds was surprised to find his brother with the rest of the pack running another stag. The second stag, a small one, after leading the chase to Morebath, returned to Halfpenny Bridge, and then made an excursion to Bampton. Eventually both stags running practically the same line were hunted down the Exe to Tiverton, where the larger stag was taken alive, and the smaller was killed in the river under the shadow of St Peter's church. The big stag had a magnificent head with brow, bay, and tray, and two and three atop, the points being most symmetrical. Large crowds on Exe Bridge and Exeleigh Ham watched the kill for it was right in the heart of the town and close to the lace factory. A few seasons ago two stags were killed near this spot on consecutive Fridays.

Nov 20th 1909

Sir John Amorys Staghound's met at the Gidley Arms on Saturday. Miller reported that he had harboured two deer in Affeton Plantation, so Mr Amory decided to dispense with the usual tufting operations and to draw for them at once with the whole pack. No sooner were the hounds thrown into cover than it became evident that Miller's work had been well done, for the two deer were quickly found, and hounds settling to work made this cover too hot to hold them. One deer came away at the top of the cover with half the hounds after him, but they were stopped and sent back into cover to help the other half of the pack who were busily running the other one. The reunited pack drove him twice round the cover and then out at the lower end of Affeton Moor and into Cottonhayes Plantation, where he was clever enough to make a double and put the pack on to the line of the other stag off which they had previously been stopped. However, Mr Amory soon detected the manoeuvre, stopped the hounds, and laid them again on to the right deer. This time there was nothing for him to do but make for the open, which he did with the whole pack hard at his heels. The chase then swept round in a big circle by Lutworthy Moors and left handed by Bealey Court and Winswood Moor into the Cheldon Valley, down the valley at best pace into Burridge Wood, where our deer relied not without justification upon finding others to take his place. Hounds ran into a herd of hinds, and it was some time before matters could be straightened again; however the pack was collected and laid on to the line of the deer, who went away by Winswood Moor and Mounticombe and back to Stone Mill across the Cheldon Valley and out to the road running between Witheridge and Chawleigh. Here she turned again with hounds close to her and made for Worlington, but hounds were driving her very hard and she turned down the valley again and about 3.30 after some interesting hunting in these great woods was killed under Cheldon. Scent was never at any time by any means good, but hounds stuck to their work well.

Nov 27th 1909

The meet on Saturday was at Knowstone and there was a large field. Mr Amory took the tufters to draw the Knowstone Woods, and the stag which was taken alive in the Leat at Tiverton recently was soon on the move. Meanwhile a good hind came out of the coverts and crossed Baples Hill, where the pack was laid on. There was a fresh find in Backstone and hounds raced their deer to Hazon Moor and through the Rackenford coverts to Sydeham. Running down the valley of the Iron Mill Stream, she turned up over short of the Bathing Ponds into Highwood, then down to the river by Five Bridges, then out over the top to Steart and down to Cove Siding, where she turned short back again over Highwood and ran up the bottom again and then out over the Stuckeridge Coverts. Near here hounds put up a stag and bustled him about to such good purpose that after a turn or two up and down the coverts he came to the water under Duvale, and hounds bayed him there for a short time. Breaking away before they could be stopped, they raced him down to Cove, where Mr Amory got up to them and whipped them off. Mr Amory took the hounds back and drew Champles and Wormsworthy, but hounds did not do any more. Scent was very catchy after the first hour.

Dec 11th 1909

It was a bleak and cold at Worlington when these hounds met there on Saturday last, but the weather improved as the day wore on. Miller had harboured a herd in Affeton Young Plantation, and tufters soon found. The pack was laid on at the bottom of Affeton Moor, and ran nearly to Worlington. The deer waited here, and were forced at a tremendous pace back to the coverts where they were found. Here the pack divided, and one section was stopped at Cheldon Bridge by one of the whips. The others ran by way of Cottonhayes, the Week Covers, and Bycott to Horridge Moor, and after running through Huntacott and across Stone Moor came down to the Dart under Chawleigh Barton. Hounds then hurried the deer up the Dart Valley through Burridge Wood to Worlington, and then back through the Young Plantation and Cottonhayes to Week School, where the deer was fresh found in the water. Running by much the same line as they came up hounds ran up to their deer just below Cheldon Bridge, and the second deer of the week paid the penalty about 200 yards from the spot where the other was killed on Wednesday.

March 2nd 1909

There was much excitement in the neighbourhood at Culmstock on Wednesday when Sir John Amory's Staghounds met at Culmstock Beacon for a days hunting. It had been known for some time past that a stag and several hinds have made their home near the monument, and they have been carefully harboured, with a view to hunt. It is estimated that upwards of one thousand persons attended the opening meet on the Blackdowns, 300 of whom were mounted on horses. As soon as the stag was separated from the hinds he led a merry chase passing Clayhidon, Blackmoor, Forches Corner, Cuhead, Church Stanton, Churchinford, Lupit, and Blackborough, and finally reaching home again via Broadhenbury, the distance covered being many miles. He proved to be a good runner for his pursuers, and survived to run another day. It is too much to hope for the inclusion of Wellington Monument or Culmstock Beacon in the regular list of meets of staghounds, but there is reason for supposing that the last has not been heard of staghunting on the Blackdowns.

January 8th 1910

On Saturday they met at the Royal Oak, Gibbet Moor. Mr Amory was again hunting the hounds, although he had to leave early in the afternoon to fulfil a political engagement. The pack was kennelled at Ash Cross, and Mr Amory drew Champles, they found near Mr Daniel's house at Stuckeridge, and ran out over Stuckeridge North down to Chain Bridge. The line then lay up the Iron Mill Stream, past Hangmans Hill, and the pack was laid on, going into Big Warbrightsley. The pack pushed the hind through Crowcombe and Sydeham, and came out on Rackenford Moor. They crossed this moor and came to Great Down, and thence to Hazon and Knowstone Moors on to Baples Hill. After running the whole length of Knowstone Wood there was a long check of about half an hour under Wolland. Eventually they fresh found her and drove her out over the top of Wolland. They then bore away to the left to Hayne Plantation and on to Bishopsnympton. They ran by the moors, through the river to Georgenympton, where they ran right through the village. At Alswear they turned right handed, and the line then lay through enclosed country, and one sportsman in crossing a ford had an involuntary bath. There was a slight check under Meeth Village where the hind soiled in the river, but she was fresh found and the end came soon after.

March 5th 1910

A three year old stag having been seen in one of General Holley's coverts near Brightley Bridge, Okehampton, several times of late Mr Amory arranged to take his staghounds to Okehampton on Wednesday last. Hounds left Tiverton by special train at 8 o'clock in the morning, and several members of the hunt took their horses down by the same train. No stag hunt having ever been arranged for the district the meet at Brightley Bridge attracted farmers and hunting men from many miles around. Strange contrasts were noticeable among the horses ridden by the farmers; some were present on cart horses, and not a few were mounted on hardy little Dartmoor ponies. Traps of all sorts and sizes were well laden with enthusiastic men and women, and there was a sprinkling of motor cars at the meet. Of foot people their name was legion. In all there were close upon one thousand people present. Plymouth, Yelverton, Exeter, Tavistock, and Dulverton contributed to the crowd. The stag was roused in Springetts under Goldburn and strode away for Broomford and thence to Inwardleigh, at a great pace. From Inwardleigh the line lay over Hatherleigh Moor to Petrockstowe and thence to Merton. At New Bridge, on Lord Clinton's estate, the stag took to the water, and after swimming about for some time he landed, and led at a reduced pace, the first two hours was very smart indeed towards Meeth, Beaford, and Moorland. Between four and five o'clock a select few – all that were left of the 200 horsemen at the meet – were making their way on tired horses in the direction of Town Mills, Torrington, when the Master decided to call hounds off. Hounds were taken back to Beaford, where Mr Amory telegraphed for a special train to meet the Tiverton contingent at South Molton Road Station. Tiverton was reached at about 9 o'clock. A gentleman who took part in the hunt from start to finish says; The country over which hounds ran was entirely new to most of us. It consisted of big woodland and moors, and we came across plenty of water. Spills were numerous. One rider had the misfortune to be immersed in the Torridge owing to the bank giving way under his horse's weight. There was further grief at a high bank with a deep pond on the far side. Several riders got well splashed here, and one horse in falling took its owner right under the water. Here and there wire was encountered, but happily it caused no accidents.

April 23rd 1910

On the last day of the season the meet was at Knowstone. Hounds found a herd in the Rackenford coverts, and the pack were laid on to some deer on Hazen Moor and ran to the Knowstone coverts where there were seven deer in front of hounds. After running through the coverts it was found they had a hind and male yearling in front of them. The male deer was eventually taken close to Bishopsnympton. The other went on over Wadham, on to Molland Station, down close to the line for a mile or two and over White

Above left: *The stag's head that was given to Sir Lewis Stucley Bart by Ian H. Amory from a run from Affeton Covert to King's Nympton Weir on September 24th 1910.*

Above right: *Close up of the plaque.*

Chapel Moors. There was a fresh find about here and hounds ran nearly into South Molton Town, then back around Bish Mill nearly to Alswear. There was another fresh find in the water, and hounds raced back to Bish Mill where the deer was set up and taken, making the 40th deer of the season.

Oct 22nd 1910

These hounds met at Gidley Arms on Saturday. Miller had harboured a stag quite close to the meet. The stag had, however, moved off a few minutes before the tufters were put into the small cover where he had been lying. The pack was laid on to his line at once and hunted steadily by Lutworthy Moors, Cottonhayes and Affeton Moor to the Cheldon Valley, where some hinds caused trouble. Eventually hounds were got together and laid on to our stag, ten minutes behind him, at Stone Bridge. From here they ran very fast by Chawleigh Barton, and leaving Stone Moor on the right hounds raced their stag into the lower end of Bycott, through this cover and across the top road as if for Alswear. He turned short back here and running by Waterloo and Ball reached Week Wood. They ran fast from here almost to Worlington, where it was found that a fresh stag was in front of them so the order was given for home. And so ended a good hunt and a very wet day.

Nov 19th 1910

Sir John Amory's Staghounds met on Saturday at Chawleigh. Miller's report to the Master at the meet was that the deer which had for some time been in the coverts between Chawleigh and Lapford had moved out of these coverts and gone towards Worlington. Orders were consequently given to trot on to Affeton Barton and to kennel the hounds there. Tufters were taken out and an attempt was made to find the hinds, but they had evidently been wandering on, and as it was now about 11.30 tufters were laid on to what was pronounced to be the slot of a youg stag. Some pretty hunting ensued, and in about twenty minutes tufters worked right up to their stag and found him lying in a furze brake in the moors below Affeton Young Plantation. The line now lay through Sir Lewis Stucley's coverts and into the Cheldon Valley where Mr Amory soon appeared with the pack and laid them on. It was at once apparent that there was a racing scent and that horses were to have all they could do to keep with the flying pack. Down the valley to Cheldon Bridge, up through Burridge, over the Chulmleigh road, right handed over the large moors and into the lower end of the Lapford Coverts hounds raced right handed again past Chenson and through the big Nethercott Coverts, at the further end of which Mr Amory viewed the stag and stopped the leading hounds to allow the body of the pack and the field to get together. Then on through Upcott, and down to the valley opposite Chulmleigh. Here occurred a slight check, and, owing to a quick forward cast by the huntsman, several of the field were left behind and had a long and hard ride to catch the pack again. From here hounds ran by Chawleigh Barton and Stone Moor to Wixon, where a very pretty bit of water hunting occurred, followed by a fresh find near Week School and a race up through the Waterloo Coverts, and down through the long Romansleigh Valley to the Mole at Alswear, and up the valley of that river to within a mile of South Molton town where at 3.15 it was killed. It proved to be a four year old deer after one of the best and hardest runs of the season. Anyone who owns a map or who knows the country can calculate the distance that hounds traversed in three and a half hours by taking only the three points – Worlington, Lapford, and South Molton. There was a large field composed with the exception of Doctor and Mrs Brown, entirely of farmers – all of whom got to the end of the great run and many of whom had a long ride home on horses that were not pulling much. Hounds had an 18 miles trot back to kennels. However, a good tea at Alswear started us all upon our various journeys in a happy and contented frame of mind, and with a steadfast determination to come out hunting again as soon as possible.

Nov 26th 1910

Sir John Amory's Staghounds had two more good days sport last week, and accounted for two large hinds.

On Wednesday the meet was at Knowstone Moor. Mr Elstone had some hinds in his covert as usual and tufters quickly singled out a good hind. The pack was laid on and rattled her back at best pace to Chain Bridge and out over the hill to Bampton, down to Halfpenny Bridge, back over the country to Wonham, across the river and up to Stuckeridge, on through the big coverts to Spurway Mill, and after a few more turns through Mr Money-Coutts Coverts, hounds brought her back to the water and was killed at 2.30 near Hangmans Hill.

On Saturday hounds met at Gidley Arms and kennelled at Bealy Court. Miller was soon able to put tufters on to the line of a herd of hinds, and they hunted very prettily up to them in the same furze brake in which the stag which gave such a splendid run the week before was found. Here a considerable herd of hinds and young stags appeared, and after some good work on the part of the tufters a fine hind was found and the pack was laid on. The line lay through Week School, into Bycott Coverts, and out over the moors beyond. This cunning hind tried every manoeuvre to throw hounds off her line and to put them on to that of some other deer, but they stuck to her with great determination, and finally she had to leave the shelter of these large coverts and make up her mind to seek safety further away. By Stone Moor and Winswood Moor, hounds ran to the Cheldon Valley, down the water to the Little Dart, and then down the larger valley, first on one side and then on the other, to the bridge by Chawleigh. Here the hounds hit the line out of the water and fresh found her in Leigh Wood. Up the valley again and away for the Lapford Coverts, hounds simply raced her, and horses had their work cut out to keep within sound of them. Down through these coverts to Nymett Bridge, then up again and away by Mr Vivian's house, as if they were going to Morchard Bishop, but a right handed turn brought us down again by Lapford Village, and down to the water where she was killed.

In 1911 Ian Amory gave up hunting Sir John Amory's Staghounds and accepted the Mastership of the Tiverton Foxhounds. There follows a letter which he wrote at the time that was printed in the *Tiverton Gazette*.

17th January 1911

Mr Lewis Mackenzie. Hon. Secretary of the Tiverton Foxhounds has received the following letter respecting the Mastership.

Hensleigh
Tiverton
Devon

Dear Mackenzie,
I think I ought now to send you a definite answer to the invitation of the members of the Tiverton Hunt to undertake the Mastership of the Foxhounds. I shall be quite glad to do this, but only because I in common with other members of the hunt know that nothing will induce Mr Unwin to reconsider the decision to which he has come. We shall miss him very much, and if I can show the country half the sport he has shown during the 19 years of his Mastership, I shall be well satisfied. I shall have to rely much upon the help of all who will give it, because my time on non hunting days will be taken up by other things which cannot be put aside. It is because I feel sure that this help will be given, and that I may rely upon the same kindly welcome and hearty co-operation which the farmers have invariably shown me for the last 30 years, first with the Harriers and then with the Staghounds, that I am now willing to accept the invitation which has been so cordially given, and follow my uncle as Master of the Tiverton Foxhounds.

Yours sincerely
Ian Amory

Jan 21st 1911

Two really good days fell to the lot of Sir John Amory's Staghounds again last week. On Wednesday the meet was at Knowstone. The tufters were drawn out there and the pack was sent to the cross roads near Mr Vesey's farm. The deer, which had been harboured early in the morning, had moved on before the tufters began to draw for them, and as scent was not at all good hounds failed to hunt up to them. Two hours and a half were occupied in drawing Knowstone Woods first with the tufters and then with the pack but no deer could be found. A move was then made to the gorse brakes on the Little Rackenford Moors, but it was not until North Hill – Mr Boles' celebrated fox covert – was drawn that deer were found. The first thing to come out was a fine fox – disturbed, no doubt, by the music of the pack. Almost immediately behind him came two deer with the whole pack in close attendance. Away past Mr Beedell's farm at Sydeham, down to Spurway Mill and on nearly to Chain Bridge, then upwards and out over the ridge towards Steart and down to the river by Halfpenny Bridge, over the river and out nearly to the outskirts of Bampton, left handed and down to the Exe by Stuckridge Bridge, across the river with hounds close to her, and away up the valley of the Iron Mill Stream, round Stuckeridge House and down by Hamslade House, back by Stuckeridge and then straight away in the teeth of a perfect gale of rain and wind by Aldridge Mill and the Bickham Moors to Swineham Hill, Knowstone Moor and Knowstone Woods to Ash Mill, where hounds fresh found her in the river and raced her back over nearly the same line of country to the Mill Stream under Town Wood. Here she was taken in the dark, and so ended a run of three and a half hours, remarkable alike for its late beginning, its extraordinary pace (too fast for most of the horses), the wetness of the rain that came down in torrents all the time, the darkness in which the hind was taken, and the scarcity of riders who were up at the finish.

On Saturday the meet was to have been at the Town Hall, Tiverton, but the hind had moved from the coverts in which she had been lying, and as it seemed quite unlikely that in the absence of any reliable news she could be found Mr Amory decided to change the meet to Templeton. A sharp frost overnight had made the ground hard and slippery, and it seemed very doubtful whether hunting could take place at all. However the meet was put off till 11, and at that time quite a large field turned up and many pedestrians and bicycles. A move was made to Witheridge Moor, and after waiting there until 12 o'clock to allow the sun to thaw some of the frozen ground, Hill Town Plantation, in which Miller had well harboured some deer, was drawn with the pack. It didn't take more than a few minutes to fine them, and a large hind singled herself out from the others and crossed Witheridge Moor in full view of the field with the whole pack close after her. She led hounds through Looseland Covert and over the moors to Merryfieldhayes – left handed by Pennymoor and Cruwys Morchard to Cruwys Morchard Mill – left handed again and back to Penny Moor and Merryfieldhayes plantation. Hounds were close to her and were making the pace uncomfortably hot for her, so she apparently made up her mind that home was no place for her, and set her face for strange lands where deer and stag hunters seldom go. Scent was good, and hounds were working splendidly. The valleys were deep and the hills were high – in some places the going was still rather dangerous owing to the frost and we were lucky when we were able to get to the top of one ridge in time to see which way hounds disappeared over the top of the next one. We soon found ourselves near Cheriton. Then a left hand turn brought us down a deep coombe under the handsome new rectory which Mr French has built for himself and his successors upon such a delightful site near Cadeleigh – then on through the park and almost across the lawn of Fursedon to Thorverton. A sharp right handed turn and a little water work up stream – a crash of music and a dripping brown body proclaimed a fresh find. Then came a race across the rich vale lands to the Exe at Stoke Cannon, a swim down stream, another fresh find and a nervous moment when deer and hounds crossed the main Great Western Railway line below Stoke Cannon Station. The field had a deep and swift ford to cross and a ride round to the level crossing at Stoke Cannon. But the hind had struck the river again half a mile lower down, and it was evident that she would never leave it. The water was high and the stream so strong that hounds could hardly face it, but at length their perseverance was rewarded, and the hind was brought to land near Lord Iddesleigh's park at Pynes after a really fine run of three and a half hours over a very stiff line of country. A noteworthy performance was Mr Hatts, for he rode his bicycle 10 miles to the place where the deer was found, rode it from there to pynes, which cant be less than 24 miles by Cheriton, Fursdon, and Thorverton, and rode it 12 miles home, a total of 46 miles, half of it being at top speed over extremely hilly bye roads.

Jan 28th 1911

Mr Amory was accorded a hearty welcome when he brought Sir John Amory's Staghounds to Tiverton on Saturday morning in the hope of providing a good hunt after a hind that was left below the town after a stern chase on December 24th. The meet was was one of the largest ever held in connection with this pack. Among the equestrians present were the following;- Mr Ludovic Amory, Mr Charles Carew, and Miss Carew, Mr W. Renton, Mr Corbett, Mr J. Chichester, Miss Chichester, Mr Harrison and Miss Harrison, Mr Campbell and the Misses Campbell, Mr and Mrs Pugsley, Mr F. Dunsford, Mr Symes (Crediton), Mr R. S. Pethick, Mrs Kelly, Dr Perry, Messrs Bostock, T. A. Chave, C. H. Spear, A. W. Rabjohns, S. Marks, A. Pring, S. Webber (Hilltop), Courtenay Haydon, S. Webber (Palmerston Hotel), J. Butt, S. Thorn, J. Goodland E. Hellard (Balsham, Cambridgeshire), Punchard (2), Sampson, A. Pring, Noon, Retallick, Holcombe, W. Glendenning, J. Farrant, W. Haydon, M. Haydon, W. Farley, G. Selly, White (Highwood), Norman (Stoodleigh), Mogford (Rackenford), Mogford (Worthy Bridge), J. Gollop, P. Pring, Yandle (3), W. Yells, Heard Jun. (Collipriest Farm), and Farmer (Cove). Mrs Ian Amory, Mr Miers, and Mr and Mrs J. W. Goddard were present in their motors, and there was a large concourse of foot people. Mr Amory took his hounds down St Andrew Street, making for the Collipriest Woods at 10.15. The deer was not to be found here, nor was she in Holwell Combe. A large party of foot people had in the meanwhile assembled at the top of Exeter Hill in the hope of seeing the deer make away towards Cullompton, as was the case when a deer was last roused in Holwell Combe. The next move was to Bingwell, whither many of the foot people followed. Not finding the deer in Bingwell Mr Amory next drew the coverts away to Thorns Copse, coming back later to Pitt Covert, and going on towards Backswood. Here a fox rose in front of hounds, but they were soon whipped off. Later in a part of Thorns Copse which had not been tried in the morning another fox was roused and some difficulty was experienced in stopping the pack. The horsemen got back to Tiverton about 4 o'clock. At least one lad, who spent an enjoyable day on foot, did not get back home till after dark. The country over which the field went was in places very boggy and there were several spills. Mr Carew's horse turned a complete somersault near Thorns Copse, happily without injuring the rider. While Miss Chichester was jumping over a bank she knocked her head against a tree and fell back over her horse. Happily the horse stood still. Mr Dunsford was nearby, and rendered the necessary assistance. We are pleased to say that Miss Chichester was little the worse for her adventure.

March 4th 1911

Sir John Amory's Staghounds met in Fore Street, Okehampton on Wednesday. Hundreds of people on horseback, in carriages and on foot turned out. Just after 10.30 Mr Amory and Ludovic Amory his brother, came on the scene with the pack which looked in fine condition. They had come from Tiverton by special train, quite a hundred ladies and gentlemen on horseback were present, including General Holley, Messrs J. D. Prickman, Luxton, Tattershall, Norhley, and Matthews, Mrs May, Dr Burd, Major Newcombe, Colonel Edwards, Messrs E. Murrin, S. Horn, J. G. Heywood, R. Parker, P. Edgcumbe, Tapson, Palmer, Weekes, Harris, Northcott and others. The Mayor and Mayoress of Okehampton and many of the leading tradesmen were also present. A move was made through the beautiful grounds of Oaklands to General Holley's woods (The Sprygnets) where the stag had been seen on several occasions lately by the keeper and others. Four hounds were put into the copse. They were soon made it known that the stag was at home and presently it was seen trotting along between the trees and bushes. Hounds were then brought out, they rattled through the copse going towards Follygate. Eventually the stag made for Bowerland, going onto Ashbury Station and to Halwill, crossing back to Northlew and Highampton on its way to Hatherleigh. Just below Hatherleigh it took to the water in the River Lew, going some way down with hounds on its track. About a mile or so down the river going towards the Torridge, the stag came to bay. It was roped and taken by a cart through Maket Street Hatherleigh to the George Hotel, and stabled for the night. The stag was subsequently released to provide sport on another occasion.

Sketch by Terry Gable

March 20th 1911

Notwithstanding the unfavourable weather a good many ladies attended the meet at Tidcombe cross roads on Saturday, when there was a big field of horsemen and a good number on foot. Miller had harboured a hind at Crosslands, near Brithem Bottom, and Mr Amory kennelled the pack at Mr Carew's at Warnicombe. No sooner had the tufters been thrown into the wood than the hind made its way towards Warnicombe, but she soon turned back to where we had found her. Tufters were stopped, and Mr Amory fetched the pack. Hounds raced her away through Warnicombe, Gogwell, Pitt Farm, and towards Backswood. Turning sharply to the right, the deer now made her way back through Pitt to Rhode Farm, where there was a slight check of a few minutes. Hounds fresh found at East Butterleigh, and raced the hind on to Shutelake and right down the valley and on to Criss Cross. Turning right handed, she was soon at Dorweek and Leigh Pool, where she ran down the Exe Valley, passing close to the Ruffwell and down to Rewe, where there was a check for nearly half an hour. Mr Amory put hounds on the line again at Hazel Barton, and the hind crossed the railway and the Culm. Hounds came up to her in Killerton Wood and she ran straight for the Culm, where she was at once taken after a most enjoyable run. Master Anthony Pugsley was "Blooded" and given one of the slots; another slot was presented to Little Miss Pethick of Plymouth, who rode a pony of 12 hands high.

March 23rd 1911

Through the generosity of Mr Ian H. Amory a large number of farmers, sportsmen, and lovers of hunting were invited to dinner at Chawleigh (The Portsmouth Hotel). About 80 people accepted the invitation. Mr Amory presided, Mr Ludovic Amory occupying the vice chair. They were assisted in the carving by Messrs E. Ford, E. Webber, and J.Tripe. Mr Ludovic Amory in proposing success to Agriculture emphasised its vast importance, remarking that much depended on its success. Owing to better prices for produce and the adoption of new methods times were certainly improving. Then Mr Thomas Baker in response, said he thought that parliament did not do much to assist agriculture. Taxes, for one purpose and another, were increasing. He considered that too much money was squandered on officals travelling the country. He trusted that in future MPs from agricultural constituencies would be influenced by the farmers union. Then Mr H. Smythe (Worlington) thought judging from the rosy faces around the table, that very little depression exsisted among farmers. They must adapt themselves to the times, and introduce up to date methods. The hunting toast was proposed by Mr John Tripe who is a great lover of sport. He contended that real sport whether it be hunting the deer, fox, hare, otter, or shooting was of great benefit to agriculturists. Vast sums of money were annually spent in the purchase of foodstuffs alone. While it gave employment and enjoyment to thousands. All present would regret to hear that Ian Amory was about to retire from hunting the staghounds owing to his having taken over the Mastership of the Tiverton Foxhounds. At the same time they were delighted to know that his brother Mr Harry Amory would succeed him. As long as any of the family came that way with their hounds they would receive a hearty welcome (cheers). Ian Amory's health was drunk with musical honours. Mr Amory in response said he had hunted with his father's harriers (15 years), and with the staghounds (16 years), never outside Devon had he experienced such hospitality and kindness as had been accorded him. No one had ever objected to his trying a covert or crossing a field. Just 500 deer had been captured in the distict since he brought down the hounds. His brother was well known to them, and he felt sure they would extend to him that kindly feeling which he had always enjoyed.

"My brother the Captain has made up his mind to give up a very good job in the Midlands in order to come home and take on the staghounds, he will keep them in the kennels at Bolam." Mr Amory mentioned the able assistance rendered by Mr F. Miller the Harbourer, who during the proceedings was the recipient, from his Master of a cheque in recognition of his services, songs were rendered by Messrs A. Cobley, E. Reed, and G. Drew, and a most enjoyable time was spent, the National Anthem brought a very pleasant gathering to a close.

April 15th 1911

At the invitation of Mr Ian Amory, nearly a hundred followers of Sir John Amory's Staghounds partook of dinner at the Rackenford School room on Friday. Mr Ian Amory (MSH) presided, and the vice chair was occupied by Mr Ludovic Amory (whip). Mrs Amory and Mr Jack Amory were also present. Mr Ian Amory said he had invited his friends, the farmers and tenant farmers, to dinner in order to say thank you before he gave up the staghounds at the end of the month. There were many present over whose farms he hunted 31 years ago. With the exception of Mr Bisset's Mastership of the Devon and Somerset Staghounds he believed he had been the longest of which there was any record (applause). For the past three years his wife had been unable to hunt with the hounds owing to an accident she receieved in the hunting field. His brother the Captain Harry Amory was relinquishing an excellent position in the Midlands under the Duke of Portland in order to come home and take on the Mastership of the Staghounds.

April 25th 1911

Last Day for Ian Amory

On Friday the meet was at Worlington, the field was probably the largest that ever assembled there, people had come from places as far apart as Exeter, Crediton, South Molton and Dulverton, as well as the usual contingent of staghunters from Tiverton. The local farmers had also turned out in large numbers, realising, no doubt, that this was the last day of Mr Amory's Mastership, and being determined to take a share in the final hunt. Miller had a deer harboured in Bycott, hounds were kennelled at Bealy Court, after the tufters had drawn Week and Ball Coverts to make sure that there were no deer there the young stag was soon found, in Bycott, and after one turn round the coverts towards Chulmleigh he made up his mind that Rackenford and Knowstone Coverts were to be his point. Tufters ran him very fast over the moors and were well stopped by Mr Tripe and one or two other good staghunters near Lutworthy Coverts. Mr Ludovic Amory had meanwhile gone for the pack laying them on the moor near the Gidley Arms. We soon found ourselves struggling over the intricate country by Creacombe, and near Ditchett Covert hounds came to their first check. They were soon put right, and sailed away over the big moors until they were again brought to a check on some newly sown fields near Beaples Hill. A wide cast round these fields put things right again, and hounds worked the line cleverly over a good deal of freshly burnt moorland into the top of Knowstone Wood, through these large coverts, and away at the lower end. Hounds had evidently got on very good terms with their deer here, and it was all horses could do to live with them for the next hour. Away Northwards over the big moors, with plenty of boggy places in them, as two or three enterprising riders soon discovered, by Kipscott to Molland Station. Then right handed and away by Anstey, Hawkwell and Upcott to Highleigh and down to the meadows under Riphay, across the River Exe, and away up through the Wonham Coverts, past Combe, almost into Bampton, down to the Exe by Halfpenny Bridge, and up the water to Chain Bridge, where hounds caught a view and ran very fast up the valley to Hangmans Hill. Then turning left handed, they ran close past Stoodleigh Village, down the long valley under Withy Cleave, and into the Exe under Hatherland. One cast down stream and hounds fresh found the deer and was killed above Worth House at 5 o'clock. So ends the season 1910-1911, the best season on record. So ends Mr Amory's 16 years of Mastership a day memorable on two accounts. First for the extraordinary amount of country traversed by what now turns out to be two separate deer. First a young stag, who came at any rate as far as Knowstone, and who there or thereabouts must have shifted his responsibilities onto the back of a very large hind, hounds therefore practically ran up two deer and in doing so hunted steadily and at times very fast over country which measured straight over the map from Bycott to Worth, taking Creacombe, Molland Station, Bampton and Stoodleigh as intermediate points. The days hunting was noteworthy also for the points of interest to which the deer led hounds. The covert in which the deer was found is 14 miles from Highleigh, a property which Captain Amory the new Master has bought. Until this purchase was made and the property had thereby assumed close connection with staghunting it was apparently of no special interest to deer, for no record exists of deer and hounds having crossed it. But within a week of the Captain's purchase, deer, hounds and fields swept over the very site of his new house. Then the last of Mr Amory's deer felt bound to visit the farm of the first of Mr Amory's staghunting friends (Tom Yandle of Riphay) the man from whom Mr Amory has been proud to learn the wiles and the art of this noble and difficult sport, the trusted friend and adviser of two generations of staghunters. It seems fitting also that the end of the day, of the season, and of the Mastership should have come within sound of Worth, the home of the Messrs de Las Casas, all four of whom have at different times acted as whips to Mr Amory in the days before the work was undertaken by Mr Ludovic Amory, who has so often and so successfully during recent years hunted the hounds during Mr Amory's absence upon other business. Since Ian Amory has been hunting the staghounds, those whose good fortune it has been to follow Mr Amory over the country declare him to be a born huntsman. More than once he has been offered the Mastership of the Devon and Somerset Staghounds. Thanks to the fine sporting spirit of the Amory family the chase is within the reach of all classes. Mr Ludovic Amory who in the past few seasons has acted as chief whip to Ian Amory will act in the same capacity for the Tiverton Foxhounds. It is not at all likely that anywhere in this country or any other there are three brothers so closely associated in any form as are Messrs Ludovic, Harry and Ian. When hunting the staghounds next season Harry Amory will carry on to run them as a private pack upon the same lines hitherto. Apart from being huntsman next season Sir John has also handed over the Mastership to him as well, making it a staggering 52 years as being Master firstly of his harriers which he formed in 1859 and still retains, but now given up the Mastership of his staghounds which he formed in 1896. Sir John Amory has put Tiverton into an enviable position in the hunting world, and it is sometimes spoken of throughout the West Country as the "Melton of the West". Long may it sustain its reputation. For the past 16 seasons Sir John's Harriers have been hunted by his son-in-law Charles Carew.

Mark Amory's Collection - Photographs by Barbara Fyer

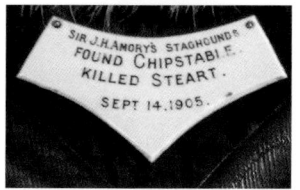

143

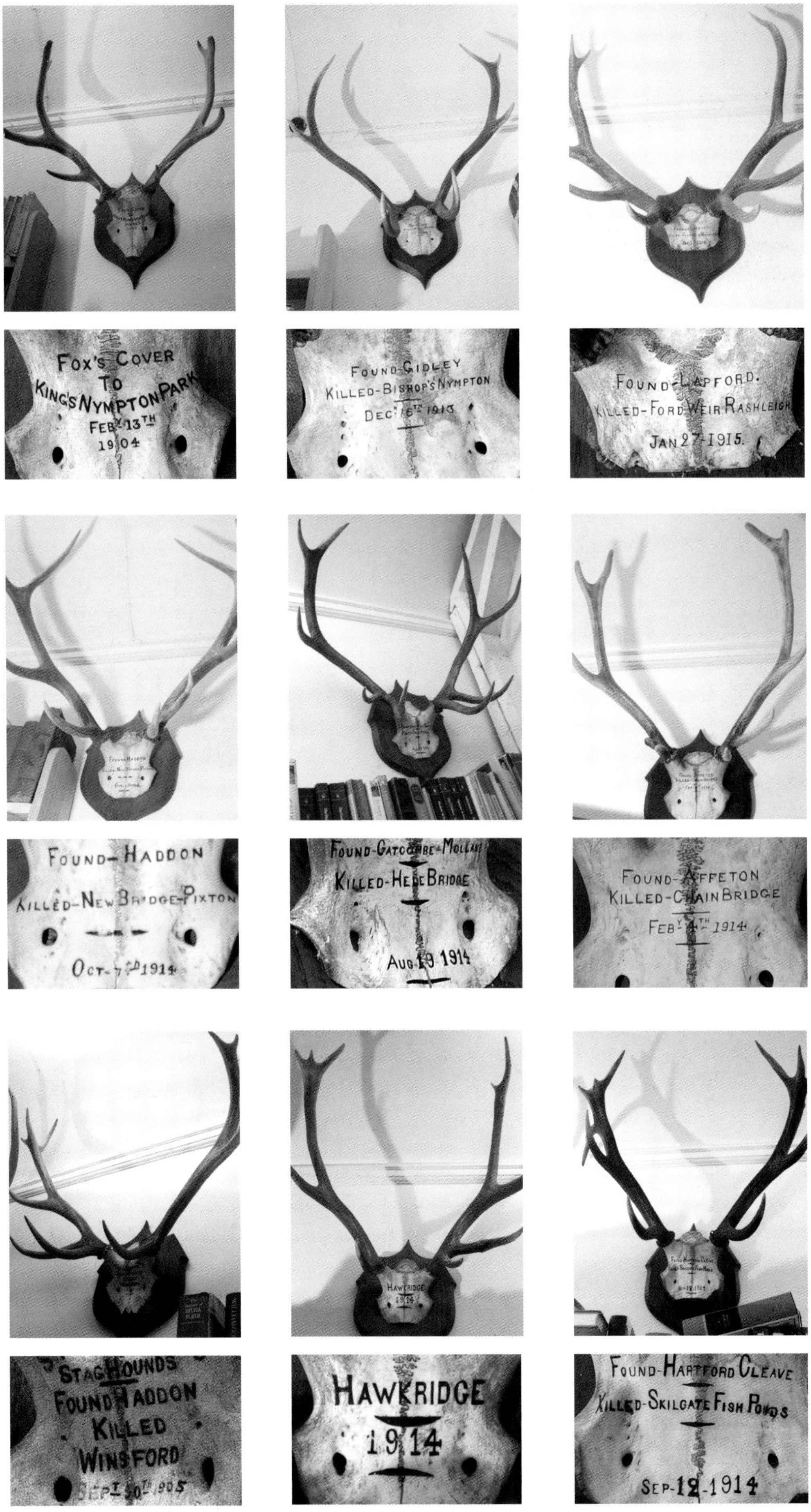
FOX'S COVER
TO
KING'S NYMPTON PARK
FEBY 13TH
1904
FOUND-GIDLEY
KILLED-BISHOP'S NYMPTON
DEC 6TH 1913
FOUND-LAPFORD.
KILLED-FORD WEIR RASHLEIGH
JAN 27 1915.
FOUND-HADDON
KILLED-NEW BRIDGE-PIXTON
OCT-7TH 1914
FOUND-GATCOMBE-MOLLAN
KILLED-HELE BRIDGE
AUG 19 1914
FOUND-AFFETON
KILLED-CHAIN BRIDGE
FEBY 4TH 1914
STAG HOUNDS
FOUND HADDON
KILLED
WINSFORD
SEPT 30TH 1905
HAWKRIDGE
1914
FOUND-HARTFORD CLEAVE
KILLED-SKILGATE FISH PONDS
SEP-12-1914

145

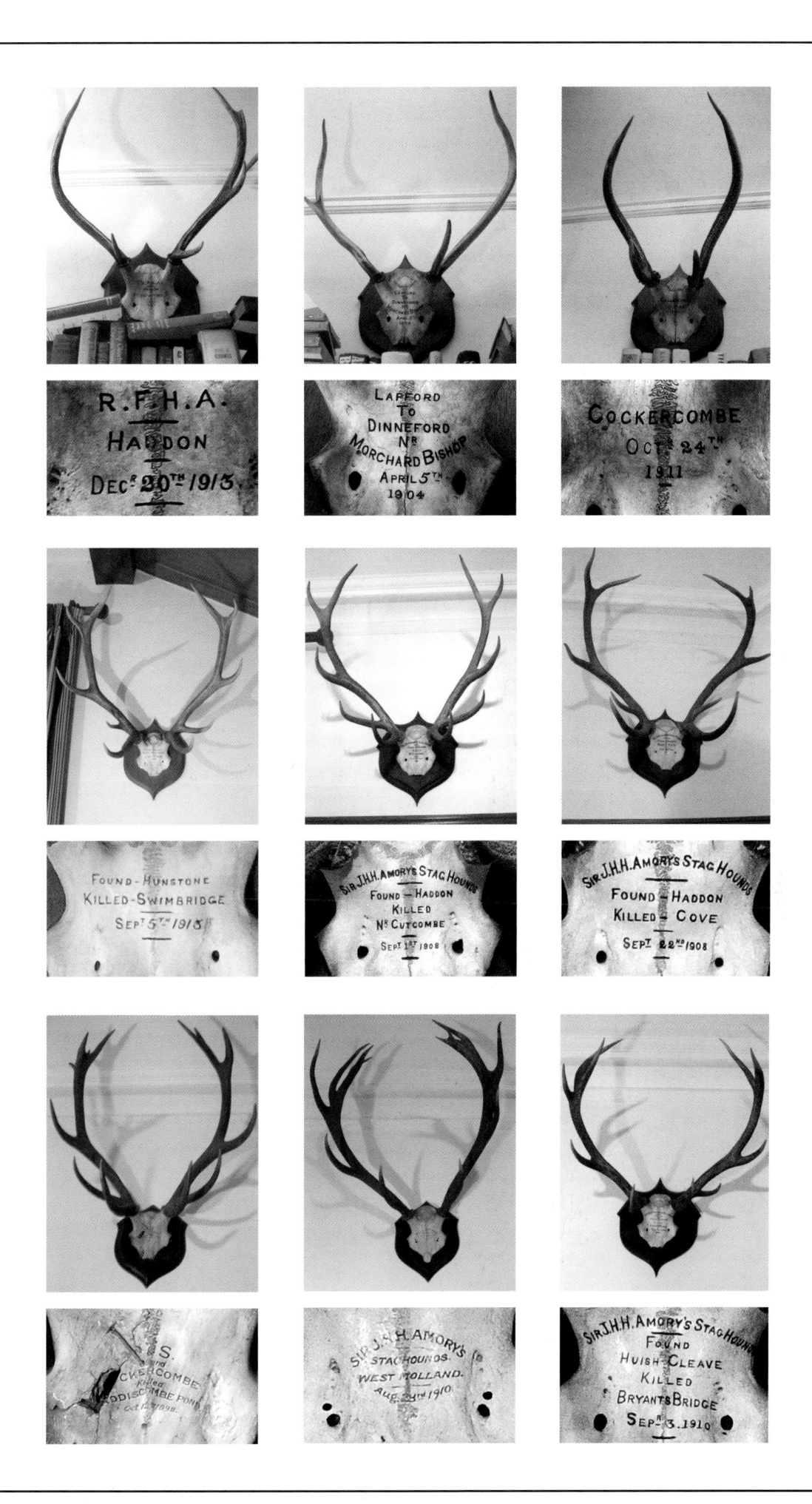

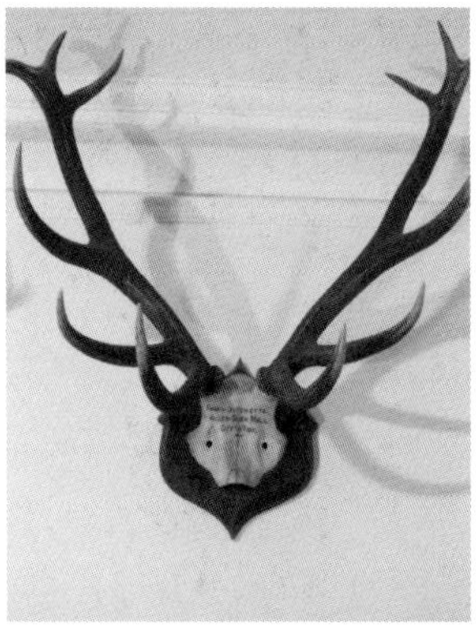
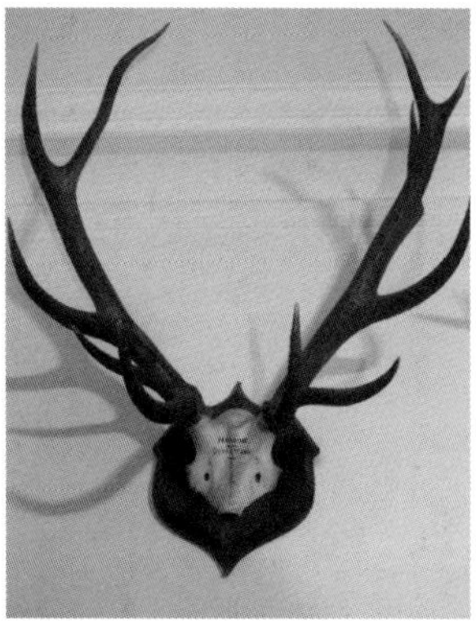
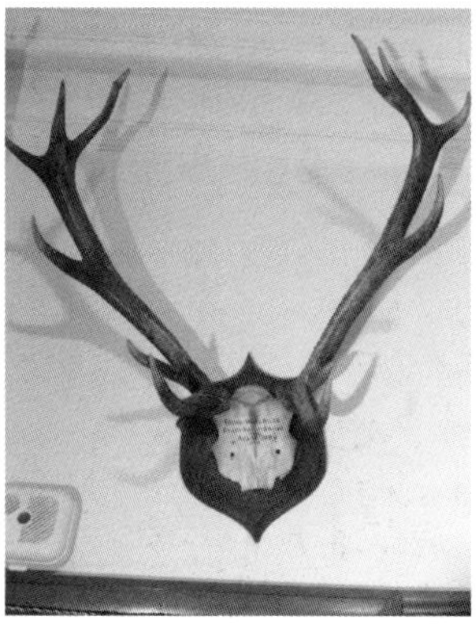

FOUND-DITCHETTS.
KILLED-BISH MILL.
OCTR 11TH 1911.

HADDON
OCTR 3RD 1911
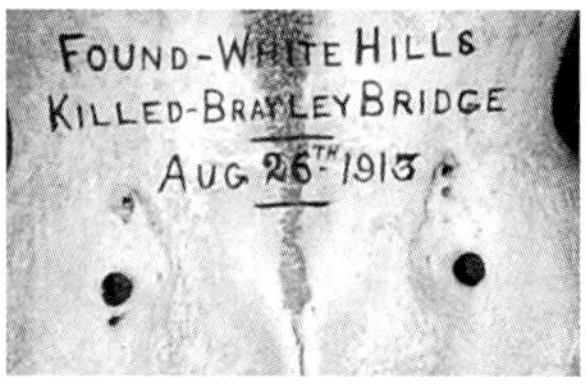
FOUND-WHITE HILLS
KILLED-BRAYLEY BRIDGE
AUG 26TH 1913

FOUND-COCKERCOMBE
KILLED-ST AUDRIES
OCTR 24TH
1911
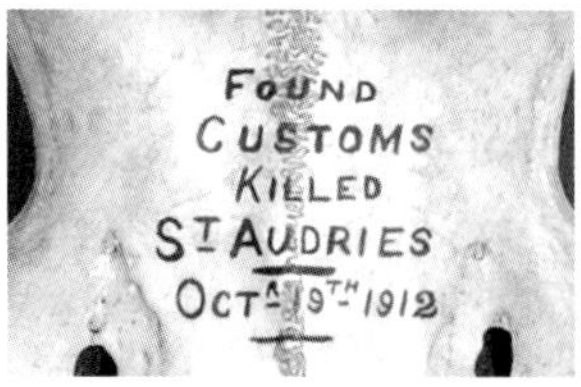
FOUND
CUSTOMS
KILLED
ST AUDRIES
OCTR 19TH 1912
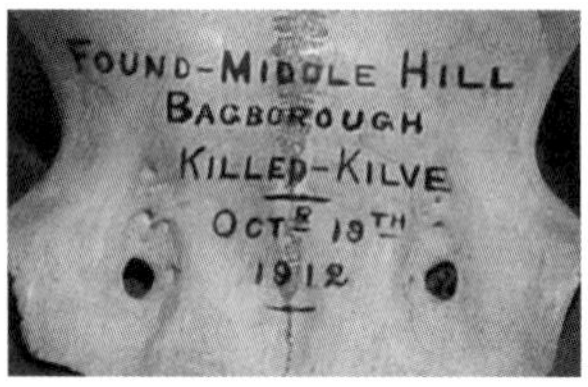
FOUND-MIDDLE HILL
BAGBOROUGH
KILLED-KILVE
OCTR 19TH
1912
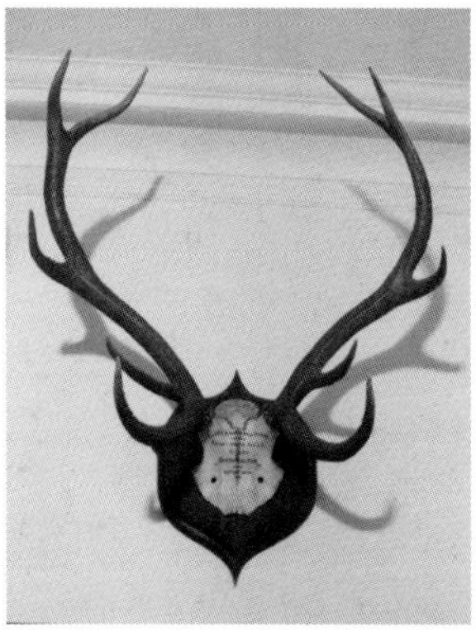

SIR J.H.H. AMORY'S STAG HOUNDS
FOUND-WHITE HILLS
KILLED
NORTH MOLTON
SEPT 19TH 1908

FOUND
LORDS BALL
Killed
CROWCOMBE PARK
Aug. 21st
1902

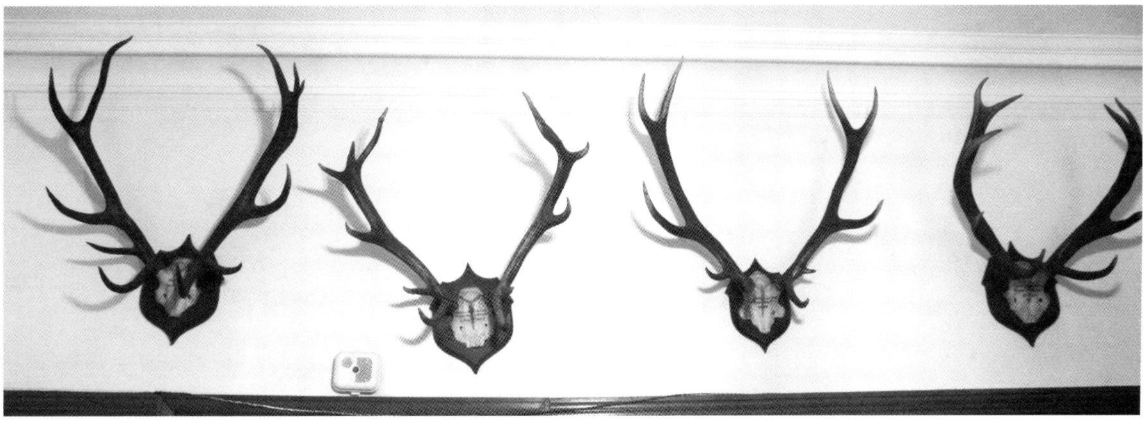

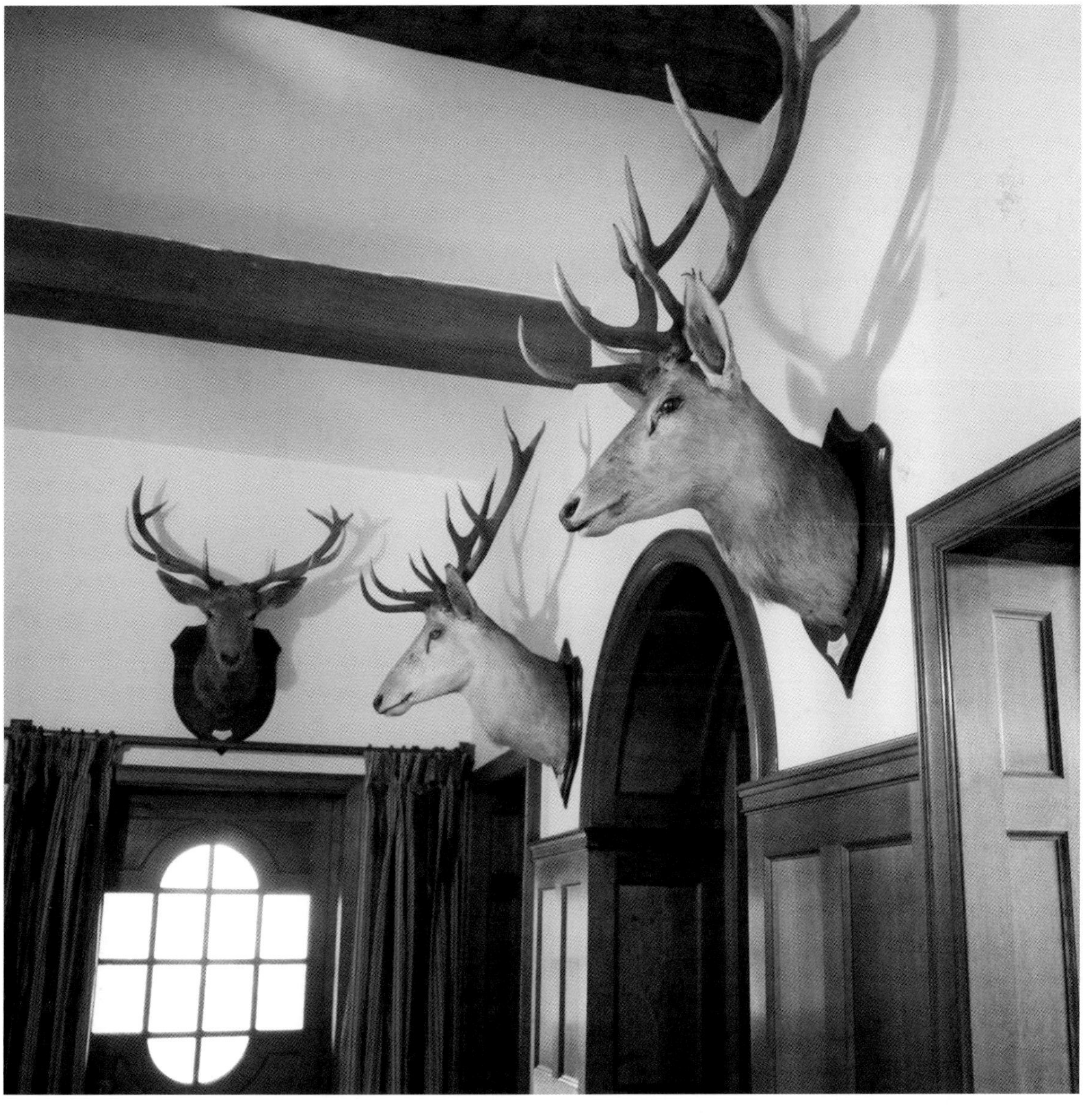

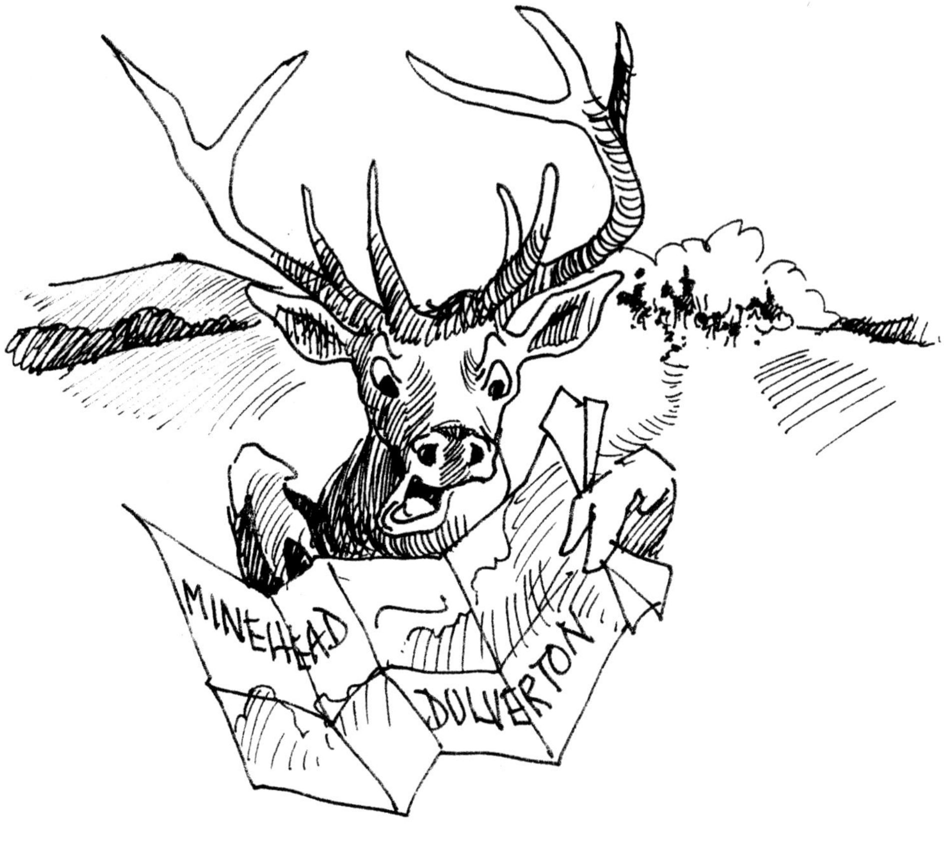
MINEHEAD
DULVERTON

Captain Harry Amory's Staghounds

Sept 11th 1911

Captain Harry Heathcoat-Amory kills his first stag

DESPITE VERY ADVERSE hunting conditions Catain Heathcoat-Amory, who has taken over the staghounds from his brother, Mr Ian Heathcoat-Amory, killed his first stag on Saturday. The meet was at Haddon and a deer harboured in Kings Wood, was bustled by the tufters into Storridge, then over Baron's Down and back to Storridge again. Nothing would persuade the quarry to take to the open, and with the countryside parched and everything even in covert as dry as tinder, scent was wretched and nothing but the new Master's dogged perseverance and the help of those who viewed the deer, enabled the chase to be persued. The deer at last went out over ther top and down to the Exe, into Exe Cleave and Bury Wood by Windy Corner, up to Harford Mill, back to Windy Corner, over Baron's Down and onto Exe Cleave again. Taking to water, there was another longish check, but Catain Amory, casting up stream again, got on terms with the deer at Barlynch, ran down stream to Hele Bridge and on to the big Pixton Wood, where in the river at 5.30 the stag was taken. He had all his rights, and two a top each side. Captain Amory was congratulated in the successful issue of the hunt.

Captain Harry Amory and his bride Miss Evelyn Mary Stanley on their Wedding Day 1898.

A photograph of the Amory Family. From left to right: Ian H.-Amory, C.R.S. Carew, Sir John Amory, Ludovic H.-Amory and Captain H. H.-Amory – at the time of this photograph Ian Amory was hunting the Tiverton Foxhounds.

Going to Sea.

October 21st 1911

Saturday was not a pleasant day for Captain Amory's opening at Triscombe on the Quantocks. Rain fell in torrents early in the day, but cleared up at noon. Still, there were quite a hundred horsemen out. Harry Flatman, who had much experience in harbouring in Mr. Stanleys days, has not forgotten the trick of it, and he reported that he had a good one in the depths of Cockercombe. After fifteen minutes of tufting, hounds put up the harboured one – a stag of eight or nine years old – in company with six hinds, and they ran from Cockercombe to Parsons Plantation, where the stag was divorced from the hinds. He rattled away to Aisholt Combe, and thence back to Cockercombe, through Ramscombe; over the Stowey road to Customs, and up to Danesborough, where tufters were stopped and gave the field a welcome ten minutes breathing space while the pack was being brought up to be laid on the line. Up to this point there had been a screaming scent and hounds had fairly raced their deer along. Hounds were no sooner laid on the line that they flashed down towards Haymans Pond, where the stag had stopped to soil. From the pond he took a course through Alfoxton and skirted the north contour of Longstone Hill and through Smith's Combe to West Hill, and thence down the gully to New Plantation, just above Perry Farm (Mr C. Weetch's). With a left turn he ran up by the fence of St Audries Deer Park where Western, an old estate man, signalled from the top of Flagstaff Hill, with a large handkerchief for hounds to come on. But they were working the line out all right. Scent was holding, and there was no need for help. Racing along keenly and swiftly they were soon up with their hunted one and pushed him over to Staple Plain, and from there he turned down through the small covert at the rear of the rectory, crossed the road, clearing the home park railings at St Audries, and with a sharp left turn went down to the duck pond below the Williton Lodge. Doubling up again, he forced his way through the throng of riders who had come clattering down the drive, crossed the park close to St Audries House, over the Home Farm, and to sea to the eastward of the slip. Hounds bayed him under the cliffs for a time, after which he went to sea, and remained there about two hours. Captain Amory despatched a message to Watchet for a boat, but by the time the boat arrived on the scene at 4.30 the tide had set in strongly, and the stag had been carried on with it past Kilve. While horsemen were holding on to the country just above the coast, one man's nag at Perry shield at something and fell into the gully – a sheer drop of about 20 feet. Fortunately – but still painfully – the horse and its rider were caught in a dense tangle of brambles. That saved their bones,

Bringing in a stag from the sea.

but didn't spare the skin. So firmly were they mixed with the brambley environment that they had to be cut out with a staff hook, neither much the worse for the long drop. Prior to the boat getting up to point at Kilve, the stag left the water and ran along the coast to Lilstock. There he turned inland and pointed to Fairfield House, but he was beaten to all the world, and as the hounds were pressing him, he again turned down to the water, and on the beach by Lilstock he was killed. He had all his rigs, three atop on each side, and a wonderful beam.

November 4th 1911

A good field met the Master on the hill above Bagborough Village in dull weather on Friday last, rain fell rather heavily as the morning advanced. A stag with two atop was soon roused in the bracken in Combe below Lydeard Hill, and he quickly made his way to Cockercombe, and in the process of operations a young stag was accounted for. Tufting for the big stag was soon in operation again and hounds moved him from Quantock Combe to Ramscombe, the field taking up their position on Stowey road. After a short wait a stag was seen to cross into the Scrubby Oaks of Great Custom Wood. View holloas and fluttering handkerchiefs brought up Capt. Amory with the pack, and there was a very pretty lay on with all the field present. The deer made as if for Danesborough, but he doubled in the cover and while endeavouring to return to Ramscombe was met by the field. He then made a wide turn and getting across entered the higer end of Ramscombe through which hounds rattled him smartly and the end came soon after by the pond at Adscombe, at the base of Seven Wells. He was found to be crippled and carried brow, tray, and upright. Capt. Amory then climbed the hills again to try to get on terms with the warrantable stag roused, but as the day was far advanced and the deer not being pressed he decided to finish, and took hounds back to kennels.

December 2nd 1911

Captain Amory's Staghounds met on Saturday at Knowstone, a fine crisp morning tempting out a large field. A hind and calf were found at once in the open, and the hind was run at a clinking pace over Rackenford Moor, and down to Halfpenny Bridge in the Exe Valley. The chase then lay by Chain Bridge, through Stuckeridge, and away right handed to Clayhanger, where the pack ran into the Devon and Somerset Staghounds. Mr Grieg, Master of the Devon and Somerset Staghounds, held up his pack for half an hour, until Captain Amory had killed his deer, and then the Devon and Somerset, with many of the Tiverton field took up thir running, after the long check, and fresh found their deer at Huntsham fish ponds. She made her way down the lowman stream, and just opposite Mr Heard's, at Cowlings, another pack of hounds were encountered trying a small covert. The pack was the Tiverton Foxhounds, and fortunately George Potter, the whip, heard the staghounds just above him, and the field saw the deer coming down stream, in time for Ian Amory to kennel his foxhounds at Mr Heard's, and so avoid complications. The followers of the foxhounds now joined the staghounds in the chase after the deer, and after about half an hour she was taken under Coombe Wood, near Huntsham. The Devon and Somerset had met at Winsford Hill, and the whole chase had lasted some five hours. One of the field remarked that some twenty years ago, in Arthur Heal's day, the Devon and Somerset killed about half a mile above the same spot. The Tiverton Foxhounds (Mr Amory's) had met at Uplowman, and had had a rattling good run of 45 minutes in the morning with a sturdy fox, found in the withy beds at Sampford Peverrell. The line lay by Sandside, Ridge, and Stag Mill, where he was lost. After the wood end coverts had been drawn and a couple of short runs enjoyed, a move was made to Bushey close to Cowlings Farm, in Huntsham parish, and here it was that the arrival of the Devon and Somerset Staghounds necessitated the kennelling of the pack. When Mr Amory unkennelled his foxhounds and again began to draw the coverts close by, the staghounds had disturbed the coverts, and it was getting late the Master made for home after a unique day's experience.

Mr Morland Greig – Master of the Devon and Somerset Staghounds whose hounds joined up with the Tiverton Foxhounds and Sir John Amory's Staghounds.

Jan 17th 1912

Last week's hunting with these hounds resulted in two good deer being added to the list of slain. The second kill followed a remarkable run of eight hours, and as it was quite dark, lanterns had to be requisitioned for the final scenes. The first meet of the week was at Bury, and the hounds were occupied nearly all the morning in Haddon hunting a fine hind which had been roused in the Deer Park. At 1 o'clock the rains of the early part of the day were followed by a fog. Hounds kept close to their hind, and after they had rattled her up and down between Hartford Cleeve and Bury for the space of about two hours they had their reward. Under the circumstances Captain Amory was lucky to kill.

Sketch by Terry Gable

Jan 20th 1912

Among the field who greeted the popular Master at Worlington on Saturday were Dr Perry, of Tiverton, Dr and Mrs Brown, of Witheridge, Mr Burgess (a brother of Dr Burgess), Messrs Yandle (2), Mr Brown, of Witheridge, and a lot of sporting farmers from the Eggesford district. Deer had been harboured in Round Wood and opposite Affeton Castle, and Captain Amory ran with the tufters through Burridge out to the Witheridge-Chawleigh road, and then back to Stone Bridge and up the valley by Cheldon, where the pack was laid on. Then followed a remarkably fine hunt. Having run by way of Winswood Moor, Affeton Moor, Lutworthy Moor, and Week Wood and Odam Moor, this fine hind backed it into Ball Covert and through Week Wood again, speeding thence over Lutworthy Moor once more to the Gidley Arms. Thence the line lay to Backstone, Rackenford, and Spurway Mill, she turned right handed up Coleford Water and then left handed over Ash Cross to Stoodleigh, and down the valley to Cove Bridge. From here she ran through Holmingham and Highwood to Chain Bridge. But though the pace had at times been very fast she was by no means done. Leaving the water she went up over to Wonham, running thence above Bampton to Birchcleave. There was a fresh find here, and hounds ran her back by Wonham House and down the Exe as far as Stuckeridge Bridge. Having landed again she went over Stuckeridge North and across Stuckeridge lawn to the Iron Mill Stream. She was fresh found again near Barrell's Cottage and ran down the Iron Mill Stream through Stuckeridge South into the Exe, and she was killed just above Chain Bridge at 6.40. So ended a run which had been in progress from 10.30 in the morning, and will be long remembered by all who took part in it. Hounds ran fast from Lutworthy Moor back to Rackenford, and hunted all day.

Jan 24th 1912

Two good days' sport fell to the followers of these hounds last week, and three more deer were added to the list of slain. When hounds arrived at Bury on January 24th the conditions were as bad as they could be. Fog and snow blotted out all the familiar land marks and hunting was out of the question in that particular locality. Not to disappoint his followers Captain Amory took his hounds back to Oakford, and having kennelled the pack at Spurway Mill drew up the valley with the tufters. In a young larch covert near Stuckeridge House a deer was roused, and tufters followed hot foot by Spurway Mill, where the pack were let go. A real good hunt followed. At the start the line lay past Sydeham and Bickham, and away over Rackenford Moor to Backstone, and onwards to Ditchetts and the Gidley Arms. Hereabouts hounds crossed the road and ran right handed down the valley, through Week, Ball, Waterloo, Bycott, and Dodyard. Thence they ran by Combe to Kingsnympton, and then left handed to Head Weir, and back over the hill towards Chulmleigh. Having been fresh found near Chulmleigh, the deer ran back to South Molton Road Station, where the the morte was sounded. From the starting place to the finish was a 19 mile point. Among those who shared in this good run were Mr and Mrs Thorton, Messrs W. Haydon, P. Yandle, and Tom Yandle.

Jan 27th 1912

The concluding meet of the week was at the Gidley Arms, and several deer were found in Affeton Young Plantation. With the tufters in pursuit they crossed Winswood Moor and Stone Moor, and then into the Cheldon Valley, where a yearling was accounted for. Continuing after the other deer the tufters ran through Burridge to the Witheridge-Chawleigh road; then left handed back through Round Covert and Affeton on to Affeton Moor, where tufters were stopped and the pack laid on. Running at good pace hounds led down the valley towards East Worlington, and then back again by Affeton Young Plantation, Affeton Moor and Cuddenhayes to Lutworthy Moor, and thence in turn to Week, Ball, Waterloo, and Bycott, away towards Kingsnympton, and left handed to Combe. Hereabouts the deer turned and came back over Horridge Moor, and Stone Moor, and decended to the Cheldon Valley by the Rifle Butts. Thence the line lay by Stone Bridge and Cheldon Bridge, through Round Covert, and a good hunt ended with a kill at East Worlington. The field included Mrs Harry Amory, Dr and Mrs Brown, Mrs Boyd, Messrs Tripe, Saunders, W. Haydon, J. and B. Yandle, and a lot of sporting farmers.

Feb 10th 1912

A good number of sportsmen assembled at the Gidley Arms on Saturday to greet Captain Amory and his staghounds at their first fixture since the recent frost. Hounds were taken to Waterloo to kennel, and tufters soon roused a hind in some gorse outside Waterloo Covert. The pack were let go almost at once, and ran by Ball, Week, Gidley Arms, and Ditchetts to Backstone, where the first check was experienced. Up to this point the pace had been fast. For the rest of the day scent was moderate, and hounds had to hunt all the way, being never out of sight. Having run up the water to just below

Captain Harry Amory slot – found Whitehills taken at Brealey Bridge August 21st 1912.

Veysey's Farm, hounds crossed Haresdown Moor, passing thence to Bickham Moor, and then left handed to beyond Oakford and up the Combe Valley, where all signs of the deer vanished. "It was a jolly hunt, and as good a one as we have had" remarked one of Captain Amory's followers to our representative.

Feb 17th 1912

These hounds narrowly escaped being cut to pieces last week by a train. During a run in the Brushford country a train came dashing up just as the pack were crossing the line after a deer. To those members of the field who were within sight it looked as though all the hounds would be killed. Marvellous to relate only one hound was found to be killed. Another had his tail cut off.

Wednesday's meet was at All Ways End, and two hinds were found in Hawkwell. The pack were let go at once, and ran parallel with the Barnstaple-Dulverton line by Upcott and down to Brushford. Crossing the line here they entered Combe, where they fresh found the hunted deer, and having recrossed the line they were soon in Hawkwell. Leaving at the top they went down the valley by Rock to Riphay and back over the hill by Hele, Langridge and East Tapps to Oakford Bridge, where the morte was sounded. The meet on Saturday was at Worlington. Several hinds were roused in Round Covert, opposite Affeton, and tufters ran down the Cheldon Valley and back again to Affeton

Moor, where the pack were laid on. After making towards West Worlington, hounds came back through Affeton Young Plantation, where complications ensued. In the meantime two hounds had taken the hind down by Cuddenhayes and Winswood Moor to water by Stone Bridge. On hearing this the Master took the pack there and hunted slowly into Leigh Wood, where there was a fresh find. From here we ran her very fast by Cheldon Village, Burridge Wood and Round Wood to East Worlington, where the second deer of the week was killed.

March 2nd 1912

Followers of these hounds enjoyed two good days' sport last week, two big hinds being accounted for, one on the Wednesday and the other on the Saturday.

On Wednesday a hard day was spent between Haddon and Bittiscombe and the Exe Valley, and the Master had the satisfaction of killing a big hind at 5.45 below Weir.

Saturday's meet was at Worlington and a fine hind was roused in Burridge. Hotly pursued by tufters she ran back to Cheldon Bridge and down the valley to Leigh Wood. Not being allowed to tarry here she went out on top and getting back on to the same line led to Leigh Wood again and thence to Cheldon Bridge, where the Master laid on the pack. Hounds hunted up the water to below the keeper's house at Affeton and then ran right handed through Round Wood and out over the top to Round Ash, Cobley, Three Hammers, Deneridge on nearly to Morchard Bishop. Thence the line lay right handed to Lapford Village and through Lapford Wood to Nymet Bridge. Up to this point hounds had run very fast. Ten stags caused some delay, but hounds hit off the line again below Chenson and ran across the River Taw, over the London and South Western line and up through Prenchard, Coldridge and Brushford to Taw Bridge and on to within two miles of North Tawton. Fresh finding here we ran back by Taw Bridge and Brushford to Eggesford Park, and the morte was sounded above Paul Bridge, near Wembworthy about five o'clock, the run having lasted from 10.30. Hounds were now 25 miles away from kennel, and they did not get back to Bolham till midnight.

March 8th 1912

These hounds met at Rackenford on Friday but as no deer had been harboured in the district they were kennelled at Mr Veysey's, while tufters went on to draw Knowstone Wood. At the bottom of the wood a lot of deer were found, and they went round and round the wood for some time. At last a hind got away over Beaples Hill; and the pack were laid on and ran down towards Rose Ash, left handed by Backstone Moor, and Hares Down Moor, right handed through Kenworthy, on through Mr Burrow's Coverts to Rackenford Moor. Then on right handed down the water by Little Rackenford nearly to the Rackenford- Tiverton road. Hounds fresh found here, and ran back through Little Rackenford on to Rackenford Moor. Then the course lay down through Bickham, Sydeham and Spurway Mill, on down the water to Burrell's Cottage at the Iron Mill Stream, where the morte was sounded. This was the fastest run of the year, despite the fact that the going was very deep. Hounds were taken back to kennel early, as for three days this week they will be in the Quantock country.

Stag in ferns.
Photo by Terry Moule

April 6th 1912

In lovely spring weather these hounds met at Chain Bridge on Wednesday. Several deer were roused in Town Wood, and the tufters ran one of them all round Stuckeridge and Wonham, back to Chain Bridge, where the morte was sounded by the Master while the field were sitting in the sun at Spurway Mill. Captain Amory then drew up the valley, but it was sometime before there was another find. At 4 o'clock a young stag sped away with tufters in pursuit by Wonham, Bampton and Morebath. The hounds were eventually stopped about 5 o'clock going into Pixey Copse.

Saturday's meet was at Chawleigh. Several deer were found at Southercott, and the pack were laid on to a young stag which ran by Nethercott, Foxes Covert, Chenson, and Lapford Wood, to Lapford Village, and back through Lapford Wood and away by Boworthy into Burridge, and down to Cheldon Bridge. Thence the line lay down the Cheldon Valley, through Leigh Wood and Chawleigh Barton Wood back to Southercott and by Nethercott, Foxes Covert, across the South Western line and the River Taw, up Coleridge, and right handed by Brushford on to Ashbridge Covert, the end coming just under Bondleigh.

September 20th 1912

Excellent sport has been shown by these hounds following the meets which have taken place this season. Fields have ruled large on most days. The venue on Wednesday was at Knowstone and a big deer was soon on foot, but unfortunately three of the tufters got away in front of the pack and ran him to Highleigh Weir, where he crossed the road.

Capt. Amory re-found him in Combehead, and after about half an hour he was taken near Exe Bridge. He was a grand deer with all his rights.

Saturday's meet was at Gidley Arms, the starting place of many a good day's hunting. A big deer was roused in Waterloo Covert and ran through Ball Covert to Week Covert and down to Cheldon Bridge through the Chawleigh Barton Coverts down to just below Chulmleigh Bridge. Then the deer turned up the valley again and ran back through the Moorstone Coverts across the river and away to Huntacott. After we had run him for rather more than four hours he got back to the Waterloo Coverts, where he managed to beat the hounds.

Feb 22nd 1913

Hounds met at Gidley Arms on Saturday last. The pack were sent to Broadmoor while Captain Amory took the tufters on to draw Bycott. It was discovered that the deer had moved, but the tufters could just feather the line, which was hunted on through Dodyard down to Horridge Moor, up over to Beacon Moor Cross, then back over Horridge Moor again, where the deer were found. Settling on to a single one, the tufters drove at a rare pace back by Dodyard, Bycott, Waterloo and Odham Moor to Gidley, where the pack were laid on and ran by Irish Combe, Vinney, Ditchetts, Batsworthy, Backstone, and Rackenford, right handed by Thorn Brake, down under Mill Brake, nearly to Queen Dart, where they fresh found and raced back to Mill Brake, Rackenford Rectory, and killed in Rackenford Village.

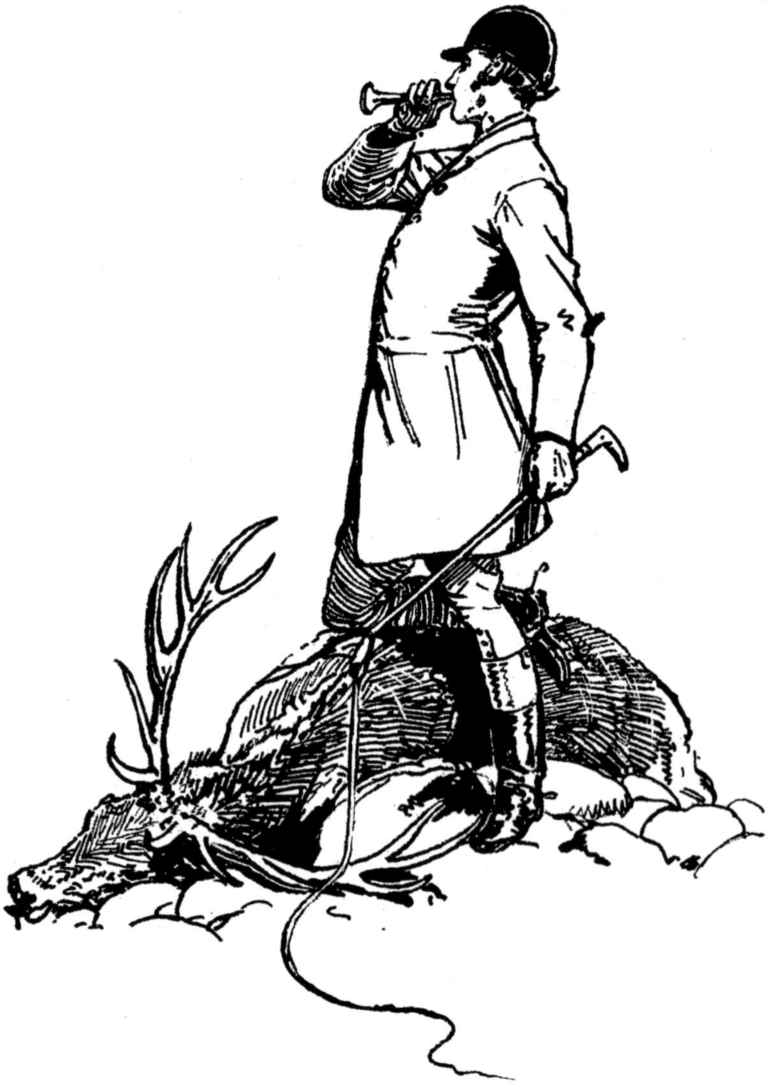